'Jason Wright has written an extraordinary book: one t and accessible to the lay reader, yet draws on complex cal ideas. Wright is at pains to walk alongside the reader, introducing key conceptual guides, for example, Bohm's implicate and engaging them in conversations on the deeper meaning of the human condition. This is beautifully crafted writing that describes William Blake's exquisite illustrations of Job, his wife and friends' journey to find true enlightenment in twenty one plates. The journey is long and arduous, and Wright powerfully interweaves it with reflections from his own experience of working with groups, their place in the community and ultimately the parallel grief, despair and trauma we face in today's complex world. But the reward for walking through the discomfort, confronting our perishing and bearing it together, is that the moment of attainment is so beautiful and pure it almost takes the breath away. This is a work of robust tenderness, and hope'.

Catherine du Toit, *Founding Director of 51 architecture and President of the Architectural Association*

'A wonderful book that approaches Blake's *Illustrations of the Book of Job* with fresh imagination. Blake's masterpiece is presented as a transition from a paradigm of false vision and exploitation to that of participation, resonance and spiritual growth. Wright's exploration includes not only the philosophical, spiritual and artistic currents of Blake's day but philosophers of the 20th and 21st centuries such as David Bohm, Alfred Whitehead, and Iain McGilchrist – to mention only the most prominent. Blake's *Illustrations* are not only a story of individual transformation but also, as presented by Wright, a collective one with great relevance to the contemporary world. Since the rational intellect has grown even greater in its power, global extension and destructiveness Blake's prophesies and visions are more important than ever.

This book is a remarkable combination of philosophy, stories of Wright's life and professional history. Of especial interest are the numerous accounts of working with addiction both individually and in groups and of relating these moving and sometimes tragic stories to Blake's *Illustrations*. For example, how people are trapped in false selves, how they become possessed by the Satan of addiction, and how spiritual experience may free them – as it did Job. The book is filled with magical and memorable phrases, for example: "Addiction is the search for something alive and relational in the dead but certain object of drugs or alcohol". As the book proceeds Wright focuses on how Blake's work illustrates the path to the Self, to use a Jungian concept – but framed in a group context. Wright's philosophy deepens and his prose becomes more expressive matching that of his esteemed philosophers… "The organising principle in the universe is a creative, organic resonance, and self in this context is an emergent experience in that process".

For all those interested in the relevance of Blake to the modern world this book, as well as being full of challenge, wisdom, and surprise, is also a great treat'.
Alan Mulhern, *author of* The Sower and the Seed *(2015) and* Healing Intelligence *(2012). Director of the Quest Lecture Series and podcaster (Vision in an Age of Crisis)*

'This is an erudite, stimulating and immersive book, expanding and enhancing Blake's vision of the story of Job for modern times. It is a triumph of hope over despair, infused with humanity and common sense. It highlights the essential interconnectedness and relational dynamics in human interaction, Seeing them as paramount in any comprehensive understanding of individual and social development. It also illuminates how self-destructive structures and ideas can lead to limiting internal and external horizons, distorting how we see ourselves in relation to others and constricting our ability to adapt and change. Gleaned from his lengthy experience as a group and individual psychotherapist, the author emphasises with poetic grace and acuity, how necessary it is to face the 'uncomfortability' of engaging with the possibility of a participatory, unfolding, emergent, co-creative process. He challenges the desire for an overcontrolling, rigid, reductionist dogma that reinforces the primacy of self-interest over altruism. The author writes: "I see in the Job a group narrative, not only for the relationship between the individual and the group, but this set in the context of the resonant and relational whole where that whole is the group, the society, the species, the planet or indeed the divine." This is a bold, accessible and, challenging work, which deserves close attention'.
Ian Simpson, *group analyst and bonsai artist. Former Head of Psychotherapy Services at a major London teaching hospital for 20 years*

Blake's Job

In this unique book, Jason Wright analyses William Blake's *Illustrations of the Book of Job* and shows their relevance in clinical psychoanalysis and psychotherapy with groups and individuals, especially while working with patients who have experienced trauma and addiction.

Drawing on decades of work in the field, this book sees Wright offer sensitive guidance to practitioners dealing with client experiences of change through the lens of addiction and offers useful insight to the lay reader. Throughout the chapters, Wright studies each illustration in depth and shows how they chart the breakdown of Job's life into a state of despair. Twinning a clinical vignette with each plate, Wright shows how these depictions can be directly applied to issues faced in contemporary analysis, therapy and addiction recovery. From Job's dissolution to his eventual salvation, Wright insightfully maps the process of change from a place of destitution to one of redemption and hope set in the context of the group. He expertly brings Blakean theory into the 21st century by looking at contemporary experience such as the impact of the 2005 London bombings, as well as looking at the importance of community, collective experience and self-identity when seeking recovery. Throughout, Wright draws inspiration from eminent analysts such as Bion, Winnicott and Hillman, while also looking to Jung, Bohm and Whitehead to support his theories on the new way of being he proposes: a collective dynamic shift from a consciousness of exploitation to a consciousness of resonance.

This book will be of great interest to psychoanalysts, psychotherapists and mental health professionals working in addiction recovery, as well as those interested in the work of Blake and its continued importance in the present day.

Jason Wright is a transpersonal and psychoanalytic psychotherapist. For twelve years, he was Clinical Director and CEO for the CORE Trust holistic addictions charity, following a career as a manager and director in theatre. He has since founded Number 42, a group psychotherapy practice in Central London, UK.

Blake's Job

Adventures in Becoming

Jason Wright

Routledge
Taylor & Francis Group
LONDON AND NEW YORK

Designed cover image: William Blake, Behold Now Behemoth, Which I Made With Thee (The Book of Job), Harvard Art Museums/Fogg Museum, Bequest of Grenville L. Winthrop, Photo © President and Fellows of Harvard College, 1943.

First published 2023
by Routledge
4 Park Square, Milton Park, Abingdon, Oxon OX14 4RN

and by Routledge
605 Third Avenue, New York, NY 10158

Routledge is an imprint of the Taylor & Francis Group, an informa business

© 2023 Jason Wright

The right of Jason Wright to be identified as author of this work has been asserted in accordance with sections 77 and 78 of the Copyright, Designs and Patents Act 1988.

All rights reserved. No part of this book may be reprinted or reproduced or utilised in any form or by any electronic, mechanical, or other means, now known or hereafter invented, including photocopying and recording, or in any information storage or retrieval system, without permission in writing from the publishers.

Trademark notice: Product or corporate names may be trademarks or registered trademarks, and are used only for identification and explanation without intent to infringe.

British Library Cataloguing-in-Publication Data
A catalogue record for this book is available from the British Library

Library of Congress Cataloging-in-Publication Data
Names: Wright, Jason (Psychotherapist), author.
Title: Blake's Job : adventures in becoming / Jason Wright.
Description: Abingdon, Oxon ; New York, NY : Routledge, 2023. | Includes bibliographical references and index. |
Identifiers: LCCN 2022061459 (print) | LCCN 2022061460 (ebook) | ISBN 9781032389868 (paperback) | ISBN 9781032407654 (hardback) | ISBN 9781003354642 (ebook)
Subjects: LCSH: Bible. Job—Illustrations. | Blake, William, 1757–1827. | Psychoanalysis. | Psychotherapy.
Classification: LCC BS1413.2023 .W754 2023 (print) | LCC BS1413.2023 (ebook) | DDC 223/.1—dc23/eng/20230419
LC record available at https://lccn.loc.gov/2022061459
LC ebook record available at https://lccn.loc.gov/2022061460

ISBN: 978-1-032-40765-4 (hbk)
ISBN: 978-1-032-38986-8 (pbk)
ISBN: 978-1-003-35464-2 (ebk)

DOI: 10.4324/9781003354642

Typeset in Times New Roman
by codeMantra

Contents

Author's Note: A Percipient Event — *ix*
List of Abbreviations — *xiii*
Acknowledgements — *xv*
A Note on Anonymity — *xvii*

Introduction — 1

1 Blake and Context — 24

2 Perishing — 49

3 Ulro: Spiritual Blindness — 91

4 Turning Point — 108

5 New Vision — 131

6 New Context — 150

7 Participation — 171

8 Endnote: Three Rituals and Two Groups — 188

Bibliography — *203*
Index — *209*

Author's Note: A Percipient Event

On 29 October 1989, I was returning home from the first week of a touring production of Antony and Cleopatra that I had been company managing. I turned a corner on the bypass to Northampton where I then lived. It had been a difficult journey, pouring with rain. After a long week putting the show into a touring house in Wolverhampton I was tired and returning to take an exam for an Open University psychology degree. Suddenly I was confronted with a new roundabout, a slippery road and too much velocity. The thoughts I remember were of the technical choices I had to make to try to negotiate this hazard, the eventual loss of control, and the suffering I was about to experience. I remember clearly the words, "this is going to hurt," and then, "this is going to hurt a lot," before I saw the roof of the car from a new angle. It did indeed hurt and was the event, the percipient moment,[1] that set in train the process which finishes in this book. I was 28.

Three years later, I had finished my career in the theatre, recovered from the spinal injuries received in the accident and taken a temporary job delivering remotely stored data to businesses across London. In the 1990s, this involved lifting a ton of paper in and out of a van on a daily basis. The physical work supported me, strengthening my back and provided a counterpart to the intellectual work, the literal changing of my mind I engaged in, as I retrained as a psychoanalytic and transpersonal psychotherapist.

One sunny morning I found myself at London University, dressed in a slightly oversized delivery driver's uniform, ascending a staircase in a Georgian townhouse in Bloomsbury. I was there to view the *Illustrations of the Book of Job* (1825) by William Blake, which I hoped to use to make a presentation to my training group. This presentation would be a plagiarised exposition of an encounter between the ego and the self, as described by the writer and analytical psychologist, Edward Edinger (1986). My attachment then was to Jungian thinking in an archetypal frame, and to some extent it still is.

In a small office several floors up I was greeted by a rather pixie-ish late middle-aged man in a green tweed suit with a glint in his eye. I mustered myself, feeling out of place and announced, "I have come to look at the Blake." He pointed to a large brown regency stripe box on the corner of his desk. I made to open it, somewhat gingerly, and he barked, "No, no, you can take them away." Surprised, but not wishing for him to change his mind, I was suitably thankful. I stuffed the box in a black plastic bag and left before he could change his mind.

I recognised this as a version recently printed from the original plates, so I didn't want my grubby fingers to make a mess of them. In the quietude of my tiny flat deep in east London, I reverently took them out. At the time I had a friend who owned a rostrum camera. I asked him to make transparencies for my presentation. I made no mention and offered no money to the Blake Society for this and came to see it as a theft, which incidentally my Blakean friends suggest he would approve of. It has followed me for thirty years. My attitude to Blake's *Job*, and what it has shown me, has changed over the intervening years, as has London and the context in which it sits. For instance, this artwork is now far more easily available to access, free, from Yale University.

Following Jung's binary form of the transcendent function, which we will explore later in depth, Edinger (1986) describes the narrative as an encounter between the ego and the self, the self being the centre and whole of the personality, conscious and unconscious, the ego being the centre of consciousness (Samuel. Shorter, Plaut (1986); Jung, CW12, 1936/1968, para. 44), the binary being these archetypal structures seen as poles. We shall explore this idea more deeply as we go forward; however, I believe this context has become more fluid, more open and more diverse much as Hillman (1982, pp. 82–85) would describe the self as one archetype amongst many, one way of organising imagination, but not the whole or the only. It is worth note that Jung nears making the same point in Answer to Job (CW11, 1952/1969, para. 757).

I would see this as the move from a modern way of seeing things to a postmodern, where there is a plurality of possibilities, i.e. not one but many ways of imagining the world. Where once there was Edinger's rigidity and Jung's binary model, now I see a more complex and diverse experience, for me a polyvalency, rather than a binary or a rigid known. My work with the illustrations, and my work as a group psychotherapist, has led to an understanding of symbol formation rooted in the individual in a group context. I have moved from an internal dialogue between ego and self, Jung's idea of the transcendent function, which is how he describes the Ego's discovery of new but unconscious components of the psyche through symbol formation, to a communitarian dialogue that recognises this process in the context of the group.

In this book, I will describe a group process of the continual revision of experience, with relevance not only for clinicians, but I hope for the general reader, who might reimagine their relationship to the context we inhabit. Ultimately this is met in the simple human trust that is needed to bear the unfolding process within and between us.

As I see it, Blake's *Illustrations of the Book of Job* (1825) synthesises an astounding range of thinking: Kabbalistic, neo-Platonic, Gnostic and Eastern, similar to the expanse of Jung's thinking. Blake clearly expresses his journey through human experience, framing a descent and return; in Jungian terms – a myth of death and rebirth. Blake's work is so full, so prodigious and so directly connected to what David Bohm (the philosopher and physicist whom we will hear more of later) would call the 'source' (1998, p. 84, 2008a, 2008c), to the 'divine', that it is possible to project many frames for imagining how we 'become' as humans into his work.

As S. Foster Damon (2013) remarks in the final introduction to his Blake Dictionary:

> Blake is a challenge to every thinking person. He is so far ahead of his times that we are just catching up to him. Many of his once strange theories are now commonplaces to the psychologist ... no reader today could mistake what Blake believed about such fundamentals as The Holiness of all Life, the Brotherhood of Man, the Forgiveness of Sins and the God within us.
>
> (p. xxviii)

Such a syncretic and synthetic journey is what I see before us and what I suggest in this book. I see it as relevant to us today as it was to the changing time of the Industrial Revolution. I hope you enjoy sharing the journey Blake has taken me on.

Note

1 Percipient occasions are Alfred Whitehead's (1861–1947) name for actual experienced events. Whitehead, a British mathematician and philosopher, did not limit these to human experience. He believed in the transmission from occasion to occasion of 'societies' (groupings) of events that generate novelty – something new in the course of the process of our becoming. So to some extent it is possible to say that meaning-making introduces something new to the ongoing process, as with Jung's notion of the transcendent function.

Abbreviations

Works by Blake

E	The Complete Poetry and Prose of William Blake (edited by David Erdman)
FZ	Vala, or the Four Zoas, 1795–1804
J	Jerusalem, 1820
M	Milton, a poem in two books, 1804–1808
MHH	The Marriage of Heaven and Hell, c. 1790–93
NNR	No Natural Religion and All Religions are One, c. 1788.
SI	Songs of Innocence, 1789
SE	Songs of Experience, 1794
VLJ	A Vision of the Last Judgement, 1810

Works by Alfred North Whitehead

PR	Process and Reality, 1978

Works by Foster Damon

FD	A Blake Dictionary: the ideas and symbols of William Blake, revised ed. 2013

Acknowledgements

For someone who has so thoroughly come to the conclusion that there is no fixed reality to individual selfhood I should thank everyone who has ever orbited near this book, or invite them to thank each other as part of a whole in movement, resonant and participant, which has resulted in words on a page. It is not a me that has done this, more an us. That aside, there are various individuals who have been specifically supportive, whom I should like to mention; their generosity and patience has been boundless. The three editors: Clare Joy, Sarah Walton and Phillip Birch, who from their different perspectives supported me and held the unfolding of the book, allowing it to open in various creative and grounded ways, holding faith when I had lost all.

    I would like to thank everyone at Number 42, who lived this unfolding as a process and now make up the community that takes this work forward. All who have passed through CORE and lived the same journey earlier in the terrifying form of ending with addiction. Carolyn McDonald, Ian Simpson, Werner Valentin and Jenifer McCabe, who have worked with the piece in group and provided the holding of 42. Charlotte Wynn Parry, whose faith in the work and reading kept it going. Carolyn, who also worked at CORE, for urging me on when I feared to give up. Alan Mulhern, Peter Schiller, Arthur Sherman and Penny De Haas Curnow, who inspired the thinking and the work over thirty years. Rod Tweedy for getting the project off the ground in the first place. Darian Leader, Anne Shearer and Nigel Wellings for readings early on and pointers to the way ahead and Catharine DuToit for such help toward the end. Not least also my family who have had to endure the tensions that have passed through it to create the work. Finally, of course, all the remarkable people I have worked with who have shared their lives with me, allowing me to love them as we explored through their creativity more deeply what it is to be human.

    I would particularly like the thank the Paul Mellon Collection at the Yale Centre for British Art for the use of their images for Blake's Job.

A Note on Anonymity

The fashion today is to form composite examples from clinical work of what one is trying to illustrate. I have mostly adhered to this tradition. This has left some vignettes seemingly blank, as I have tried to exclude detail that might cause too much of a sense of identification. Some details are often poetically telling in the work and of use to understand or have a sense of a context but may lead to a direct identification which is not my conscious intention. The group vignette after the bombings in 2005 is my recollection of that event, anonymised as far as possible. Others may not recognise the meeting in this form. I have tried to remain truthful to the poetry which the people I have worked with met their unfolding lives. I remain, as I have always have been, astounded at the courage, ingenuity and beauty which has been brought to the work and that I have been privileged to attend to.

Introduction

From Exploitation to Resonance

In this book, I will use Blake's *Illustrations of the Book of Job* (1825) to describe what I see as a move from a consciousness of exploitation to a consciousness of resonance. I would like to encourage a movement from the assumption that as individuals and as a species we can exploit the context in which we live, to the understanding that we are a participatory component in a wider process of becoming, a perceived fragment in that process, but reflexive of, resonant and coherent with it as a whole. I hope this has relevance not only for therapeutic work, particularly work with addiction, which has formed a major part of my work for many years, but also more generally.

The Job story can be read as a struggle with our separation from a previous, more participatory experience of becoming. Mulhern (2015) suggests the Job narrative expresses the change from the worship of nature gods to one father god, and that it addresses the fears of a shift away from a participatory embedment in the process of becoming towards our current perception of separated beings acting upon an objective and material world. We should re-examine this myth as we come to a point where the problems with our success as actors within a system present as symptoms, psychological and ecological. I will explore the symptom of addiction, which I see as central to our life in this context as we enter what is being called the fourth industrial revolution – the digital revolution – and a period for the earth in which we crown ourselves ruler, giving it the title of the Anthropocene.

The Job story appears in the Old Testament and is dated to 600 BCE. It is subtly altered by Blake to represent his perception of becoming in the early 19th century. We will explore how Blake uses this narrative through various theoretical views: Carl Jung, who formed his own analysis of the book of Job in his 'answer' to Job (CW11, 1954, p. 355) and provides an imaginal frame not dissimilar to Blake's; James Hillman, who offers an example of neo-animism, with his archetypal psychology (1975a, 1983b, 1994; Hillman and Moore, 1989), which gives us an imminent means to imagine a way to participate in the becoming of the whole; Alfred North Whitehead, who's speculative philosophy offers a model for articulating a process of perishing and becoming that I see as congruent with Blake's imagination

DOI: 10.4324/9781003354642-1

and this piece in particular; and David Bohm (1980; Bohm, 1998), who offers a deepening of Whitehead's thought into the perpetual unfolding and refolding of life in which we are participant. These theorists all point to a life beyond material rationalism, as of course does Blake, one in which our experience is both a reflection and a component of a wider whole. Crucially, through his notion of dialogue (1996), Bohm offers us a practical means of engaging with the change in sensibility that brings together not only the theoretical approaches I outline but roots this in the context of our shared lived experience.

We will also consider other thinkers who have commented more directly upon Blake, particularly Katherine Raine, the poet and Blake scholar, who links Blake to Neoplatonic thought (1982, 1968, 1979), and Sheila Spector, who emphasises a Kabbalistic reading of Blake's work (2001a, 2001b). She argues that he developed his mythic narrative over his lifetime and brought it to full realisation in his final great composite works, *Milton* (1804–1810/1811: Bentley, 2004, p. 120), and *Jerusalem* (1804–1820: Bentley, 2004, p. 176) two epic illustrated poems. These were completed just before Blake met John Linnell, the artist, patron and friend who assisted him in embarking on the Job and then the Dante illustrations. This meeting was a turning point for Blake, which saw a flowering of his work and recognition late in life. I see it as the world finally coming to find him, as somehow it could begin to bear what he had to bring.

As you might guess this will be a journey of the imagination – how through symbol and metaphor we can come closer to the experiences we live and their divine roots. It will also be syncretic – the bringing together of differing schools of thought or religion. Blake believed all religions at root were one, and at the age of thirty-one he produced the work 'All Religions are One' (1788), from which this quote is the beginning:

THE ARGUMENT
As the true method of Knowledge is Experiment, the true faculty of knowing must be the faculty which experiences.

This faculty I treat of:

Principle 1
That the Poetic Genius is the True Man, and that the Body or Outward Form of Man is derived from the Poetic Genius. Likewise that the Forms of all things are derived from their Genius, which by the Ancients was call'd an Angel and Spirit and Demon.

I believe this to be true, but I take a more secular and metaphorical view, akin to Whitehead's model of Pan-experientialism, the idea that the divine whole is the divine whole. Like Bohm and Blake I propose that we are coincident with it, though our perception of it varies with our experience and imagination. I favour a more participatory model of 'one ocean many shores' as Ferrer (2002) suggests, rather than a more traditional metaphor of one mountain with many paths. As Blake remarks in Principle 7 of 'All Religions are One':

Principle 7
As all men are alike, tho' infinitely various; so all Religions: and as all similars have one source the True Man is the source, he being the Poetic Genius

We will explore through the ideas put forward in this book how there is in each event this resonance. However, as David Bohm suggests, following his personal experience, his work with quantum mechanics (1980) and his dialogue with Krishnamurti (Bohm, 2008c; Peat, 1996, pp. 195–197), through the idealisation and reification of thought we hinder the apperception of deeper, more subtle components and orders of our experience. This I would see akin to Whitehead's 'fallacy of misplaced concreteness' (PR 7; Cobb 11–12), the mistaking of an abstract idea for a concrete notion, and of course Blake's visionary perception.

To quote Yeats from his writing on the works of Blake, 'Vision, or imagination', writes Blake, 'is a representation of what actually exists, really and unchangeably. Fable, or allegory, is formed by the daughters of Memory'. 'A vision is, that is to say, a perception of the eternal symbols, about which the world is formed, while allegory is a memory of some natural event into which we read a spiritual meaning' (1893, Vol. 1, p. 307).

During my work as a therapist over the last 30 years, I have come to see Blake's *Job* as not only descriptive of what Jung would see as an individuation narrative, but more interestingly as a narrative for how we might re-examine the context in which individuality sits: in terms of the group, wider society and physical and spiritual contexts. Jung (CW11, 1952, Para 648,650) focuses on the Job narrative as a pre-figuration of the Christian myth. It is through Job's experience that God is changed. The Job narrative, as Blake constructs it, offers us a return to the participatory experience of becoming prior to the advent of the one father god, but contextualised for today's experience with the conscious awareness we have garnered through the suffering of this journey. It is a volitional re-embodiment, a re-enchantment with the context in which we sit – personal, social, ecological and cosmic – but awake to the transient and tragic nature of this becoming, as we must recognise that we are coincident with the infinite divine, however, much we remain condemned to a limited and endlessly perishing consciousness of it through our day to day experience. We must think less that we change God, but that we are coincident and dialogic with the whole. This, for me, leads to a resonant rather than an exploitative experience of our becoming; to set us back in the context we inhabit as a living and lived experience rather than a separated objective and dead one, searching for an objective divinity that is forever over there and to which we must aspire. The concomitant of such alienation without faith will eventually be denial. This faithless denial Blake refers to as 'Ulro' – spiritual blindness.

Blake would conceive this participatory perception of our life as an internal and real experience. He has a number of names for this: 'Jesus the imagination'

(FD, 2013, p. 195), the 'True Man' or 'Poetic Genius' (pp. 330–331). Following Emmanuel Swedenborg's lead, a Swedish theologian, mystic and philosopher, he conceived it as a direct internal connection to the divine life of the whole, which he clearly expresses in the later plates, particularly 18–21. Blake offers us an imagination of a process of internal psychospiritual renewal. His eternal falling away from the 'Error' of rigid certainty to be recontextualised as a new perception. For him, in the context of the True Man, our divine internal being. As Tobias Churton (2014), the mystic and academic, so beautifully articulates:

> For Blake, Imagination was not simply a faculty, a kind of creative tool … Imagination was divine life itself. Imagination retained the link between earth and heaven, matter and spirit … Blake, with staggering idiosyncratic audacity, would refer to 'Jesus the Imagination' because traditionally Jesus had opened that link, descending and ascending with the angels, and in His being constituted that link ('I am the Way'), that 'golden string' Blake would come to celebrate in his epic *Jerusalem*.
>
> (kindle location 1347)

It would be sufficient to choose Blake's *Illustrations of the Book of Job* because of its beauty and accuracy; however, as I describe in 'The Author's Note' it resonates with the work of Jung and particularly with the archetype of death and rebirth (something perishing to give space for something new to grow) and the transcendent function (1916,1958; Miller, 2004).[1] This frame of renewal, of perishing and becoming, as a dialogic mirror between the finite and the whole, has been ideas I have used consistently to imagine my work with patients, and the changes people have made during our work together. However, this mode of thinking has implications for my approach to selfhood. I see self as an event in becoming, as an organising and mutable symbol for the interplay of experience as it is constructed in the moment. As Nietzsche (Barresi & Martin in Gallagher, 2011 pp. 43–44) has described it, this is 'a necessary fiction', not a reified and static fact of our psychological existence. Insofar as, we treat the image of our selfhood as fixed, we are in trouble.

Blake lays much store by the image of 'Satan of The Selfhood' as error as the reasoning mind 'the state of death and not of human existence' (J49:67. E p. 199; FD, 2013, pp. 335–338; Raine, 1982, p. 51), a rigid and dogmatic image of selfhood which is transcended as we form a new sense of self in the wake of wider experience. Perhaps because of his historical context, or more likely because of a deeper construct in human experience, he links this to a hegemony of reason, particularly as expressed in Enlightenment thinking of the 17th and 18th century that led to the Industrial Revolution Blake lived through. This is an egocentric selfhood rather than a more open notion of the Jungian archetype of the Self, which is the centre and the whole of the personality at once, rooted in the collective unconscious.

The *Job* can be seen as the condensation of Blake's whole mythic vision into one work at the end of his life. It is clearly a narrative for the human condition and the fluid and perpetual process of change. It comes at a point where humanity starts on its greatest hubris to date of mechanised industrialisation. I have argued elsewhere

(Wright, 2014) that the symptom of addiction as we currently experience it is rooted in this time and reflects the social and cultural changes that the industrial revolution generates. We will focus on this symptom as an illustration of the process of perishing and becoming that I have described, an expression of our dilemma in context. To overcome addiction one needs to recontextualise one's life and be open to its relational needs. Perhaps we might see this symptom as a canary in the coal mine that warns of what is to come. I would use a Hillmanesque understanding of 'symptom' (1964, 1976; Hillman & Moore, 1989) that sees it as a window to the soul, to some deeper process within to imagine the event. This is born out of my thirty years work with groups and individuals and my ten years prior to that in the theatre.

I see that Blake's image of our becoming is full and pertinent to this thesis that through the relational, both personal and collective, we can form a dialogue that supports an apperception of our context and place within it; a perception of the timeless noumenal within the unfolded phenomenal. Bohm would describe this as the 'implicate' (1980), the whole and full context of becoming that we experience subtly, enfolded within the explicate; the revealed moment experienced. Bohm suggests through dialogue in a group a novel experience of the whole can be perceived and participated in. As I see it Blake suggests through these illustrations, and particularly in the final plate 21, much the same.

Symbol, Whole & Divine

Symbol

I will use the idea of *symbol* and *symbol formation* throughout this book. My approach to symbol is rooted in the thinking of Jung (Samuels, Shorter, & Plaut, 1986, pp. 144–146; Sharp 1991), Bohm (1998) and Whitehead (1927). I see a symbol as an arising event, as imagined, as I think did Blake. I would see that any symbol contains at its heart the ineffable connection to the whole. Jung can also be read in this way, rooting symbol in an archetypal context. This has resonance with Bohm, who sees the whole implied, yet hidden, within the explicate, unfolded, superficial event in hand. This idea of Bohm's could be understood as a holographic image which contains a reflection of the whole however it is divided. When questioned as to whether there was a correspondence between the implicate and Jung's notion of the collective unconscious, Bohm (2008a) said it could be looked at in that way and some Jungians he knew saw it as such.

Bohm has said the whole is implied in each particle of light. He suggests the explicate and the implicate orders are mirrors in which reflexive consciousness is formed (2008a). Echoing Whitehead's understanding of symbol formation as the relationship between the sensually perceived world, 'perception in the mode of presentational immediacy' (1927, pp. 13–16), and the way we make sense of that world through our experience of it, 'perception in the mode of causal efficacy' (1927, pp. 30–59). These modes of perception relate through 'symbolic reference'. In so far as, there is a mismatch between the symbolic reference and perception in the mode of causal efficacy there is room for imagination. For me, this is the window to the divine, what is whole beneath our perceived events, filled with a quality of the unknown and the possible which we receive into life. Blake more poetically addresses this in his famous lines from 'Auguries of Innocence' (1803).

> To see a world in a Grain of sand
> And a heaven in a Wild Flower
> Hold Infinity in the palm of your hand
> And eternity in an hour.
>
> (E, p. 490)

Whole

I use the word *whole* throughout this book. I have deliberately tried to shy away from overusing a term like 'God' or 'pure awareness', which point to traditions in religious thinking, what the evolutionary biologist David Sloan Wilson would call 'meaning systems' (2015, p. 157). When I have used God I have tried to keep it within the tradition it is set, be that from a Christian, Blakean or a Whiteheadian context. I am not a theologian and I do not propose to present coherent theological arguments, rather I am rooting my experience in the context of psychotherapeutic practice with a transpersonal and psychodynamic flavour.

The *whole* I would see in the context of Bohm's 'holomovement' (1980, pp. 189–194), an undivided and unbroken whole or implicate beneath the explicate of presentational experience. One could call this an 'infinite' subject (I) beneath the fragmentary objective habitual patterns of thought that generate an object (me) (Bohm, 1994, p. 160). This whole may have many frames, for instance that of 'myth' or 'group' or 'physics'. Bohm points to an experience of 'immeasurability' beyond a literal known thought, one that is in my view experienced apperceptively. This I see resonates with the contextual gestalt of McGilchrist's right brain perspective (2009) and the experience of the Vajrayana Buddhist teacher, Reggie Ray's 'emergent soul' (2008b and c), as the sense of the creative universe felt in the spine. For Blake, this image is the 'True Man' or 'Jesus the imagination'.

In practical terms, it is this to which we appeal in the dynamic and creative field, within and between humans and the world and out of which our symbols form. As I sit with a patient, it is in this co-creative space I wait and, perhaps appeal for something novel to form. This is holding in the receptive sense that Whitehead (Mesle, pp. 72–79) articulates, waiting and listening and holding until something forms, a reception into the becoming moment. The key to this kind of experience is where and how one pays attention.

The Divine (God)

Our principle frame for imagining is Blake's visionary myth and its context. Blake sees imagination as the core of human experience and gives divine access to the whole. He educated himself with the Bible, so takes many references from there, however, to quote from the introduction to *Jerusalem*, Chapter 4, where he speaks to Christians as deists and materialists, Blake says:

> I know no other Christianity and of no other Gospel than the liberty both of body & mind to exercise the Divine Arts of Imagination.
>
> Imagination, the real & eternal World of which this Vegetable Universe is but a faint shadow, & in which we shall live in our Eternal or Imaginative Bodies when the Vegetable Mortal Bodies are no more.
>
> (J.77 E, p. 231)

For Blake, the imagination gives access to the divine resonant experience of the whole and is where life is fully lived.

As I have articulated I perceive that we are collectively shifting our focus from the exploitation of our environment to a contextual relationship with and within it – a resonance. My perception of environment is not only the ecological and planetary, but the environment we make and perceive socially, psychologically and spiritually. Whitehead would see that the meanings we make, or the symbols we form, arise in us as novel experience in the context of the whole, which then informs the whole as a new component in the ongoing process. His interest is in novelty. Bohm would see how fragmentary and literal thoughts can inject incoherent 'meaning frames' into this process, unless we recognise the context in which they sit, and how that context has a sense of wholeness, a divinity, to it. Blake would reference this as the priesthood standing between God as an experience of the whole and the human, a denial of the experience of poetic genius.

Alfred North Whitehead (1861–1947) was a secular mathematician, physicist and philosopher, but he was brought up in an Anglican household. His father was a vicar in Ramsgate. He describes the context of the whole in terms of God, articulating the 'primordial' and 'consequent' nature of God (Cobb, pp. 71–75). He understood the primordial nature of God to be the valuing component of the whole for the perishing moment as it is being received into life, the coming event – the consequent nature of God is the collapse of event that is consequent upon that valuing. He remarked that the felt experience of this is the experience of the love of God. Like Blake this God is not classically Christian, but idiosyncratically Whiteheadian, where God is creativity (Segall, 2013, p. 59) 'the universal of universals' (PR, 21). Whitehead chooses the word God because at root our experience is met in a subjective sense in a universe of experience; his pan-experiential whole.

> The contemplation of our natures, as enjoying real feelings derived from a timeless source, acquires that "subjective form" of refreshment and companionship at which religion aims.
>
> (pp. 31–32)

This universal creativity accords with Bohm's view. Whitehead sees this process as secular and receptive. At root we receive the new into life, we don't make it (Mesle, 2008, pp. 72–77). I have some sympathy with this construction. I am interested in the mystery of our existence, what it is to be a 'me' and how does that fit with other 'me's', and the contexts physical, social and spiritual we inhabit. Although I may have fallen in love with almost all of the traditions for articulating this, including the secular and humanist, I cannot fall wholeheartedly into any one dogma. I have learned and experienced a syncresis, a dialogue between experiences, thoughts and meaning systems, that lead for me to a root experience of our humanity, much as I see in Blake's work. Again, this is born out of experience with people and their differing imaginative ways to resolve the problems life brings them. It has never been what I think I know, and whatever meaning system that I might apply that has allowed room for change, but my capacity to bear and wonder, to pay attention and relate, looking for the emergent creative possibility between us. I can no longer sustain a self as isolate and objective, and I don't see how we can sustain an isolated position without resonant dialogue, and stay free from mass violence. For me, it is just the ideation of our objective individuality that gives rise to the fragmentation, objectification at root in conflicts we act out so brutally. If we dialogue we are able to bear between us the polarised self experiences that come from our fragmentary attachments to thoughts.

The change in perception from exploitation to resonance I understand to be driven by the number of us that there are on the planet, a function of our success as a species. Altering not only our view of our context but that of the system in which we are embedded, bringing more clearly to consciousness our place in the system as a whole. It is a mutual negotiation, between the particular and the whole; a mutual reception, if you like, widening how we see our capacity for symbol formation and setting it in the context of the whole that we are component. In its simplest terms, the more of us there are the more there is the possibility for new imagination, new ideas and new thinking, how we effect this is the question. This is the recognition Blake offers, that the divine is inside us, and in dialogue within and between, Bohm's 'infinite subject', the implicate beneath the explicate moment in which we can participate.

The Transcendent Function

Edinger (1986) discusses the Job series in the context of the Ego-Self relationship. In this context, it is not the ego of the egocentric, or of Buddhism. It is the Jungian analytic ego, the structure in the psyche that experiences consciousness and whose archetype is considered to be the hero (Samuels, Shorter & Plaut, 1986, pp. 50–52); this is 'the central complex in the field of consciousness' (Sharp, 1991). I would not directly equate it with Blake's 'Satan of the Selfhood', the accuser that leads us to enlightenment, although Raine (1982) makes this link. I would see that figure as akin to our ego defences, particularly narcissism. Transcendence of these structures leads towards that experience of oneness. I link this to Bohm's construction of me and I, the objective projection of selfhood, 'me', out of an implicate subject 'I' (which for him is coherent with the moving whole). There are differing concepts for how this oneness is experienced with different traditions. Lancaster (2004) elides Kabbalistic and Buddhist thought, rooting his thinking in cognitive neuroscience and perception which I have found helpful to understand my experiences.

I may be taking a particularly rigid and personal position with concepts for the ego, but I see it as having a set of functions: memory, thinking, feeling, perception; certain executive functions and the capacity to reflect, this to some extent owes something to the functions of the ego outlined by Fordham (1958/1985). I would not see this reflection limited to ego consciousness. There are the defences of the ego, primary and secondary, which protect the ego from uncontainable experience, internal or external (McWilliams, 1994).[2] A primary concern though is to keep the integrity of the ego so that the conscious perception in the world can be maintained in form that is coherent with the ego's perception of the unfolding of that world set, to my mind, in a socially agreed conception of that context.

The Self in Jungian terms is the centre and whole of the personality 'an archetypal image of [one's] fullest potential and the unity of the personality as a whole' (Samuels et al., 1986, p. 135). The relationship between the Self and the ego is that between mover and moved.

Edinger (1986) describes the relationship between Job and Yahweh as the relationship between the ego and the Self; 'an encounter with the Self', as he says. This I have addressed, as developed in Jung, with the idea of the transcendent function. In this model, conflicts appear in the psyche and are expressed as confrontation between the ego and the Self. The experience of life at this point is often full of conflict and confusion, for Job it is loss, seeming persecution, betrayal of self and other and sickness. For some one suffering with addiction, it will be the crisis that arises when the using no longer conceals the underlying wounds to the psyche. During this crisis, a synthesis is formed in the Self, in the wider unconscious, generating a new symbol that is born into consciousness through the ego. Miller (2004) describes this process as having twelve stages and that it is dependent upon the ego's capacity to bear the changing symbolic content of the unconscious as to how comfortably this process is experienced. In so far as the ego has the elasticity to bear the production of a new image, it will allow the new inner synthetic, psychic experience to come to consciousness. In so far as it is unbearable, new psychic experience will be defended against.

In the context of Solms' (2021) work this can be seen as a processing of the up rush of experience from the body stimulated by the external world, which is the function of the ego that is associated with reality testing. So in this model the transcendent function is how we grow psychically, an ongoing synthesis between the conscious and unconscious life, and although derived from the work of Schiller, it is highly reminiscent of a Hegelian dialectic model, also reminiscent of the transcendent quality of *aufgehoben* that McGilchrist (2009, pp. 203–207) links to the synthetic process between the left and right brain. I would draw an analogy to dialogue in group that this process is reflected in dialogic group work somewhere within and between the relaying minds of the whole group, from which the synthesis of a new symbol can occur. The event may arise in Job but is an event in and with the group.

Jung suggests that the first half of life is about building ego strength and finding one's way in the world. The second is about realising what a shoddy job one has done and deconstructing the structure that has been built to be more open to the totality of one's perceived experience, the individuation process. I would see that we are widening this process to see it not only individually, but in the life of the group, which becomes a co-creative process in and for the group, as we will outline with Bohm and Whitehead's work below.

I have approached some of the research for this book through workshop and shared experience. After one such workshop a group analyst pointed out to me that Job is not alone in the images, he is accompanied by his wife, and either his family, the comforters or members of the community in which he lives. This simple comment struck me as profound and led to me in great part viewing this set of images in the context of the work I have done with community formation.

Theorists and Thinkers

A central conceit of the book suggests we are experiencing a change to the relationship between the individual and the group,[3] a re-focusing of an assumed separateness to a wider perception of our experienced individuality as resonantly connected. Here, I am using the Group Analytic idea of the group as put forward by Foulkes (1983), Bion (1961) and Patrick De Mare (1992) that postulates the individual as a nodal point in the matrix of the group, familial and social. In this context, there is a dialogue between the needs of the group and the needs of the individual. I see that this re-focusing away from our assumed separateness does not preclude our subjectivity, nor a sense of personhood, but widens it to perceive, or apperceive[4] more deeply the interdependent and homeostatic context within which that selfhood sits.

The term 'apperceive' was first used by Descartes and taken up by Kant, Leibnitz and then further developed in the Western philosophic tradition. There is a range of definitions: medical, psychological and philosophical, which point to a wider conception of experience than the merely sensory and include a contextualisation of experience in relation to a sense of I-ness. According to Sharp (1991), Jung differentiates between passive and active apperception. Active apperception is the ego grasping something new and coming to terms with it. Passive apperception is forced on consciousness from the outside, through the senses, or from inside, through the unconscious processes; an example might be the 'transcendent function'.

I am using the word in this book in the context of a gestalt in the moment, a synthetic perception of experience in the here-and-now. Involving introspection, 'proprioceptive experience', in Bohm's terms (2004, p. 75), as well as felt and perceived experience in the context of experience and memory, but it goes beyond – in the way that Sharp suggests – to something new.

David Bohm worked with De Mare and incorporated many of his ideas into his work, particularly that of the large group, where phenomena arise that are more socially focused than in smaller groups. However, Bohm did not think that there would be a social solution to this problem, and pointed, as does Blake, to a far more radical change in the context of how we perceive the world. Although Blake is seen as politically radical, by 1810 he changed his belief that the solution to the ills of the world he inhabited were social.

Neuroscience

Through his neuroscientific and philosophic exploration of left and right brain functioning, Iain McGilchrist (2009) describes a reflective and dialectic process of becoming that is in keeping with the ideas of change I have outlined. He proposes that the left and right brain function differently, the left being linear and reductive, and the right being contextual and expansive. The dialogue between the two functions is through negation, each refusing each other's perception and then acting upon that not as a direct refusal, but a 'yes, but…'. McGilchrist suggests that the right brain first perceives experience in context, then refers to the left to process this gestalt; once processed the left brain refers back for recontextualisation, 'reintegration' as McGilchrist sees it (2009, pp. 203–207). He suggests that when this process is working well there is a sense of uplift, as a new experience and perception is formed. It is a raising of consciousness. He refers to a Hegelian *aufgehoben* (uplift), which is particularly relevant in the context of Blake as a proto-Romantic. McGilchrist grounds our current thinking about a process that Blake articulates, as Tweedy (2013) so eloquently argues in his book exploring 'Urizen', Blake's figure for hegemonic reason.

McGilchrist suggests that the Romantic philosophers of the 19th century recontextualise some of the linear simplicities of the Enlightenment philosophy of the 16th and 17th centuries (p. 352). The Enlightenment's rationalism is the philosophy against which Blake railed. I also note that McGilchrist's recontextualisation, reregistration is a matter of reception, not of outright refusal: a *yes but*, not *no*. We will see later how Whitehead focusing on this relational reception of perpetual becoming as opposed to the fixity of rigid being opens the door to the resonant possibilities of the emergent process I see before us. Bohm's approach to thought as limited and fragmentary offers the same view, not unlike the way Blake's challenged enlightenment rationalism, as a useful component in becoming, but only a component. Reason is not the be-all and end-all, but a participant in a wider overall process.

In a wider context, Reggie Ray (2016) uses McGilchrist's brain lateralisation thesis to articulate his experience of Vajrayana (Tibetan Tantric Buddhist) meditative practice, embedding the sense of our becoming in a participatory and collective frame, rooting it in the body, for him the right brain experience is the body. This is my experience in meditation and as a psychotherapist – the changes we make are made in our body and are received into life. Thought may offer insight and discussion, but the actual change is a corporal and relational event. We will explore this through clinical vignettes.

This neuroscientific frame is a material image for an internal division of perception that has psychological and spiritual roots and reflects the dual context of matter and experience that Whitehead articulates. Blake, Bohm, Whitehead and Jung can all be seen to have panpsychic[5] perceptions of experience, although Whitehead is better described as pan-experiential. This perception recognises that the mind fundamentally penetrates the world. I frame this in the tradition of dual aspect monism,[6] the belief that spirit and matter are different sides of the same coin, as do Bohm and Jung. Although Blake would be more thoroughgoing and see all experience as internal to the psyche.

> Rivers Mountains Cities Villages,
> All are Human & when you enter into their Bosoms you walk
> In Heavens & Earths; as in your own Bosom you bear your Heaven
> And Earth, & all you behold, tho it appears Without it is Within
> In your Imagination of which this World of Mortality is but a Shadow.
> (*Jerusalem*, 1820; Plate 71: 15–20, E, p. 225)

The evolutionary biologist, David Sloan Wilson, takes a more rationalist and traditionally scientific view, which might seem out of place here in a book which essentially has mystical roots. However, he explores the nature of altruism in groups (2015) fully pertinent to the argument I am putting forward. Evolution progresses through altruism at the group level. Whether we look at a group of pond skaters, a virus, cells in a body or humans, it does not matter; it is their working together as functionally altruistic that is important. He suggests as humans we do this through symbol and goes on to remark:

> A single biological species spread out of Africa and inhabited the globe, adapting to all climatic zones and occupying hundreds of ecological niches, in just tens of thousands of years. Each culture has mental and physical toolkits for survival and reproduction that no individual could possibly learn in a lifetime. Then the advent of agriculture enabled the scale of human society to increase by many orders of magnitude, resulting in megasocieties unlike anything our species had previously experienced. The human cultural adaptive radiation is comparable in scope to the genetic adaptive radiations of major taxonomic groups such as mammals and dinosaurs. What else is required to conclude that symbolic thought functions as an inheritance system comparable to the genetic inheritance system?
>
> (p. 56)

A group is more successful if its individual components function for the good of the group. This I have experienced in the groups and communities I have come to form and lead and points towards the resonant shift I perceive we are trying to make.

However, it is not only thought-led, as the quote above might suggest, but context-led, as Bohm, Whitehead and Blake identify. In Sloan Wilson's frame of multi-level group organisation the primacy of selfhood is weakened. Coupled with the thoughts of Bohm, Whitehead and Jung this offers a powerful frame to think about how we could become more open to what Blake sees directly.

Participation

Both Bohm (1996, p. 87) and Ray (2014, pp. 35–40) suggest for the last 5–10,000 years, particularly in the West, we have come to see ourselves as separate from our planetary system, acting upon it and the other life forms we share it with, as though it were inferior or dead. Mythically and historically, this shift can be seen as rooted in the changes humanity made to engage with our environment, particularly when we became farming cultures. However, this omnipotent perception of our separate identity would appear no longer to function well as we become increasingly aware of our impact upon and within the system that sustains us. I suggest we are experiencing a return to the apperception of the whole, but with a more conscious and volitional experience of that context; particularly in the context of the group. Anxieties at this changing perception are expressed psychologically, socially and ecologically all around us. As we come to recognise more consciously how we are coherent with a systemic whole which is altered through and with our symbol formation and the actions that follow. This is exactly the experience Job has and Blake articulates so profoundly. It is the dialogue between Job and the community in which he is embedded, personal and divine that allows for a new perception to be formed.

I would argue that a rigid perception of our separateness dissolves as we become more aware of this context. It is not an annihilation of self but a liberation. The idea of a fixed self becomes 'a fallacy of misplaced concreteness' (PR, 7), 'a necessary fiction', an abstract notion we concretise which falsely objectifies a fluid and continual subjective experience. Here Whitehead, Articulates this experience in the context of soul, the Platonic precursor to Lockian 'Selfhood' (Barresi & Martin in Gallagher, 2011):

> We ask for something original at the moment, and when we are provided with a reason for limiting originality. Life is a bid for freedom: an enduring entity binds any one of its occasions to the line of ancestry. The doctrine of the enduring soul with its permanent characteristics is exactly the irrelevant answer to the problem which life presents. This problem is, how can there be originality? And the answer explains how the soul need be no more original than a stone.
> (PR, 104)

Our focus upon our perceived singularity and single organism homeostatic boundaries works against our inhabiting of a constrained but symbiotic context. I suggest more attention needs to be paid to the context and perception of self, and the complex frame in which this self as a symbol of singularity sits. In proposing, along with Whitehead that self is an emergent property of the whole system, a different systemic and emergent orientation to selfhood arises, one that gives primacy to *becoming* over being. A shifting and altering symbol in relation to the context is then formed. Ultimately, this perceptual change not only deconstructs the singularity of self and reveals its social, psychological and ecological predicates and dependencies, but severely alters any notion of centrality to that structure, both individually and as a species. The point is not the objective *me* and its fixity, but the fluidity of the process behind the subjective *I*, which we can understand as a momentary image within the event.

VIGNETTE

As an example of what I mean, there was an architect who attended one of my groups, who had manifested a compulsive addictive behaviour that was experienced as betrayal in his relationship. He worked to understand the symbols of his actions and the impact that had on his relationships, not only with his significant other, but more widely in his practice and his social life. He was also able to grasp that they somehow beautifully represented the unconscious dilemmas of power and powerlessness that reflected his early life. He was re-experiencing and denying a symbol for his struggle. This insight and the work that followed it changed the symptomatic expression fairly quickly, but also built a space between us and within him that he could reflect upon the emerging moment and allow it to unfold rather than impose an action, like the using, upon it.

This was experienced in the room. As an architect he was able both to see the processes of matter and its use and formation to create inhabited space; he would also draw that sensibility more widely into that of planetary becoming and the ecological struggles we face – our inhabiting of and coincidence with the planet. As we became able to reflect, often in silence upon his unfolding experience and in his practical life in the formation of space for his clients and the creation of space in his close relationships so as to allow a deeper connection and relationship he began to perceive this as a whole process in action. There was a relinquishing of the active self for a wonder at how the creative new can be received. Needless to say this enabled an inhabiting of a genuine authority born of experience that was of greater use than the fabricated self that existed before, improving both his personal relationships and his working life.

These ideas are central to my work as a therapist. I may have many fantasies about the people I work with and how they might reimagine their lives to be more full and creative; however, telling them this, or telling them what to do, is not the solution to their woes. My role involves being able to bear with them the suffering that the symptom they bring engenders and allow for us to imagine together a new emergent symbol that will open up possible pathways in their lives. This is not an act of will but an act of reception; I would say a mutual reception that focuses upon the emergent and valuable in the context of the work.

To see this in Whitehead's grammar, we are component in a series of nested symbiotic ecosystems, from the subatomic to the cosmic. We negotiate through these ecosystems with emergent images and symbols, one of which is the self. He is arguing against the idea in Western culture of self as an individual actor, that as we develop from babies to toddlers to children and young adults, gradually separating from our mother's womb, we are a homeostatic corporal and psychological system that only acts upon and usually takes from a social, psychological and spiritual context. Whitehead proposes a different conception: the self as an emergent image, perpetually shifting and responding to the context in which it unfolds. This resonates well with Sloan Wilson, and for me points to the reification and objectification of the fixed individual self as an abstraction, as 'misplaced concreteness', a limited perception which now is proving destructive. It may have been useful to separate self from its context, and for that context to become better known, but now that knowing needs to be inhabited, participated in recontextualising that selfhood and its implicate roots, building a frame that can creatively receive events into life.

So here, we have a picture of the particular – the self, in the context of the whole – the world that is relationally fluid and mutually receptive. Job in relation to Yahweh as expressed in the story of Job and contextualised by Blake for his time. He draws on ancient Western exoteric and esoteric traditions which are directly relevant to ours, taking a psychologising, synthetic and syncretic frame, perceiving the image of self as emergent in context, focusing upon co-operative and co-creative processes, as expressed between our individual perceptions. In this, I would include the context of 'no self', of emptiness (Wellings & McCormick, 2021), as understood from a Buddhist and a mystical perspective, a state of mind that transcends self and leads to an experience of the whole in the process of becoming.

> Emptiness is the English word of choice to translate the Sanskrit word 'shunyata' – and enormously rich and complex notion that has been unfolding in meaning for almost two-and-a-half thousand years. A notion that is the opposite of our own usage – for to directly and fully experience emptiness is the experience of unbounded bliss.
>
> (p. 80)

Blake articulates this process through his illustrations, Whitehead and Bohm through their process-orientated ideas, and Jung describes this in the context of the 'transcendent function', the self as part of the events it experiences, so that individuation is a whole life journey. All of these are images for a synthetic, and, as I would see it, syncretic process of emergent becoming in which every fibre of us participates.

Places

The CORE Trust

I came to London after I had recovered from the car accident I describe in the author's note and began to train as a therapist. I also became involved in the mythopoetic men's movement and through that found a placement at the CORE Trust, a holistic treatment centre in Marylebone. It was not long from my arrival there as a volunteer that my management skills from the theatre became useful and I progressed to become chief executive and clinical director. The founders of the project were Jackie Leven and Carol Wolfe, both of whom had worked in the music industry and were recovering addicts. Carol I did not know but Jackie I knew well and came to love deeply. He was a mercurial figure and it was difficult to tell what was factually true and what was constructed to form a story that served the emerging moment as he perceived it. He was charismatic and managed to build with Carol a form of treatment that could operate as a community. Today much of what they formed is commonplace, but then it was radical. He used to say that what we do will go through these phases: the joke, the threat and the obvious. Indeed it did.

However much the project might have seemed out there at the time it gave people a place to belong when they wanted to stop using. We developed the project into something that could provide a place of belonging whilst people also made the changes they need to return fully to the community they had lived in, now free from using. This took two years on average and required work at some depth to bear the change.

I will refer to this project through the book, not so much from the early times when we were building our model, but later when it was established and functioned with some degree of success. As a holistic project that was founded in the 80s it offered a range of therapies, psychological and complementary, structured around a day programme. The two principle therapies were acupuncture and psychotherapy, and the community was held together using the archetypal thinking of James Hillman, augmented with group analytic ideas. We offered three groups a day, individual psychotherapy (sometimes twice a week), and acupuncture, then a choice from a range of therapies: Chinese herbs, Qui Gong, Reiki, Homeopathy, Western Herbs, Nutrition advice, Cranio Sacral therapy, Felden Kreis, Zero Balancing, Alexander Technique, Reflexology and others at different times. This pluralistic structure was also held together in a communal and narrative way, looking at the symptom and soul in context. Drawing together the root of these healing models was complex and a joy. Trying to square the eastern correspondent logic of acupuncture with the rational deductive reasoning of psychoanalysis could only be addressed through human experience and the attention and intention with which one soul brings to bear on another. I will show how Whitehead provides a frame for thinking about this form of integration in receiving the emergent moment into life through value. However, this is a post-hoc understanding for the work as I only met Whitehead after I finished with the project. At the time, I used Hillman's ideas of soul and intention to bring together, in pluralistic context, a synthesis of the models used. This for me was a poetic endeavour and not a scientific one. So it might be seen here why Blake's revelatory understanding of our becoming is attractive.

Jackie and Carol were at heart practical and did not structure the project in the context of the academy. There where charismatic and strong leaders, which often caused tensions, but provided a holding for the project and those who were letting go of using. We gave it more rigour but remained truthful to the emergent, perhaps chaotic and plutonic spirit that gave life to those who attended and the project as a whole. The crucial question was how to choose life in the face of death. Of course, this choice is faced directly in Blake's Job.

Number 42

I worked in CORE for just over twelve years, spent a period in the wilderness, and then founded a practice with approximately seventy psychotherapists that work along similar communitarian lines. I will reference the work at CORE principally, but Number 42 appears later as an example of group and community work.

Narratives

The Job Story

The Job narrative is quite simple although Blake makes some crucial alterations and focuses particularly upon the beginning and end of the piece. Job is one of Yahweh's most faithful servants, obedient to Judaic law, pious and faithful. In a confrontation with Satan, Yahweh's gives him Job to test his faith. Satan robs Job of his wealth, his health and his family. Misfortune was considered the fault of sin and Job is challenged that he has disobeyed God. This he denies, however, he remains faithful to Yahweh and calls on him for justice. Eventually Yahweh reveals to him his creation and its context, renewing Job's faith at a deeper level and restoring his health and fortune.

Blake's alteration of this narrative we will explore as we progress through the book. However here, it is useful to see that he draws a much more internal narrative, emphasising the relationship between Job, Satan as a 'Satan of the selfhood', and Yahweh, as the God of 'I am that', which for me personifies an idea of Bohm's implicate. When Satan falls this image is internalised, drawing the infinite God in to an internal experience.

The Lurianic Myth

I will argue like Spector that Blake uses the Christian Kabbalistic myth of Mercurius Von Helmont (1649–2012). This is based on the Lurianic myth, which I outline below.

The teaching of tsimtsum, the Lurianic myth that God limits himself to form creation, is rooted in the will of Ein Sof[7] (the limitless transcendent nature of god) to be known, not for his benefit but of the benefit of creation. A gift and act of generosity is the core of Ein Sof. Here, we might recognise a resonance with the creativity of Whitehead or Bohm. However to give requires a limiting. Lancaster suggests nothing can arise without a 'dynamic of difference' (2005), which I see as resonant with Blake's contraries. Ein Sof's limiting leaves a space into which a single ray of light penetrates, forming Adam Kadmon, the primordial Adam, a template for creation.

Light then emanates from Adam's eyes to be gathered in the ten sephiroth to further build creation. The vessels break and the fragments fall with some light to create the hierarchical order. Lancaster (2005) is interesting here, suggesting that it is the matter of limitation and an excess of judgement that brings about the catastrophe, placing the responsibility squarely in the realm of the divine. God is all, the generator of evil as well as good.

This cosmic drama is resolved through tikkun – a rectification. Humanity as beings of the lower realms are responsible for clarifying the light, and form the shards of evil so that it may be restored to the source. This is the work of the Kabbalah and is achieved through the correct practice of mitsov, which has evolved into orthodox Judaism today.

The Plates

Blake's illustrations are engraved on copper plates which are now held in the British Museum. To divide the book into chapters, I have divided the plates into groupings which fit with the story I am trying to tell. I have followed to some extent the frame of Andrew Solomon (1993). Foster Damon (1966) gives a different framing, matching the plates to the Elohim of the Frontispiece, but Solomon's grouping serves the purposes of our narrative well, articulating the perishing and becoming I wish to focus upon.

Chapter 1

Blake & Context

The Frontispiece

Here, I discuss the context to the book and introduce Blake. The image of the Frontispiece can be seen as the whole journey Blake will describe. I will use clinical vignettes to illustrate the ideas and experiences I bring, but I have gone to some length to anonymise any particular person. This takes the form of condensations and composite experiences, so that no one event is wholly expressed. The people I have worked with have found more imaginative ways to bear their lives than I can express here, but I hope I give a flavour of the beauty they bring to their becoming.

I am using the word 'beauty' in a particular way, not as a social construct, as it is mundanely understood, but a resonant experience of relational coherence. The example I tend to use is of a moment of beauty in the work, a shared event, an interpretation, or an experience of mutual understanding when the resonance is beautiful. I have worked with many people suffering with addiction, and many of the vignettes in the book will reference this work. Each 'user' has to come to terms with letting go of the using, the process or substance that they have clung on to as a pastiche for true relatedness, so that they might bear relation when they have enough experience to be able to do something with it. The point when one is ready to do this is one of utter nakedness and betrayal in the face of death. I will make reference to several of these moments, but it is always beautiful, not just to witness but to participate in. One is challenged oneself at that depth: why, in this moment, should I choose to live? I suggest it is only one's humanity, one's own capacity for life that can meet such a moment. However, if you show up, it is breathtakingly beautiful when you meet someone as they begin to turn to life and relate. This is not a social construct but a resonant fact of shared becoming.

Chapter 2

Perishing

The first ten plates depict the downfall of Job at the hands of his own self-righteousness. This section splits into two – The Fall and Ulro (Blake's term for spiritual blindness).

Plates 1–6

THE FALL

In this section, we will explore Bohm in the context of dialogue, Blake's Kabbalistic roots as described by Spector (2001a and b), and the link to Whitehead's idea of co-evolving organisms and the way current neurobiological thinking might support these notions. However, to sustain the linear narrative that Blake offers, we will look at the narrative of addiction and how it develops, its meaning for cultural and personal experience, and as a symptom for our time. This is an illustration of the process of human opening that I am outlining.

The first six plates depict Job's destruction, his fall from the exalted position he has held, and the breakdown of the status quo. Kathleen Raine (1982) emphasises his smug self-righteousness, which I would see as an accurate description of Job at the beginning of the story, and is Blake's description of Hell: 'Hell is all self-righteousness'. Also I would see this as inhabiting a consciousness of isolation and separation, the dualist experience of subject and object – in other words the consciousness of exploitation. He and his community are dogmatically faithful, not *inhabiting* the life they are leading. There is a destructive relationship with the context he inhabits on a personal and collective level based on the omnipotent and ultimately flawed obsession with Enlightenment dogmatic rationalism, akin to an ego-defence of rationalisation rather than reason. This I see as akin to Bohm's ideas of the fragmentary nature of thought that confused and abstract idea of becoming with the participatory whole experience of becoming. During these six images, this self-righteousness is stripped away until there is nothing left.

Chapter 3

Plates 7–10

ULRO

Ulro is Blake's perception of spiritual blindness. His response to the Enlightenment was essentially Platonic, in that there is a falling into sleep as the soul descends to earth. Enlightenment rationalism perpetuates this fall beyond sleep to a death of soul into a reasoned selfhood. This is separating matter form the soulful and spiritual as the materialists had in the enlightenment bringing about in Blake's eyes a spiritual blindness. We will explore the plates and their relevance to the narrative of addiction as an experience of semi-death.

Chapter 4

Turning Point

This is the point that the old perishes and the new begins to form. We let go of the old idea of life and begin to leave space to receive the new into becoming, receiving the fragments of the past into life through value in the present.

Plates 11–12

This is the point that Job alters his experience, his relationship with Yahweh and his relationship to his context changes. He is able to accept and receive the creative new into his life. I illustrate this as akin to the moment one stops using and re-enters a full life. I will explore Bohm and Whitehead and their perception that creativity is at the root of our experience and the unfolding of the world, how in the death and rebirth cycle the perishing of the old image, which has been witnessed so far, cannot be avoided, before the new can be perceived.

Chapter 5

A New Vision

Plates 13–15

Although Job has allowed for a shift in his experience, he is yet to embody this and change fully in response to his new vision. In these two plates, he orientates his experience of Yahweh, seeing him first as terrifying, in Plate 13, and then as ordered, in Plate 14. This plate particularly sets out the order of the universe as Blake perceived it, owing much to Kabbalistic imagery. From an addiction narrative point of view, this is the point when first one stops and feels that everything is chaotic and confusing, then the orienting and processing of the experience, and what led to the using, starts to take place.

In Plate 15, we see the historic context, participatory and profound, in which Yahweh shows Job his creation and his place in it. This is the anxiety that Mulhern (2015) points to in the original Job narrative, exploring the change from nature gods to the one father God, a recognition of the context we actually inhabit and in my view the point of recontextualisation that we face in the relation to the whole, involving the remembering that precipitates the shift from a consciousness of exploitation to a consciousness of resonance. There is a return to a remembering of the participatory and dialogic that Bohm describes.

Chapter 6

A New Context

Plate 16–17

Here, we see the core of the transformation that Job goes through. In Plate 16, we see the fall of Satan, Blake's 'Satan of the Selfhood', a change to the context of self in relation to the whole, a fixed and old narrative perishing to reveal a new vision. In the context of addiction, this is the death of the user, the using mindset and the compulsion to use, and the opening to a flexible and human relatedness to those around us and our environment.

In Plate 17, we let go of an external image of a god, not unlike Nietzsche's idea that when he went to meet God and found him dead he also suggested there was a loss of self. Blake presents this in reverse order. Blake does not believe that either God or self is gone, just the divided dualist frame. He believes that we are coincident with God, with the whole. From an addiction narrative point of view, it is letting go of addiction as an abstract identity and reforming identity in a truly human image

Plate 18 is the full experience of the context of our becoming – one with the universe, the 'moment of enlightenment' as Raine (1982) puts it, or the direct conscious reception of the divine. In the personal sense, it is the momentary epiphany of the consolidation of change, after Blake's burning up of error, which is witnessed in the first half of the journey.

Chapter 7

Participation

In this section, we examine how we transcend our previous experience and inhabit something new, the recognition that we are not separated from the whole but coincident with it. In terms of addiction, this is beyond using and is entry into an engaged and full new life.

Plate 19 is the experience of receipt and return to connected relationship, both in a proximal and human sense and in the sense of a more transpersonal interconnectedness. Whitehead perceives creativity as a receptive thing. Life is received in to becoming, moment by moment, actual event by actual event. This relational reception is becoming, which perishes into the next moment. Bohm frames this as the explicate unfolding out of the implicate, the whole, in one moment of participatory perception, 'a kind of showing' (1980).

In Plate 20, which Blake worked on again and again in watercolour, and for the engravings, we see transmission, the direct expression of the unfolding process as we experience it in the moment to an active sense of relation in consort with the receipt into life of Plate 19. It is past self and time and an expression of congruent participation in Bohm's implicate.

Plate 21

CONCLUSION/WHOLENESS/PREFALL

This is the final plate of the series and resonates with the first. I see the images in the plate also point to a fully participatory co-creative becoming, inhabited in group. I would call this the relational consciousness of resonance and as such is the completion of the transformation I am articulating. Although the transformation is held by Job it is for the entire community, witnessed and felt as such.

There are two figures in the bottom two corners, a sheep and a cow that could almost act as keys that lock the first and final plates face to face, pointing towards as a cyclical process. It is from here we fall again. To fall – perish – again, into an unknowing, so that a new event becomes inhabited.

Chapter 8

Endnote. Three Rituals and two groups. Here, I give extended examples of the process I am articulating.

Notes

1 Jung's understanding for how the ego and the deep unconscious interact forming creatively novel symbols to bear developing experience was published in two forms in 1916 and 1958.
2 McWilliams offers a comprehensive Psychoanalytic Diagnosis of the ego that I see as pertinent to the Jungian conception of work with the unconscious and formed quite a foundation to my practice. However, it is less likely to meet the second half of life as constructed by Jung in terms of individuation, or Hillman (1996) with his teleological approach pointing towards what we are developing into as the driver to our becoming.
3 When I refer to 'group' throughout the book it is usually in the context of group analytic thinking. This group can take many forms: 'large', which is over sixty, according to De Mare (1992), small, which would be eight or so, or median, which would be somewhere between the two, say fourteen – thirty. The bulk of my work has been with

median groups; however, I have also worked with large groups in a wider context, both corporate and social, and I have formed communities working in a therapeutic context. Following the work of De Mare it can be understood that differing dynamics come to the fore in differing group structures. Group analytic theory considers how social dynamics and 'primitive feelings' – those from early life – are more likely to come to the surface in the large group. I have also employed the mythological, archetypal and communitarian thinking of James Hillman (1989 Hillman & Moore) to my work, so now I take a synthetic position between these two philosophical viewpoints, reading the group not only in the social, but also the mythological context. For brevity, when using this word I will not define each time which frame I am referring to and hope that the context in which it sits makes it clear.

4 Webster's dictionary describes 'Apperception' as 1 : introspective self-consciousness; 2 : mental perception; especially : the process of understanding something perceived in terms of previous experience.

5 *Panpsychism is the view that mentality is fundamental and ubiquitous in the natural world. The view has a long and venerable history in philosophical traditions of both East and West, and has recently enjoyed a revival in analytic philosophy.*
Stanford *Encyclopedia of Philosophy* article (May 23, 2001; Jul 18, 2017)
The principle view I take is set in Whitehead's speculation that experience is at root a becoming as much as an perception of matter. Matter is only perceived as we perceive it because of experience. He proposes a 'panexperientialism' which sees all creation as symbiotically evolute. Evolution for him is not only a biological process but works down to the smallest energetic relations the universe co-creates. From Bohm's point of view, this is experience of what he sees as the implicate (interconnected and resonant whole) beneath the explicate experience of the everyday.

6 Dual aspect monism is a theory of mind that accepts that there is essentially one sort of stuff that is experienced as both spiritual and material that these are two sides of the same coin. This tradition is seen to begin with Spinoza (1632–1677) and is present in the Jung Pauli conjecture (2014).

7 EIN-SOF (Heb. אֵין סוֹף; 'The Infinite', literally that which is boundless), the Kabbalist name for the transcendent God, His pure essence: God in Himself, separate from His relationship to the created world (Jewish Virtual Library, 2022). Brian Lancaster says God is Ein Sof (without end), a term intended to convey the infinitude that is paradoxically both ever-present in the world and yet utterly transcendent (2004).

Chapter 1
Blake and Context

Healing

I am not a mechanism, an assembly of various sections.
And it is not because the mechanism is working wrongly, that I am ill.
I am ill because of wounds to the soul, to the deep emotional self
and the wounds to the soul take a long, long time, only time can help
and patience, and a certain difficult repentance
long, difficult repentance, realisation of life's mistake, and the freeing oneself
from the endless repetition of the mistake
which mankind at large has chosen to sanctify.

D.H. Lawrence

Eternity

He who binds to himself a joy
Does the winged life destroy;
But he who kisses the joy as it flies
Lives in eternity's sun rise.

William Blake (Note Book 43: E, p. 470)

An Introduction to Blake

William Blake (1757–1827) was an extraordinary figure of the late eighteenth and early nineteenth century. He was all but ignored in his time, but has been highly regarded since, and has much to offer us now. He is an outlier, separate from the main artistic cannon, outside of contemporaneous artistic and philosophical trends, although he developed in response to them. He was polarised against the rationalism of the Enlightenment, holding at the core of his work the ancient spiritual roots of our becoming. Our response to him can be complex but he is a powerful figure today influencing many. I have attended two large exhibitions in London over the last twenty years and both were packed from start to finish. Many focus upon his politically radical thoughts, but here I am more interested in his *vision and understanding of our becoming*, both exoterically and esoterically.

He lived in London during the flowering of liberal economic and social cultures and the Industrial Revolution. During this time, the population in London almost doubled from three quarters of a million in 1760 to 1.4 million in 1815. Between then and 1860, the population was to more than double again to nearly 3,200,000 (Old Bailie proceedings website). This was driven by migration as well as an increase in fertility and health.

I see that addiction as we now experience it is also linked to these social changes, which I am sure is more than coincidence. The first great outbreak of 'using' was the gin craze of the early 18th century, resulting in the Gin Acts of 1729–1751, and was driven by glut harvests. This symptom could be seen as an outcome of the changes brought about by many people leaving the land and moving to the cities, thereby becoming subject to the needs of capitalism and industrialisation, the mechanistic breakdown of agricultural communities and the atomisation of previously formed cultural structures. There is contemporary research that highlights the connection between broken attachments and addiction (Gill, 2014). Addiction in this context I see as the material relation to a dead object, an object we consume in place of a reciprocal relatedness we long for, personal and spiritual (Wright, in Gill, 2014). Blake clearly offers us an image for the renegotiation of this struggle in his Job narrative.

Blake was holding the position of the historical and spiritual, the revelatory and esoteric, in contrast to the rationalist Enlightenment values he was born into, when reasoned materialism burst into life and led to industrialisation. He has been called the last prophet, exemplifying the impact and influence of direct inspirational experience, which is the root of his work and lived experience. He is seen as a proto-Romantic, presaging the thinking to come. I suggest that his thinking is still profoundly relevant to us today.

The scientific and secular changes that Blake witnessed evolved out of 17th-century thinking, exemplified in Cartesian dualism (1641) and the rational mechanistic science of Bacon (1561–1626) and Newton (1642–1727), both of whom Blake railed against. There are similarities between Blake's time and our own, such as the liberal economic political organisation and a fourth industrial revolution, shifting from manufacture to the gathering and manipulation of consumer information, automated intelligence and the development of a virtual world that is becoming more habitable (at least in fantasy). This revolution may well offer us as much disruption as the one Blake witnessed. I see that this is facilitating a change in the way we perceive the world and our place in it, driven by the rapidly increasing number of us and our developing capacity to symbolise and communicate en masse through technology. As Harari (2014, 2016, 2018) argues these changes do not come without threats and impacts upon what might make us human as we identify yet more with the metaphor of mechanism and the machines we create from that spiritually blind but pervasive idea.

Blake experienced the naturalisation of the self (Baressi & Martin in Gallagher, 2011, pp. 38–40; Martin & Baressi, 2000) through the thinking of Locke and Hume. There was a movement away from the idea of a soul, and a more participatory medieval consciousness, toward the rationalisation of selfhood into a mechanistic structure of thought. Blake protested against this spiritual blindness, in his terms 'Ulro', and a hegemony of rational thought, to the detriment of the person as a whole and their divine being, or the 'True Man'. According to Solomon (1993), Blake devotes Plates 7–10 to this experience of Ulro. Tweedy (2013) eloquently discusses this rationalist hegemony through the 'Myth of Urizen' in the context of McGilchrist's thesis of the hegemony of the left brain's rationalist, partial and mechanistic experience of the world, so prevalent in the 18th century and also, McGilchrist would argue, today.

Blake's *Job* can be read as focusing upon the individual, drawing God inside as an internal felt presence, his 'Jesus the Imagination'. He would go further, seeing the world entirely as an inner experience and the external world as illusory. From a psychoanalytic viewpoint, Britton (1998) sees this as an expression of a 'true self' in the context of the psychoanalyst and paediatrician, Donald Winnicott's work. This is a connection to a true self within that is the source of life. One might link it to Bohm's implicate subject. In a Winnicottian context, a true self is the centre of life. It would be seen in opposition to a false self that forms as a life-destroying carapace to defend the true self against assault. Kalsched (1996) offers an interesting analysis of this structure in an archetypal context, postulating an internal archetypal spiritual defence mechanism that protects a traumatised inner true self.

The Job narrative can in this context be read as a breaking down of false self structures to reveal the true self. This is an individual narrative and as far as it goes accurate. However, I see in the Job a group narrative not only for the relationship between the individual and the group, but also set in the context of the resonant and relational whole, whether that whole is the group, the society, the species, the planet or indeed the divine. I see Blake's whole inside as referential to how we relate to the divine whole, much as David Bohm (1992, pp. 160–164) would suggest that there is an infinite subject (the I) that is buried behind an objectified self (the me). I would argue that a rigid sense of internal and external is a socially negotiated construct that we have reified overly and continue to do so through our pursuit of what McGilchrist refers to as the left brain hegemony and ubiquitous rationality (2009, pp. 428–462).

McGilchrist is not hopeful that we are able to shift away from this hegemony of the left brain. In fact he believes we push ever further toward a destructive and categorising mind, as witnessed in the 18th century. I am not so gloomy, but I would frame the changes needed in the context of an addiction, that we have become addicted to knowing in a rigid, rationalist, mechanical sense that excludes doubt and the complexity of our relational becoming. I fear we favour the repair of a mechanism over the receipt of a possibly disruptive new life.

From my experience, working with people suffering from addiction it is only the ability to receive life in its open and full context that allows the addiction to be let go.

I am, however, anxious as to the heat that might accompany any change we need to make or even the realisation that change is needed. People suffering with addiction will pursue to destruction a line until bare and empty. They have to appeal to a faith that new life is possible and utterly re-contextualise their thoughts. What cost, then, to change our collective current trajectory. This context I frame spiritually, although it is entirely possible to conceive of this as secular and relational. It is not the dogma that is important but the action. It is why I see the metaphor of addiction as key to our time, pointing to that which is missing, as I do in this Job narrative; the relationship between the individual and the collective, the particular and the whole. I see that Blake expresses this struggle clearly through his mythic vision.

Blake's polarisation against the Enlightenment and mainstream society of his time was expressed as railing against the dogma of the Deist church, materialist science and reason, particularly that of Newton, Locke and Bacon. The Deist faith perceived God as the divine engineer, sitting between the old church that promoted the link between God and soul, and sceptical atheism, which became the prevailing narrative of the Enlightenment. This led to clear alterations in a sense of selfhood. Blake was seen at best as eccentric, and probably mad, by the time he came to make this work and was progressing toward a death in poverty. I interpret him simply as pursuing his spiritual path. I do not see him in any way mad, but clearly visionary, and in touch with the experience of life as revealed and imaginal. He was capable of bearing this experience and articulating it so vividly that it still speaks to us today. Today, there is often confusion between the emergence of spiritual experience and the way it disturbs a fixed sense of reality and a psychotic breakdown. A category for this kind of experience was published in the DSM IV called Spiritual emergency and DSM V(V62.89)[1] called Religious or Spiritual Problem.

I see that Blake had mostly given up on the world by this time, at the age of 61 (1818). He was content with the rich inner experience and direct knowledge of the divine; however, at seemingly the last minute, he began to be more recognised and appreciated, as indeed the world altered its thinking, turned toward Romanticism, and society came to meet him.

This appreciation was much due to John Linnell (1792–1882), a successful portrait artist and landscape painter, who was introduced to Blake in the summer of 1818. He introduced Blake to Samuel Palmer (1805–1881) and the small group of artists who styled themselves 'the ancients', who admired and supported him for the rest of his life (Bentley, 2004). It seems that by this point Blake was at an extraordinary stage of spiritual development, having resolved his mythic and visionary journey in the context of the time he lived. I am reminded of a quote from the poet and artist, Theodore Roethke, who suffered deeply with his mental health: 'what is madness but nobility of soul at odds with circumstance' (Roethke, 1966). Blake was certainly at odds with the circumstances in which he found himself.

Ronald Britton (1998) saw Blake as an 'epistemic narcissist', i.e. someone having to form and stand by his own philosophy; however, if you see him holding the historic tradition of prophetic experience, particularly in a kabbalistic context, this is less sustainable.

I see him as a truly noble soul, but not mad, simply ahead of his time and at odds with the dominant philosophy. Churton (2014) describes Blake's experience as clearly imaginative and points the Moravian church of his mother as a primary inspiration. Higgs (2021) points to synaesthesia and a broader construct for the perception of reality. I think that his visions are simply mystical and aligned to the context in which he lived, such as those experienced by Hildegard Von Bingen or Julian of Norwich. Not a rational and reasoned structuring of experience but a revelatory imagining; less a left brain experiences than a right brain condensation of a myriad related experiences. We could think of this as an approach to symbol formation akin to Whitehead's (1927) notion of symbolism. The substructure of Blake's visions is interesting and might point to the context he experienced, which we will explore.

The approach I have taken to psychosis in my practice is to see it a confusion of meaning between internal imagined experience and external experience, which may or may not be a shared reality. This I would see as an archetypal frame, or taking a more psychiatric view, an inability to differentiate meaning, so there is either an excess of meaning or no meaning at all. On both counts, Blake would not appear either to be undifferentiated in his meaning or unaware that his perception is part of an imaginal construct, all be it an esoteric, deeply spiritual and developed one. As Spector suggests mysticism is 'the interaction between an expanded level of consciousness and an elevated plane of reality' (2001b, p. 12). Thoughts about the limits of imagination and the nature of reality I don't propose to address here, but clearly I take a broad view of the nature of imagination.

The Illustrations of the Book of Job was commissioned by John Linnell in the last years of Blake's life and completed two years before he died. Ostensibly, the commission was offered and taken to support him when he was in penury. There are two previous commissions of watercolours, one set for Thomas Butts in 1805 and a second for John Linnell in 1820. The contrast between the two is interesting, not only in terms of the differing coloration with access to new materials but also in the contrast in tone, which offers an insight into Blake's changing experience at this profound time in his life.

The *Job* can be seen as a condensation of his entire personal myth, formed over his lifetime and completed in the years leading up to 1820. According to Spector (2001a, 2001b) this mythic journey from linear exoteric Christian myth to cyclic Kabbalistic was completed in *Jerusalem*, his final and extraordinary but difficult prophetic poem. Spector's view that this is the completion of his journey toward a Kabbalistic view, suggesting his myth is rather traditional, and not merely an invention out of nothing, is to my mind coherent, and evidences the deep spiritual and esoteric journey embedded in the wisdom acquired from a lived life.

There are clearly references to Kabbalistic and hermetic ideas throughout this work, which we will see as we progress through the images. It is difficult to know what access he had to Kabbalistic thought. I don't know whether he could have met any practising Jewish Kabbalists. It would have been more likely that his work is structured in a Christian Kabbalistic context. We will see reference to this in the imagery in the frontispiece. However, between Plates 12 and 14 he makes a shift in the lateralisation of the plates by swapping the images of Orion and the Pleiades at a significant point, as Job's alienation from God is relinquished. This swaps the lateralisation of severity in Orion's belt and Mercy with the Pleiades and would suggest to me that he knew both as this lateralisation is swapped between Christian and Traditional Jewish Kabbalah.

He knew well the work of Jacob Bohme (1575–1624), the Christian mystic and Paracelsus (1493–1541), the Swiss physician, alchemist and philosopher through the work of Emmanuel Swedenborg, and can be seen to be profoundly moved by or at least congruent with Bohmeist thought (Fischer, 2004). Blake will have had access to the Hermetic Tradition and the neo-Platonist philosophers such as Plotinus, Proculus, Porphyry and Apuleius translated by Thomas Taylor (1758–1835), who he knew when he was thirty; so there are influences congruent with the Kabbalistic tradition that run through his work.

Blake & Self

Our main interest in this book is with Blake's imagery in the *Illustrations of the Book of Job* and the co-evolving process between Yahweh, Job and Job's community. We are looking at this from a 21st-century viewpoint, 200 years since its production. I see it now as an expression of a change in consciousness brought about through the number of us alive. It is easy to recognise it as an expression of the individual journey through our becoming, the changing of selfhood in the face of changing circumstance. However, I focus on this particularly as an expression of the relationship between the individual and the group, as a constant poetic becoming that we inhabit as groups and individuals co-evolving in a layered process that is relational, participatory and fluid. How in the context of our clearly related interconnectedness do we find our place in the order of things?

Blake offers insight into this changing relationship and articulates how we can reorder our relations to accommodate a new perspective. Far from looking back I see he looks also forward to the evolving context we now inhabit, which of course needs to include previous understandings of this unfolding process of change. This sits well with the idea that there is a shift in our perception of the context we inhabit, akin to the process of individuation in the Jungian canon and to transcendence of the ego in the Buddhist and Eastern – the realisation that the differentiation of subject and object is a false distinction. In this work, we are principally addressing that idea through Bohm's ideas. I see that the Blake illustrations offer a template for this that resonates with both an individual and group context. This is the move I conceive of from a consciousness of exploitation to a consciousness of resonance; in other words a receptive becoming resonant with the whole, which receives action into becoming through participation, rather than an exploitative imposition upon a partially perceived event. This is addressed directly by Blake at the end of this work, from Plates 18 to 21, and only fully expressed in the last plate before we return to the beginning of the cycle to repeat the process iteratively.

We are at the point where the understanding or experience of the divine is open to dialogue, particularly in the secular West. God as we have understood 'him', as an image of a fixed being, has changed. Blake was not faithful in this context. His divine was an internal experience of 'divine humanity' in the tradition of Swedenborg. I see we are living in a time of dialogue between faiths, including secular atheism. We are in search of a syncretic narrative that is resonant.

The man gods that preceded the hegemony of the one father god have taken on a new form, as Hillman (1975a, 1983; Hillman & Moore, 1989) suggests, through his polytheistic and poetic approach to psychology, re-emphasising a neo-Platonic frame and reviving the notion of psyche as soul. The gods have become psychologised, that is to say internal and relational. Pointing to the advantages of a polytheistic frame of imagination, and relation to a becoming beyond rational thought, Hillman emphasises this polytheism in the context of metaphor; not the reified literal living god as an object, but image as a participatory relation to a co-evolving process felt in the body. This leaves us with the question – what does this mean for me as an individual and how is that me considered? Not, who am I? But *what is me*? Hillman suggested to me at a workshop in 1992 that "the 21st century will not be about who am I but what is me". I was too young to take in his meaning, too deeply entrenched in my own self formation and the repair of others, wrestling with a pastiche of self-actualisation. Over time it has stayed with me as a thought, until now it seems prescient and clear. We are more in the frame of Bohm's 'infinite subject' than the objectified Lockean self. Blake's me is the internal divine, the 'True Man', not the rational or empiricist self, but a direct internal connection to the divine whole.

This has serious ramifications for both the narrative of self and how those narratives are to unfold. The question of 'what is me?' focuses us on a process we are a part of, as opposed to the mechanistic self, acting in time. As Barresi and Martin suggest (2011) following from William James' consolidation of self to its postmodern disintegration. How then do we find our place in the order of things; orientate our becoming in the context we live? Bohm and Whitehead look to the orbits of emergent events, the act of valuing and creating perceptually in the context of a creative whole, reframing our experience not as separate, as subject and object, but component of and connected to a whole, which itself is intrinsically creative. Our experience as part of a whole, broader than just the image of self, becomes orientated toward coherence, a congruence with the becoming structure we inhabit. The aim then would be to become *more coherent with the emergent unfolding process of the whole*, a spiritual experience not unlike that expressed by Blake's internal human divine, or the perspective of the right brain, as discussed in McGilchrist (2009, 2021) and Ray (2016).

Mystical thought such as Hermeticism, Alchemy or the Kabbalah have always considered such experiences. Bohm articulates this in the context of quantum dynamics, postulating an explicate order (time and space as we experience it) as a projection unfolding out of implicate quantum interconnectedness. Blake's image of seeing heaven in a wild flower, the world in a grain of sand or eternity in an hour, is an apperceptive and poetic expression of the implicate beyond and between the revealed moment. Hillman and Jung come to this through the world of imagination and hermeneutics, symbol and relation, rather than fact and matter, which is embedded in embodied experience. Symbols arise in and between us.

In the *Book of Job*, it is what happens bodily to Job, the physical hardship and loss he experiences in his community, including the divine Yahweh that is important. He is the occasion of the event, but what happens is for the whole community. There is a whole system we inhabit, broken into components, the experience of a lived life, but the breaking down into components is not the fragmentation of the rigid thought frame. Components are always given context by a whole.

Communal Vignette

As an example of the event arising within and between a group, I would like to share an experience from 14 July 2005. At the time I was leading the CORE Trust, a community-orientated project working with addicted people in central London. This was the week after four suicide bombs were detonated on the London transport network, one of which had exploded within 500 metres of the project. It was a meeting of the whole community, described as the 'house meeting', the designated space where we addressed the issues for the community which came out of the experience of the community.

It was a beautiful and sunny day. It felt as if the contrast had been turned up. There was a period of remembrance, standing in the street in silence, as a marking of the trauma, before the group met. This had an aggregate quality, much like Hopper's fourth basic assumption (2009), following the work of Bion (1961). He describes how a group can collapse into a basic assumption process between aggregation and massification; aggregation is self-focused and can look like an inchoate collection of individuals trying to reach out to each other but unsure and confused. Hopper's image for this is of whitebait on a plate. Massification is the other pole, rooted in the group turning away from selfhood, as if all members are mashed together. In either case, where members are isolated (aggregation) or merged (massification) no real relating is possible. Bion's basic assumptions fall in to three forms: dependence upon an imagined leader (BaD), pairing between two members of the group who will produce something the group can be interested in and follow (BaP), and fight or flight, where the group in fantasy takes flight from or attacks an external enemy (BaF). The remembrance on the street was aggregate and uncomfortable, so the group that followed had the quality of a mass, certainly at the beginning.

I will not go deeply into the process, but the theme of this particular house meeting was violence within and to the larger community, a fear of madness and powerlessness. This experience was not unsurprising, given the personal, political and social context we were experiencing as a City. This was a significant moment on the trajectory to the complex and confused politics we are currently experiencing.

The group explored these anxieties through a threat of violence between two members. Less mention was made of the violence close by, at Edgware Rd tube station. That had been discussed in other forums throughout the week. But it was brought into context in a real way through the symbol of a member's threat of violence – a taboo for the community. The internal tension was high and there was real fear that the community could not be contained or safe. The discussion was about how life, and indeed the life of the group, could be made safe, what were we to do and how were we to do it. There was an appeal to the staff team to provide containment and boundaries and calls to take events into their own hands – an expression of BaD. The tension rose in the group as no one could address directly either the external threat or the internal. I felt the tension both to want to do something, to set the boundary, to exclude the one seen as mad or violent, and to contain the experience, to allow for compromise and working through. The conversation continued skirting round the central issue of violence, internal and external, raising the temperature in the room.

Finally, a powerful member of the community leant forward and said "I do not feel safe. And I cannot stay here if I do not feel safe". This is a recurrent theme in all communities, particularly of course in the context of addiction and using, when the psyche is in such turmoil and there is such distrust and betrayal of the self. This was the point at which the tension reached its height. It felt as if the bomb had gone off in the room, and indeed as if it had gone off inside me.

My experience in these moments is to try to remain both coherent and thoughtful, to allow, to be aware of the experiences I was having internally and externally, not to collapse thought, but to feel and allow thinking to unfold out of the experience, to receive the moment into its own becoming. It was intense, deafening and terrifying. I was not sure I could contain the experience, certainly not sure what to do or how I would do it, even if I could figure out what that was. I knew, or at least felt, that I had to come up with something. That would seem to be my structural role in the project. But what? I could not make this safe. We could make it safe enough together, but I could do nothing. This is an example of what the leader can experience through BaD and the feelings that go with it.

A colleague came in just when I could not: "That is the point. It is not safe and we can't make it safe. Together we can do something to help each other, respect each other, help make it safer. But it isn't safe", and then, as if to drive home the point in our particular context, "particularly when we are using". This opened the group and the explosion was not in me but in the room. It was a relief to find that it could be contained by the group, with each individual held in context, a balance between the individuals and the group in relation. This communal sense developed as it was thought about and felt and discussed and borne together. This of course was not the end of the ramifications of the experience of the bombings, but a community trying to bear what had been an intentionally terrifying experience in the context of political and social difficulties unfolding in London and indeed across the world. I saw it then as a new post-modern form of war bringing itself in to our lives.

The focus in this group was on integrity of being, without retaliation for insult, to name that and not pretend it was safe. Life is not safe. Death is ever present. Of all people, those suffering with addiction are some of those who know this most acutely. However, for the most part it is the little death of the proximal self, the specific adaptation in and to context that is borne, not literal death, until of course it isn't and life, or at least this mortal life, stops. I could not make it safe and it was not safe. However, we as a community could bring light to those fears and try to work with them, the context they were from and which formed them. We could go round and round the social, personal and in this case political conflicts that arise within and between us, and try to bear and understand them, allowing them to move, to change and to be understood. For me, this is the key in group, if we can create sufficient space to make the unbearable bearable; alone this is profoundly difficult.

Later, in a supervision group, much of the staff team were more interested in a regulatory frame that would provide rigid and authoritarian containment. They wanted to move toward a rule as a defence against the horror of our broken humanity. In the project, we had deliberately kept rules to a minimum to avoid just this polarisation, so that we could explore the possibility of building our own boundaries. I was aware of the limitations of this, given the nature of the internal process and its unpredictability in the collective context. Rules could do nothing to meet addiction and its, only a tolerance and the willingness to explore how change might take place, perhaps allowing for a choice to live. At that point, boundaries could be developed between people as they began to cohere to the unfolding process of their lives. The members of the group knew this, but the despair and defeat, rage and outrage was palpable, and there was little place for it to go except a reactionary and regressive ossification to rule. We felt the group disintegrating, like the experience depicted in the early plates, and we could only just hang on to the capacity for growth through imagination. This experience is clear in Plate 3.

In the context of these meetings, it was my responsibility as the leader of the project to take a particular role and hold a particular frame during this process. It is one that I am familiar with, so I felt as comfortable as one can under the circumstances, but there is a negotiation between the needs and integrity of my own psyche, and that of the group, that the role affects. They are co-created between the members and mutually negotiated, I would say, received. It is why I could not speak, and my colleague needed to. I could not act authentically as rigid authority. I could only hold the communal despair until something more true and real arrived. This is a clear example of the idea that I am trying to articulate of the negotiation of the boundaries between the group and its members, and the symbol formation necessary to facilitate that dialogue. For me, this was not to collapse into a fixed image or idea but a bearing of the images of fear and threat, and an appeal to the collective to hold this process.

The interplay between the individual and the group, the symbolic negotiation between various needs and images in dynamic flow, unfolding in a developing context, is what David Bohm (1996) describes as dialogue. I will say more of this as we go through the plates, but the state of mind required to engage with it is an attention that experiences a transcendence of the proximal meaning frame to the context in which that meaning is embedded. I hope the example above shows that by not collapsing the event into a framework where rules are offered, and something supposedly known about how to keep the group safe is forced allows for the exploration of what was really there: in this instance the existential fear of violence, self-destruction and hate. These are feelings we need to incorporate in a communal context, both as individuals and a community of individuals in relation. We were able to form the relational capacity that can provide for the containment of experience. To collapse it is to deny this possibility, which we arrived at as a group. It was a creative solution to a terrifying problem.

I read Blake's *Job* as an expression of this experience. Through his suffering, he is able to transform his own experience and that of the community in which he is embedded. This transformation takes the form of a transcendence that recognises the divine roots of our experience. Bohm's implicate beneath the explicate (1980); Jung's collective unconscious beneath the individual unconscious (Samuels et al., 1986) and Whitehead's primordial nature of God (PR, 344). This is valuing the proximal event of becoming that we witness, which is a process of creative coherence with the unfolding moment and its archetypal organisation. There are many forms that the proximal image can take but the felt sense of the coherence is humanly consistent. Cultural adaptations may differ but the functional experience is the same.

The Evolution of Coherence and the Felt Sense

Now, we face a time of development and synthesis, as evolutionary processes fall into the timescale of human thought. They are no longer boundaried by biological processes taking many centuries, even if those have been perceived as divine intervention, graceful or otherwise. Evolution is a function of human culture in context.

Sloan Wilson (2015) argues that religious cultural development is evolutionarily adaptive. This adaptation forms functional groups that can interrelate, achieve tasks, manage resources for the good of the group and sustain altruism. He argues that from an evolutionary point of view altruistic groups are more successful than groups full of selfish individuals. He cautions that this is a functional process. It is the altruism at the root of group coherence which is the issue, not the proximal adaptation that might evolve; not any one dogma, but the altruistic outfall of that structure. This is congruent with Whitehead's perception that the universe is built out of symbiotic organic processes of evolution. Religious insight can then be seen as an adaptive structure for organising groups; it offers a means of considering the nature of human experience as we adapt and co-evolve with a creative universe. Whitehead would suggest that it is the consequent nature of God that provides the ultimate value, the creative value of the whole for the particular event. It is the felt experience of the divine in the moment of experience that allows for the valuing of the most creative event to come in to being. He suggests that this experience is felt as the love of God. Here, he shows his Anglican roots but also gives insight to the felt sense that goes with a move towards coherence.

The choice for altruism has a felt component as much as a rational one. For me, this felt component, in and beyond the symbol, is the more important part of becoming, as Whitehead suggests with his model of a symbiotic universe that is felt. This relates directly to Blake's lived experience of our divine nature, the ineffable beyond the material matter of fact, which he expressed through his visionary capacity to imagine. We live first and think later. Life is experience-led, not abstracted, although meanings and concepts as abstractions inform experience and become events in themselves. Meaning arising out of event then informs the future connections of those events, which is the resonant and relational experience of consciousness. One of Whitehead's key speculations is that 'experience goes all the way down' (Mesle, 2008, pp. 35–70; Whitehead, PR, 116). Like matter, it accrues from the quantum level of probabilistic relationships. Feeling accrues to experience from the lowest sub-atomic level. However, Whitehead gives primacy to this feeling. For him, the world is an experienced phenomenon – pan-experientialism – not a phenomenon of matter.

In so far as the proximal adaptation, the dogma is identified as the function, we run the risk of reification of that function, the 'fallacy of misplaced concreteness' – to see meaning as fixed and consistent over time rather than an emergent product of the events that surround it. This is to see as necessary what is in fact contingent. I believe this as true for self as well as religious narratives; both are fictions. Bohm points to this idea when he discusses the fragmentary nature of thought (Bohm, 1994) – any thought is only a partial representation of the instant in hand, this idea is present, for instance, in the confusion between the archetype and the archetypal image: i.e. that the archetype is not concrete whereas the image has a solidity to it. The image is not the archetype but a cypher for it. This differentiation is essential for the place in which we find ourselves negotiating our symbolic life. The symbol contains within it the felt sense of experience, but the image around which that constellates is like a map; not the terrain of the actual experience, but a representation. Bohm uses the ideas of Korzipski (1879–1950), the philosopher who coined the phrase 'the map is not the territory' (1933) and importantly for Bohm (1987, p. xvi–xvii), 'what you say a thing is, it is not'; it is not the word but something beyond the word that the word alludes to which we experience.

This of course has implications for the nature of self and the narrative we form to perceive that structure as coherent, which is represented in Blake's *Job* as 'Satan of the Selfhood', a reified image that becomes redundant as the process of becoming unfolds. However, it is the scaffolding through which we come to know our life and all too easily identify with and cling onto. Its reification and collapse becomes the road through which we open to a new life, as is shown throughout *The Illustrations of the Book of Job*.

Again, we return to the primacy of Hillman's question – what is me? not, who am I? I see that Blake's *Job* not only questions assumptions about self, but offers a frame for imagining its processes of change, both incremental and proximal, profound and transcendent. I see these processes not only in an individual frame but also in the group and social context in which the individual frame is embedded.

This process of a changing perception and experience of self I believe evidences the shift from a consciousness of exploitation to a consciousness of resonance: the conscious recognition that we are component in and acting within a wider context, and that we have to receive resonantly our experiences in community, perhaps in communion. We must not act out of a rigid historic thought frame, as we will exploit and objectify the environment, most likely from the seductive aim of making it safe. This is the relation of infinite subject to infinite subject, not object to object; the life-affirming and creative experience between Winnicott's true selves.

We have reached the point where our evolutionary development has overtly and consciously altered the context within which we live; we are now clearly actors, if not the main actors, within the system that we experience, and not simply subject to it. The world as we now create it is perceived as intersubjective and consciously dialogic. The differing proximal adaptations for common pool resource group formation are openly in dialogue and tension experientially and volitionally. There is a search for an image that can contain this process and bear this function. The regression to fixed and tribal images of power is clearly not the answer. I see that Blake's *Job* provides such an 'image', in that it offers a view where one acts altruistically from an understanding of the context inhabited; the opening to receiving experience into becoming received in the fluid frame of a sense of 'I' as the orientating subject.

So, not withstanding both Bohm (1996) and Ray's (2008a) referencing of the hunter-gatherer's world experience, we have in some sense become masters of our environment, material and psychological, leaving us with the despair inevitable in that realisation and the concomitant impact on ideas of self. To use a psychoanalytic model – separation from and need for mother, indeed a fixed idea of mother and mothering, is now a conscious struggle on a global scale, as we form new group relations in a limited and finite environment, and re-imagine our place in this context. The imagination of a separate and masterful object that can operate on a blind system no longer will do; it will and is driving us to destruction.

One could see that we have been in co-creative dialogue with our environment since time began, but now this is clearly conscious and has implications for how we recognise our humanity. Importantly, I see this as an expression and a reflection of the system as a whole, as Rilke's thought 'that it is inside human beings where God learns' (1924). How do we 'right-size ourselves', as those in the Twelve Step Movement might say, recognise *our* place, our sense of self, in the context of this process? How do we find our place in the order of things and consciously become coherent with the system as a whole.

In short, we have become so powerful a component in the system of the planet we can no longer approach it as an infinite objective resource. We need to alter our perceptual and relational experience to recognise our place in the system, which is a co-creative, intersubjective and relational place. This process is in train, but uncomfortable, as it challenges the way we see ourselves. I suggest that Blake shows us a way to re-imagine this context individually and together, but alters the context of our own self, away from a fallacy of misplaced concreteness to see ourselves as individual object to a fluid sense of our becoming and participating in the process in which we are particular expressions individually and collectively. This is finally expressed in Plate 21 as the cooperative whole is experienced, before the fall into the next perishing of an iterative process.

Our Psyche

It is worth noting, as Harari (2016, p. 11) and Sloan Wilson (2015) both point out, that the speed of our evolutionary development has taken us to the top of the food chain in only a few thousand years, rather than the millions that it had taken up until now to embed an apex predator in an entire reciprocal ecosystem. Harari argues we lack the majesty to manage this responsibility; the co-evolved structures of limitation are not there. Lions had two million years evolving within their environment to fill their niche and have a matching confident psyche and ecosystem. We are still encumbered with the middle of the food chain psyche of feeling as if we have not got enough and the resultant kill or be killed, eat or be eaten underlying fantasies are the source of anxiety and neurosis. We have the underlying psyche of meerkats, who, it would appear, cute as they are, have a capacity for murder greater than our own.

Harari argues that our ability to cooperate in large numbers, brought about through consciousness, cognition and our capacity to symbolise, gives us power beyond our imagination. The management of this has to be found culturally, as we take responsibility for our place in the order of things. If there is one thing we can do with this adaptive facility, it is to adapt successfully to our environment, to use our capacity to symbolise, to transcend our paranoid psyche. It is indeed inside human beings where God learns, or, to follow Blake, where God now lives. We now have the responsibilities that we ascribed to that idea, and I am arguing we have them relationally. I am wont to turn this image on its head and look at this from the context of the whole. Our imagination in this context is at the evolutionary cutting edge of the system in which we live, but for that it is not ours alone, but a function of the entire system. The individual self in this context is an ever-changing narrative, born out of a complex and auto-poetic system, working toward homeostasis. The internal imagination of the whole, the 'True Man', as Blake offers us, gives us the apperception of this context as a context of reception. How can we receive into life the divine whole in all of its resonant beauty?

What I see in the Job story, and particularly in Blake's expression of the narrative, is the re-introduction of this contextual awareness, but in a different form. One might call this the functioning of McGilchrist's right brain (2009), expressing, at a point of great cultural omnipotence, our relationship to the context in which we live. I offer an image for reframing that relationship as a cultural shift from exploitation to resonance. However, and to me most importantly, his insight is based upon his own deep personal experience of the process, of becoming as a human creature alive to and participant in an eternal process.

Blake's work is not academic, but experienced and felt, and the better for being outside of the academy, particularly in the context of his day. Blake brings to the ferment of reasoned omnipotence the voice of the revelatory, the voice of God. Not a God of grace and ransom, omnipotent and salvationist, but a God of relations and participation. This is Jesus the Imagination inside of us, reflecting the co-creating universe and of course that presence in others. By ransom, I mean a construct of Jesus saving us through his divine grace, rather than a relational approach to redemption through our actions as beings; the humanisation of God's image into a relational and intersubjective dynamic. Self in this context becomes an ambivalent thing. What we think, we think for the world, and we have to accept responsibility for the symbolic context in which that thought takes place – the context of the whole.

Blake articulates his vision framed in four platonic levels with its divine context in a letter to Thomas Butts (1802) thus, we will explore these levels later in the book:

> Now I a fourfold vision see
> And a fourfold vision is given to me
> Tis fourfold in my supreme delight
> And threefold in soft Beulahs night
> And twofold Always. May God us keep
> From Single vision & Newtons sleep

The Frontispiece

This image sets out the journey Blake and Job are going to take us through in its most condensed form: we are shown the descent into incarnation, into the particular and the return to resonance with the whole, the fall into becoming that can be seen across Blake's art, and then an uplifting of our felt experience to the divine apperception of the whole. Blake will describe the process in detail over the next twenty-one plates, depicting Job's encounter with Yahweh; finite humanity's encounter with the infinite divine, and, for me, humanity's part in the context of the whole.

From a Jungian perspective, this process has the fundamental archetypal structure of the death and rebirth cycle which will be seen in this book from the perspective of self-formation. In volume nine of *The Collected Works*, *The Archetypes and the Collective Unconscious* (1939), Jung discusses the archetype of rebirth often also framed as: Metempsychosis – the transmigration of souls, Reincarnation, Resurrection and Re-birth within the span of one life (which he divides into two forms – a renewal with and without change to the personality and finally participation in transformation). Towards the end of the paper he focuses upon 'natural transformation [as] individuation', the natural processes in the unfolding of an individual life where we might consider that changes in self could be seen as a death of an old form and renewal of a new. For Jung, this is the process of unfolding into the greater internal unconscious personality – the Self. In this book, I am interested in psychological and spiritual transformation, following Whitehead's (Cobb, 2008, pp. 75–76; PR, xiii–xiv; Segall, 2013) doctrine of perpetual perishing and becoming, similar to the archetypal notion of death and rebirth described by Jung, and the fall and return of Blake's Job.

Job's journey is a descent myth. This will be set in relation to the group and to the whole that the group is embedded within. I have worked with this process in communities, where individuals and their processes of change are reflected and contained in the group. From this point of view, the death and rebirth cycle can be seen as an exile from community, an encounter with death and a return to the community to be witnessed as changed. We used this idea extensively when working with addicted people at the point of change. I will articulate that process as we go forward through Whitehead's (Cobb, 2008, pp. 75–76; PR, 21–22) creative emergence of perpetual perishing and becoming and Bohm's (1980, chapter 7) unfolding and refolding of implicate becoming.

I would describe this condensed image, showing the whole in relation to the particular as the 'poetic moment', following Whitehead's metaphysics, the resonant relation of nested organic and inter-relational systems in which I see self as contextualised. These processes of experience and becoming reach down to the smallest levels of creation to the quantum. This presents an emergent frame for the perception of becoming. In my experience, this is felt in the body, a particular intense attention to our subjective experience which transcends our perceived separateness, our understanding of self and other.

This could also be seen as a 'transitional space' (Winnicott, 1971) the intersubjective, or the co-created experience, the space between and within where the emergent and relational becomes manifest. David Bohm 's (1996) work on dialogue in group, and participation in the ongoing process of becoming, describes an explicit experience formed, or unfolded, out of an implicate and interconnected whole, beneath and within which the particularity of our lived experience is contextualised. I believe this perspective offers us an opportunity to perceive non-hierarchical, linear or mechanical frames for the unfolding of experience. Blake perceives this as a journey of participatory incarnation, as shown particularly in this work the 'Vision of the Last Judgement' (1810) and 'The Sea of Time and Space'[2] (1821). He also sees it as a perpetual and cyclic process, almost as I would see it with each breath.

The clouds which we see at the foot of the image represent for Blake the veil between the divine and the worldly, suggesting this process is happening in the divine realm, which for Blake was within, an internal perception of the creative universe. The figures we see are the Elohim, the builders of creation, ending finally in Christ, Blake's image for 'Jesus of the Imagination'. For Blake, this was a real and extant object. According to Foster Damon (2013), these figures are 'the whole course of human thought' in search of an ideal by which to live. The first is Lucifer the egoist; the next three represent the infernal system of Justice: Meloch the executioner, who annihilates all opposition and fails through impatience; next is Elohim judge and definer of guilt, who creates Adam and Satan, then Shaddai who fails through anger. This leads to Paschad, bewilderment, then Jehovah as the bringer of the law, and finally Jesus who subverts the whole system though forgiveness and is sacrificed to Satan. (FD, p. 134). Foster Damon (1966) also notes that this structure is represented as a descent and return through the characters of the Elohim that are seen on the frontispiece. The correspondence is Lucifer, Plates 1–2; Molech, 3–4; Elohim, 5–6; Shaddai, 7–8; Paschad, 9–10; Jehovah, 11–12; Jesus, 13–14; then in reverse: Jesus, 15; Jehovah, 16; Paschad, 17; Shaddia, 18; Elohim, 19; Molech, 20 and Lucifer, 21.

These thoughts chime with McGilchrist's perception of brain lateralisation (2009). He proposes a right brain whole perspective contextualising a left brain linear processing, the dialogue between which achieving action in the world. Using McGilchrist's brain lateralisation, Tweedy (2013), a Blake scholar, stresses the tension between the linear and mechanical nature of left hemispherical perception and the right holistic and contextual view in Blake's work.

> Indeed, one of the main significations of the 'left' in Blake's work is to denote unconscious, automatic, or mechanical processes. Rationality is conscious of the universe but unconscious of itself: the figure of Newton, bent over, analysing his own ratios and figurations, is a potent embodiment of Blake's dictum that 'He who sees the Infinite in all things sees God. He who sees the Ratio sees himself only'.
>
> (pp. 297–298)

Here then, Tweedy points to the recontextualisation of self that I see in terms of the poetic moment, self as a perceptual tool for the homeostatic coherence of an organism in relation to and a component of an undivided whole. It is here perceived by Blake as an individual relating to and perceiving the divine within and through the iterative process of fall and return, death and rebirth, perishing and becoming. I believe we can see this in the frame of the group, the fall into event and then a raising back to poetic resonance as a group process, also as processes for the group and the individual members in dialogue, a context then that is personal, social and systemic-cosmic in Bohm's terms, all of which is perceived in the context of an open fluid and perpetually reforming relational subject, which is perpetually transcended. This adventurous shift in perception offers the spiritual freedom that Blake presents to us as vision and poetry.

The Poetic Moment

> META
> Metaphor happens in the body
> The resonance of things are
> Digestible not decidable
> Like the touch we share.
> The space between and
> The space within oscillate
> With divine intent.
> The Holy action of becoming
> That engenders all living.
> (Wright, 2019)

I have chosen The Poetic Moment as the title to this section to reflect my particular perspective of the synthetic and creative experience of psychotherapy. When we sit as therapists in a room with individuals or groups we have to think and feel on many levels. I see this as similar to the process of reading or writing poetry. I have shared a poem from 2019 that is trying to understand this experience and articulate it. Also, perhaps, this title is a nod to Blake's idea of Poetic Genius. I see our work as a process of becoming, as co-created and emergent, set between two or more subjects, and the context within which they are formed.

The image I am presenting is one of the emergence of creative symbol through which we participate in the becoming of life. In the West, where I live, this is attached to self. I suggest self as a tool of perception and of apperception, where the process reaches beyond its proximal construction of experience to something new. I perceive we are at a point of some collective change in this context. I see it in my practice and in the world at large. I see a collective shift synthesising everything we have thought, felt and experienced so far into a new perception. Perhaps it was ever thus but now it appears we are experiencing a shift from a consciousness of exploitation to a consciousness of resonance, notwithstanding the regressive eddies of particular events, occasions and social movements. We are exploring this through Blake's vision and Bohm and Whitehead's thinking, who all see the whole of life reflected in the individual event. As therapists I see we sit with this experience open to it and try to allow for the most creative event to unfold. We use a myriad of theories but at root I think this is what we do. Theory here is a useful word as its roots are the same as theatre, so there is a show, a metaphorical exploration of the event in hand, exactly as Bohm describes the explicate (1980).

We experience our unfolding life with a general sense of the onward march of time, an interior and exterior, a narrative, a sense of self in relation to others and the world and for the most part, with autonomy. Differing cultures will and do emphasise differing components to this frame and differing contextual relationships, but as a general image it is consistent across humanity – people in relation to others and their environment.

It is also clear to me that most of these structures become illusory as we move toward the edges of our experience. Time, for instance, although perceived as linear and entropic, breaks down at the very small. Subjectively psychological time differs from dream time, from social time, from mythic time, from clock time, from a lifetime, and a spiritual sense of time. In the realm of physics, mechanical, Newtonic, rigid, abstract time and space has given way to a flexible and curving Einsteinian space-time amalgam, and at the quantum level, wave formations replace matter as probabilities, not measurable points. Bohm and Peat makes the same point about time, self and thought (1987, pp. 102, 223–227), as does Whitehead with regard to creative advance (PR, 35). Nothing is fixed, but a series of probabilities which accrue together through continued emphasis. In this context, our self narrative breaks down under linear scrutiny; is it in the body, mind, feelings, thoughts, relationships, social context, habitual repetition of an imagined idea; all of these or none of them? Is it a fluid, socially negotiated narrative, or a fixed object? Bohm answers this with the paradox of the observer and the observed; the observer and the observed are one. The subject 'I' and the object 'me' are one.

Particularly in the West, we perceive a self in context, which acts in its environment and is acted upon, a 'being'. This idea can be brought back, in a Western perspective, to a Platonic and Pythagorean root; through, for instance, influence on the Christian church. Plato's construction of 'Soul' or 'Psyche' is as the essential self, which Socrates argues for in the *Phaedo* (387–386 BCE). There are many ways to construct the notion of self-formation. I am taking a depth psychological, transpersonal and emergent sense of self, which I would set in a narrative context. This is self as a necessary fiction, in which I see a receipt and orientation emerging out of the process of our becoming, but not fixed or real. From a Buddhist perspective, this individual illusory perception can be transcended to perceive beneath the creative process of becoming in play, the creative universe reflecting upon itself, what is called pure awareness. Something like this is also true with Blake, a perception beyond individual selfhood to something greater. Shown in the later plates as the image of god is internalised in Plate 17, an apperception of our becoming is perceived and experienced. However, as Shelia Spector suggests he uses a more western Kabbalistic model. I am not intending to say these are the same experiences because they arise through differing metaphors, but I would see a correspondence and that correspondence is human.

From a group analytic perspective, this self is context driven and socially negotiated, a nodal point in a social matrix. I perceive that we hold this narrative together, creatively, through a poetic resonance. I believe the fixity of rigid being is illusory, notwithstanding the work I have done to support these structures in people's life development. The bringing together of experience and its symbols to create something third, something new, a novel symbolic event, separate from, but incorporated in and resonant to, the components that form it. Approach this perception with too much linearity, too much literal identification, too much of the attitude of the mechanistic and of course it will disappear in a mass of contradictions. However, hold oneself lightly, present and open to experience, and the whole context unfolds into life joyously and imaginatively, just as Blake's visions unfolded.

There is a tension at the heart of Platonic philosophy between being and becoming, which Whitehead addresses (Mesle, 2008, p. 50), reversing Plato's implicit focus on being, found in the *Timaeus* (360–347/8 BCE) and *Phaedo*, to a perpetual becoming and perishing. Whitehead conceives of a perpetual and ongoing process which generates 'events' and 'occasions' out of previous events and are then themselves precursors – predicates – of possible events to come. The fixity of rigid being, in this context, is illusory, a passing moment in an ongoing flow of becoming and perishing. We hang on to our rigid identifications to these past events at our peril. The image for self that is formed through and with these events shifts as these events shift. For me, the way he conceives an event in this process is crucial. It is not through the action of the past upon the present, but a reception of the past into the present. The new event is received into life through value in the present. This valuing then informs event and the events to come, which are all part of an unbroken whole. Blake shows us this experientially through the passage of the plates.

This speaks to me of the bearing and shared valuing that is experienced in psychotherapeutic practice and offers a radical perspective for the relational nature of becoming. Whitehead's perception sits on the edge of the mechanistic Newtonian universe and the thinking of the new physics. He sits between the two, on the cusp of the Quantum. Some see the conception of actual occasions as the building blocks of life, materially and experientially as analogous to quantum events (Garre, 2006). As a theoretical physicist, Bohm takes a more directly quantum perspective, describing the explicate emergence of event out of the implicate whole beneath, and within the unfolded experienced moment. Both Bohm and Whitehead point to a receptive and creative becoming though which we apperceive. The self then would be a reflection of the wider whole, not an owned and discrete event separate from that whole.

For me, this has practical relevance to the work I do; it is not what I do to a patient that helps them come to terms with their experience, but the capacity I have to receive their experience and value it that creates the possibility for some new adventure in becoming, in which they may participate. I do not do to, but whatever is done is done together – a mutual reception. This is clearly reflected in the Blake plates, particularly as we see in Plates 11 and 12, where the old is challenged and a new context is indicated, and in Plate 19 where the benefit of a new relation is received into life.

This reception is perceived for me through imagination. The world is seen through the images and the symbols we generate, the juxtaposition of events creatively and socially negotiated. These symbolic events then accrue to philosophies, myths and stories, which inform and recreate perception. I see that ideas, myths, symbols and people that form them are a fluid system of experience, inter-relating and in dialogue. In some real sense, the symbols we create take on a corporeality, if, however, abstracted from the event in which they are formed. They sit within and between us, like Winnicott's[3] transitional phenomena, events in experience, alive and becoming.

This receptiveness and imagination has resonance with McGilchrist's perception of the dialogic process between the left and right brain, both mutually receiving the other's perspective in a critical context. The right brain offers contextual perception, which is deconstructed and codified in the function of the left brain, then returned to and recontextualised as a function of the right. At its best, this is a circular dialogue, which McGilchrist suggests is not dissimilar to a Hegelian dialectic, or for that matter Jung's notion of the transcendent function (1958), the relationship between the conscious ego and the unconscious Self. Blake developed a complete and functional expression of this dialogic process, founded in the Western esoteric tradition and Kabbalistic thought.

A VIGNETTE

As an example of what I mean with an individual, I would like to refer to a moment experienced with a performer and a poet who has a belief and imaginal system, which would be congruent with the esoteric components of Blake's work and what the poet and Blake scholar, Kathleen Raine, refers to as the underground river of Western thought (1979, p. 2). They contextualise much of their life in this frame, with an interest in the medieval, and how it might inform our current culture. This could provide a deep understanding for the changes we have experienced during the early modern times and the kind of linkage Francis Yates[4] (2001) makes between medieval philosophy and science. They also have an understanding of Hillman's work, which takes a similar perspective to Blake, seeing imagination as the glue between spirit and matter.

During our work together, they came to the point of remarking that they were not afraid of death: 'it is simply a moving from one plane to another, you do this and you do that and then...'. I replied immediately that 'this was always denial', even within the traditional Platonic framework of metempsychosis, of souls passing in and out of this plane of existence, which would be at root in this esoteric metaphor.

What had come to mind was the experience of working with addicted people when they are beginning to try to find something to have faith in after the horror, self-betrayal and the semi-death of use. At this point, the denial of death is broken. It is a stark and naked moment in front of actual physical death as a present possibility. The choice to live has to be made actively. Blake articulates this moment between Plates 11 and 12, where Job's shattered life is reset and something in him dies. For Blake, this is Job's self-righteousness and the context of his life is changed to open into a new world view. For me, what is surrendered is the fixed image of self that no longer bears accurate witness to lived experience. This is seen to unfold into the process of the contextual, between Plate 12, a new realisation, and 16, the surrender of Blake's 'Satan of the selfhood'. In this moment, when faced with utter loss and self-betrayal, the hollowing out of selfhood that using engenders, there is only a moment to moment faith, and thereby the possibility of renewal. It is a terrifying defeat. This patient had experienced this level of loss and self betrayal in their life, and it was referenced in the percussive nature of my response. However, what is less frequently articulated is that this choice is with us perpetually, as Blake suggests in his view of the last judgement, as a perpetual fall and redemption; this also was resonant in the timing of our shared experience as they met this response.

My personal experience working with people is that this is a constant truth, redolently seen with addiction, but a truth with every breath for all of us, mostly not consciously engaged with, but habitually glided over. Unless confronted with the difficulty of harsh experience, which brings our attention to this letting go, the renewal goes unnoticed. For me this reaches to the core of our suffering, and is what arose in my response to my patient: a confrontation of the stepping over of the moment when the old perishes.

So I see we perpetually face a death, a death of a self, for a new sense of self to emerge in its place, born into and from the context we inhabit. At crucial moments in our life, such as the ending with addiction, it becomes starkly clear. My experience of any shared moment of becoming, like this, is receptive. It is a process of value, of actual relational and experiential care in context. The genius of Whitehead's conception for this moment is the receipt into value that precipitates an event into becoming, an active allowing not an acting upon the world. The world exists and it is the value in the becoming moment that defines the event of that moment. This is for me more an experience of beauty than construction.

I was surprised by my sudden response and its percussiveness. They too were taken aback. It probably hurt. I felt some guilt, and felt that I had been clumsy, drawing attention too closely to the gap between their idea of their self and the actual event. I clarified my thoughts in the context of the Platonic soul leaving the body and the grief that might engender, as this seemed an appropriate metaphor. Death as the loss of finitude, event and experience. The finitude, the limit of the body, which offers the possibility of event, and then how finitude might reflect in a moment to moment way, as we set boundaries between ourselves and others.

In the context of the psychodynamic process, the event was able to help them understand something more grounded of the boundaries they needed to develop in their life; boundaries between themselves and others, and within themselves, so as to make sense of what was and wasn't their responsibility, to challenge omnipotent defences of loss and fear of abandonment, behind which often lurks the fear of death. This all points to the perpetual perishing of a fixed sense of self, to which we so easily cling, past its usefulness. This is self-righteousness, as Blake sees it, and we will follow his treatment of this through the plates.

How this reflects upon the Job narrative is something we will develop as we go through the book, but I hope this vignette picks up on threads that are important. The ideas of death and rebirth as a cycle and present in all moments we live, implicit if not explicit. This is a Blakean theme, in the context of his 'A Vision of the Last Judgement' (1810) which is perpetually with us. Addiction as a symptom expresses accurately this struggle in our collective and individual life. However, the point that I would like to emphasise is this poetic moment co-created between this poet and I, which brought together many things that in Whitehead's terms of process are rooted in previous experience and seed those to come. We could go further in Bohm's terms to the implicate whole beneath the explicate event, and see them actually reflected continually, in the unfolded moment of experience set in a body.

I have tried to articulate this shared experience in the poem below, which assumes a notion of the platonic soul.

The great loss

The moment comes
She all Suffering
Falls away.
The angels sing for joy
At your return.
One with source.
Infinitude beyond
The cellular.
Orbits then fall away
To their habitual probabilities
Marching Newton's matter to
The crack of doom.
With such loss the infinite
Is no consolation.

No repair for
Her generosity.
Limit beyond time
The lived, the shared, the
Event of our mortal frame.

Notes

1 V62.89 Religious or Spiritual Problem. Diagnostic and Statical Manual of Mental disorders 5th edition. (DSM-5)
   This category can be used when the focus of clinical attention is a religious or spiritual problem. Examples include distressing experiences that involve loss or questioning of faith, problems associated with conversion to a new faith, or questioning of spiritual values that may not necessarily be related to an organised church or religious institution. The new diagnostic category came from transpersonal clinicians worried at the misdiagnosis and treatment of people in the midst of spiritual crises.
2 Blake's condensation of Porphyry's (234?–305? C.E.) myth 'The Cave of the Nymphs', a description of the soul's Journey into incarnation and a moment in the 5th book of the Odyssey (Raine, 1979). Porphyry was a Neoplatonist philosopher born in Tyre in Phoenicia. He studied with Longinus in Athens and then with Plotinus in Rome from 263–269 C.E. and became a follower of the latter's version of Platonism (Stanford encyclopaedia of philosophy).
3 'Transitional phenomena refer to a dimension of living that belongs to neither internal or external reality; rather it is a place that both connects and separates inner and outer' (Abram, 1996: 311).
4 Francis Yeats 1899–1981 (1979/2001) links the beginning of modern science to alchemy, neo-Platonic thought and the mysticism of the late medieval and renaissance through Mirandello de Picola and Marecello Ficino. It is worth noting here that John Maynard Keynes, the economist and brother of the Blake scholar, Geoffrey Keynes, links Newton's discoveries to his alchemical work, and acquired Newton's black box of alchemical writings for Trinity College, Cambridge. This draws a line back to the thinking of the medieval that is hidden under our more modern thought and re-emerges in the Blake images, and for instance in Hillman and his interest in neo-Platonic thought.

Chapter 2

Perishing

> I have chosen the serpent for counsellor, & the dog
> For a school master to my children…
> My heavens are brass, my earth is iron, my moon a clod of clay,
> My sun a pestilence burning at noon, & a vapour of death in night.
> What is the price of Experience? Do men buy it for a song?
> Or Wisdom for a dance in the street? No! it is bought with the price
> Of all that man hath – his house, his wife, his children.
> Wisdom is sold in the desolate market where none come to buy,
> And in the wither'd field where the farmer plows for bread in vain.
> (FZii 398: E, p. 325)

In these few lines from *The Four Zoas* (1797) Blake sets out what I have taken a whole book to articulate.

In the first ten images of this piece, nearly half of the work, Blake describes the fall from self-righteous fixity to Ulro, spiritual blindness. We see Job's destructive downfall, the perishing of a fixed self-identity, as the context changes, then we experience the horror, despair and grief of Ulro – a life absent of spirit. To read this sequence as a description of individuation through contact between Job and Yahweh, or the ego and the Self, is in its small form an everyday iterative process gradually leading to deeper and deeper insight. However, in its grand form it is, as Raine (1982) describe, a map for the enlightenment process leading to unity with the whole, which for me is reminiscent of the left brain right brain recursive model of McGilchrist (2009, 2021).

I suggest that this can be read as a group process, but also from the point of view of the individual individuating within the group, who is also contained by the group. We can equally see the process reflected in the group, as it forms of its own sense of identity and culture. De Mare et al. (1991, p. 47) and Bohm (1996, pp. 78 & 141; Bohm & Peat, 1987, pp. 252–253) focus on dialogue. De Mare et al. take an analytic model, setting the formation of a group identity in the context of Freud's Ego, Super-Ego and Id, mapping them on to the group structures he names as ideoculture, socioculture and bioculture (1991, pp. 182–185). He imagines these interact in the way psychic structures do in the personality, to form a group culture.

As we will see, Bohm brings his framework of the implicate and explicate order, the apperception of the infinite whole unfolding through group dialogue into the explicate event. Both Bohm and De Mare focus on larger groups, between 15 and 60 people, when it is impossible to accommodate everyone's feelings, thoughts or assumptions. If approached with good will the polarising tensions that arise can be ameliorated by the differing positions of other members of the group and lead to creative thinking.

In these ten plates, we see the breaking down of the old order that is no longer coherent with experience, so the breakdown of rigid and fragmentary thought that Bohm (1992; 1996, pp. 48–61) sees as representational of the whole, and can be confused as such but in fact is only a component of that whole. He cautions against identification with this representational fragment as it fogs the mind to the implicate beneath. This grasps in a nutshell McGilchrist's (2009, pp. 93, 429–434) concerns with left brain thinking alone, without the recontextualisation held in the right brain. In the last plate, Blake shows us just this recontextualisation and roots it in the divine whole as one event.

Destruction

Plate 1
The Status Quo.
Thus did Job Continually

At the foot of this image is an altar inscribed with the words, "The Letter Killeth, The Spirit Giveth Life. It is Spiritually Discerned". Blake is bringing together the full weight of his experience and learning in the Job narrative, what he saw as a universal condition of human experience relevant to his moment and ours. In choosing the Job story, Blake develops the way that it speaks to our collective fears and guilts and uses it to show us our place in a fluid and uncompromising world. I read him as setting an individual narrative in a group and transpersonal context, which is also a struggle with the notion of divinity or spiritual context in a materialist world.

Raine (1982, p. 11) like Spector see that Blake spoke in the register of Old Testament prophets, which, following Swedenborg's thinking, addresses the inner spiritual core rather than the Enlightenment voice of reason, bounded by 'Newton's ratio'; this is the five senses separated from the divine and inter-connected presence of the world, or McGilchrist's left brain functioning. It is worth noting that in this image everything takes place inside the cloud of smoke from that altar, symbolising the inner life Blake so valued. I suggest that this internal order is what McGilchrist (2009, p. 93) describes as right brain functioning.

In this first plate, the family look happy and everything seems well. However, they are in a dangerously unstable place. The patriarch and his wife are dependent upon the holy books whose law directs their lives. They do not have an inner connection to their faith, and they are reliant upon the dogma contained in those books. The family is attentive and Job is wealthy – there are many sheep, a settlement and a church. However, the sheep and the dog are sleeping, not aware of the danger that is to come or the cause of it.

Raine (1982, p. 35) sees the wording on the line-drawn altar as an adaptation from St Paul's first epistle to the Corinthians, and the clearest indication of the fall to come:

> Which these also we speak, not in the words which man's wisdom teaches, but which the Holy Ghost teaches; comparing spiritual things with spiritual.
>
> But the natural man received this, not the things of the spirit of God: for they are foolishness unto him: neither can he know them, because they are spiritually discerned.
>
> But he that is spiritual judges all things, yet he himself is judged of no man. For who have known the mind of the Lord, that he may instruct him? But we have the mind of Christ.
>
> (1 Corinthians, 2.13–16)

Raine suggests that Blake held St Paul in high regard, because he saw in his writing the Swedenborgian teaching that the true man is not the natural body but the spiritual body. She suggests that Blake believed this was to know the mind of God (p. 35). The experience I bring to this is steeped in today's thinking, for example, the practice of Qui Gong and meditation. I would not see that the material and spiritual body are split in this form. The presence of spiritual experience is for me coincident with the physical body, which through its perishing provides limit to the unlimited experience of the subject, offering the capacity of consciousness in the form we experience it, the paradox that Bohm (1994, pp. 210–213 & 237–238; Bohm, 1996, pp. 69–71), refers to as the observer and the observed. To literalise too strongly either way, with matter or spirit, is to falsely concretise something that is fluid and reflected in its components. I offer throughout the book images and models for understanding this experience imaginally and practically, but to my mind and in my experience the whole is ineffable and beyond description. Blake's communication of what is a revelatory experience is direct and astounding and has accompanied me for thirty years without growing dull. Here in this plate are the indications that all is not right, that Job is stuck within the letter of the dead law, unaware of 'Jesus the Imagination', which as we know is Blake's divine internal spark of unified being. This is his 'Poetic Genius', the 'True Man', that is the source of the derived outward body and all religion.

Spector argues convincingly that Blake had an understanding of the Kabbalah and adapted his myth to meet this understanding over the course of the development of his art, moving from a linear exoteric Christian myth to a cyclic Kabbalistic one. The Kabbalistic myth is one of exile and return, as described in the introduction above (p. 17–18). Creation becomes manifest through the divine will of Ein Sof and falls, through an excess of judgement, into the material hierarchy we currently experience. It becomes humanity's responsibility to make contact with the divine, and repair this catastrophic fall through the reparation of the broken Kabbalistic tree, separating the shards of the vessels of the sefirot from the original divine light.

There is some debate as to how Blake's Kabbalistic knowledge might have come about, whether it is through the work of Jacob Bohme (1575–1645) or another source is not clear. Raine makes continual reference to his understanding of the 'Jewish mystical tradition'. Spector's meticulous studies show that Blake is informed by the Christianised version of the Kabbalistic myth (2001b, p. 12), which follows from the Lurianic myth of the 16th century briefly described above. She argues that the myth alters over Blake's life and that you can see this process through his composite art. Finally, the cyclic myth is realised in the composite work, *Jerusalem*.

In this plate, we could see many Kabbalistic symbols, not least of which is the tree central to the image – the Kabbalistic tree of life – a pictorial representation of the connection between humanity and God. Although here it is perhaps better thought of as the tree of knowledge, Solomon (1993, p. 79) makes the important point that the Jobian journey is from the Tree of Knowledge to the Tree of Life, articulating Blake's thesis that the only sin is the hubristic sin of knowing good from evil.

This image then represents the knowledge of law, but without the lived experience that Job is about to gain, which enlivens the tree and the connection to the divine. There is the sun and the moon, laterally distributed. The number ten appears as the number of sons and daughters, which is the number of sefirot that descended from Ein Sof to form the Kabbalistic tree. This structure is an emanatory structure, like the neo-Platonic model, although the description and process are not similar. Job is depicted as having only the human wisdom of the 'natural man', correspondent to the lower levels of the Kabbalistic understanding of life, and Blake's level of Generation and Ulro, the natural man of Locke, Newton and the worldview of the natural sciences. The Natural Man to Blake is devoid of spiritual life, his church is the Deist church 'they behold what is within now seen without' (FZii 54 E, p. 314). Crucial to the understanding of Blake, whose felt experience of a whole life is to be coherent with the internal subject, this is the subjective 'I' not the projected object of Bohm's 'me', which is nearer to Blake's 'Satan of the selfhood'.

A cloud separates Job from Beulah, the world of the soul and the divine world of Eden. He is trapped then in his material existence, without a known connection to the divine. I see Blake as not particularly dogmatic in his approach to wisdom traditions, but more inspired by differing traditions and their expression as a means of apprehending his own experience, a synthetic model, exposed too many images for change and development over a lifetime. Blake created for himself a symbolic language to express his fourfold image, much of which draws upon the work of Emanuel Swedenborg (1688–1772), Thomas Taylor (1758–1835) 'the English pagan', as well as Platonist translations of neo-Platonic writings. We will meet this more fully in the next plate.

The caption, 'Thus did Job continually', can be seen to be as a reference to ritual sacrifice, which Blake opposed, not only literal animal or human sacrifice, as in the Old Testament, but 'penalties and punishments of all kinds accepted by moralistic religion' (Raine, 1982, p. 36). 'Little Boy Lost' from Songs of Experience (1789–1797) can be seen as an example of a child being spiritually sacrificed to the Deist religious ideas of his parents, which was no less terrible to Blake than Isaac's sacrifice by Abraham. These penalties and punishments of morality can be seen, for instance, in the form of self-limiting toxic shame, the shame at the root of addiction and the compulsive behaviours we adopt to defend ourselves from the experience of the difficult aspects of our lives. The 'Calvinist soul' that Raine describes is not only at the root of our humanist philosophy, but, as Weber (1904–1905) suggests, the liberal capitalist economic model that we have adopted, leading to the idealisation of commodity, market and the means of exchange over relational exchange. This leads all too easily to the erosion of value into empty coin and monetary worth, or the separation of spirit and matter and the deification of that matter.

Here again, we see the sacrifice of our humanity to the ideological dogma of the day, and here I am most identified with Blake. Humanism has given us much, but for me has thrown something out with the bathwater – a more interconnected and resonant world in which we are component. Instead, we see ourselves as objects separate from and acting upon a system, rather than part of a world in which relational engagement can take part in and alter the whole. Blake sees a relational becoming which is dialogic and participatory, however perceived internally, a self of perception and reception rather than a self that directs and acts upon. This image can be seen as depicting the beginning of the process of transcending the subject and object structure, being separated from the whole through self-righteous ignorance. For Blake, it is the experience within, the 'True Vine' connecting all that was the true and eternal life. Following Swedenborg's thought that, it is the innocence of 'Songs of Innocence' (1789) that was the true measure of the 'True Man', not merely the experience of the five senses of the empiricist hegemony expressed in Songs of Experience (1794). The coherent and relational whole is expressed from Plates 18 to 21. I do not mean to say the centrality of human experience is unimportant, or wish to deny the importance of self, but to see humanity and the self experience in the context of the wider system. I see the next stage in the world's development as human, as does Blake; however, as he is about to show us, if we do not alter our concept of the context in which humanity sits, we are bound to suffer at the hands of our own narcissism. For me, this is not to throw out all that we have learned but to build a wider imagination that can incorporate all these differing narratives and tensions. Blake shows us this as a process. Bohm and Whitehead articulate a similar process.

The entire first image could be seen as sacrifice, of the old way, the old life and the habitual deadening dogma that must be given up for the generation of something new. What is it that we have to give up, to destroy, to allow for new creation? This has direct relevance to our current experience. Through addiction it can be seen in literal form, but also in resonant group relations, when we have to give up something of our identity to negotiate our place within the group. This accommodation between self and group is essential to the dialogic negotiation of group functioning. Something of our selfishness, our narcissism has to be sacrificed. For Job it will be his self-righteousness, so piously captured in this image; the thing he most cares about is to be taken away – his idealised relationship to God.

If we follow Raine's (1982, p. 35) suggestion that to know Christ is to know the mind of God we come to the point where self is transcended and we are at one or indeed zero: nothing, empty, no self. This is the Pauline notion of oneness in Christ, which from a Kabbalistic perspective would be coming to know the mind of God, so we become one with God. Blake believed that we were coincident with God. For Blake, Job's piety was indicative of a false relationship to God. Job was self-righteous and overly pious, a pillar of a dogmatic society unconnected to its true context, so for Blake this is not the traditional God of Christian obedience but the eternal creative that Blake saw in imagination.

A Modern Day Example of Job's State in Plate 1

An example in the context of addiction might be 'the dry drunk', someone who is able to ingest, for instance, the dogma of the twelve step process, follow its rules to the letter, but never let go of the need to use. The use is waiting there, in Blake's terms Satan, often for thirty years or more, waiting to return to governance of behaviour. For me the key to the twelve steps is not the dogma, but the deep spiritual challenge the steps offer to bring about change and new relationship to the whole.

One might see this as reflected in our current struggles with our impact on where we live. We look back for an answer to the difficulties we face from our success as a species and imagine that some of the ideas we have used are not those that can take us forward. We look to idealised concepts from the past to find a new communal and spiritual balance to understand how we can experience this new life as a whole, whilst we also find ourselves in the position that our ideas of God used to occupy. We have the capacity to alter ourselves and our environment in ways that we could not previously have imagined, and before us we envisage yet more power for change and manipulation of the material environment. This material power has not brought with it the capacity to understand the interconnected ramifications of our actions. It is as if each component of the system sees only from its own viewpoint and operates on the world from that perspective. Blake points to a means of bearing this struggle and bringing it into a coherent alignment with the whole. However, it will not be done with rules, or at least rules alone, but with an acceptance, surrender, to the process of the whole in which we are engaged.

The instruments in the tree are an important symbol for Blake, who sees the divine in art and music as a means of connection to, and expression of, God – the God of collective human imagination. Here, they are accessible in potential. Only the protagonists are blind to them, isolated and asleep, heedless of the possibility of their experience. This is how we live today – addicted to commodity and repetitive processes such as gambling. A yoga teacher once told me that the positions are not the important thing; they were simply the method observed when people made the changes to their being that yoga brings about. The same could be said of the Twelve Steps. They are not the important thing but a way to get there. What is needed is the intent and the giving up to apperceive the unfolding process which is being lived.

For Blake, Gothic architecture was a symbol of spiritual religion. Early in his career he had a deeply moving and visionary experience in Westminster Abbey (Bentley, 2004, pp. 16–17) and came to see that 'a Gothic church is a representative of true art' (VLJ. 82 – 4.E 559).[1] Here, the church is disappearing in the setting sun, indicating the coming darkness and alienation from the True Man, and the onset of spiritual night, or the dark night of the soul. In the margins of the page, a line-drawn universal tent, or tabernacle, surrounds Job's family, to symbolise divine protection. Above is the cloud of unknowing, which separates the world of generation from the upper, spiritual worlds of Beulah and Eden – the upper worlds in Blake's quaternary.

Raine reminds us that, 'For Blake, as Plotinus the neo-Platonist, the fall of man is not into sin but into oblivion or sleep, Ulro, the sleep of spiritual blindness'. Job's apathetic look and the sleep of his flock and family take on a different hue in this context. 'Blake intends us to understand that Job is in a natural state of virtue but of spiritual forgetfulness' (p. 39). This is a story to provoke spiritual awakening, an awakening to whichever context in which we are embedded, be that purely relational or, as Blake suggests, connected by the eternal vine to the ground of divine being.

This is a self-righteous man asleep in his self-righteousness. Raine describes the danger in which the self-righteous find themselves, 'because whereas a sinner knows his own shortcomings and in this very recognition acknowledges God, the morally virtuous man is self-sufficient and likely to become ever more firmly entrenched in his own ego' (pp. 39–40). I think this is a description of the spiritual narcissist.

> Of all types of ego, the righteous ego is most perilous because so convincing both to its possessor and others. In its self-righteous virtue it assumes the likeness of God, a terrible mimicry that Blake represents and describes in the figure of the resentment of Satan himself
>
> (p. 38)

Job's dogmatic and literalist interpretation of the law, connected to righteousness, is how 'Satan of the Selfhood' enters his world and destroys his life. It is through faith that his life is restored, not faith in dogma, but faith the perpetual process of becoming. For a new life to be formed, the old has to be let go, although the imagination of a journey between a known self and a new self is often too painful to bear. We so cling to the self of the past in the hope that it will offer us what it had before. This is the key to addiction: clinging to a habit that will kill you but gives you what you know and, even if painful and destructive, is comforting. It does not need to be a full 'habit' – work, the takeaway, the television or the media, is enough.

So in this image, we see that Blake shows the struggle with the imposed, external order of the material Enlightenment, 'the natural sciences' which dominate over the internal, spiritual world. Raine points out that Blake believed it is because of mankind's loss of access to 'the divine body' (p. 41), or divine image, that Mosaic[2] law, the law of Moses and the Ten Commandments, has become necessary. For embodied relationship, in Blake's mind, the divine is also necessary.

Humanity's original, lost divine image, the likeness of God, innate in the Everyman, would be a perception of the right and left brain working together – a Kabbalistic restoration. This for Blake and Swedenborg is the incarnation of Jesus who gave the 'new law'. Job lives in the church of the dead letter. Man has lost his connection to, '[All] God's creatures' who act from innate instinct. This is a direct challenge to Locke who sees that there is no innate knowledge or divine inspiration. The moral code of any materialist philosophy is necessarily based on the five senses, since this philosophy knows no other source of knowledge. In this plate, the use of the term 'self-righteous' describes any code based upon the fallacy that 'the true man' is generated from natural sciences. For Blake, the challenge of Thomas Paine, Voltaire and Rousseau was that man is a 'natural organ subject to sense' (NNR. E, p. 2).

> Many persons, such as Paine and Voltaire, and some of the ancient Greeks, say: "we will not converse concerning good and evil; we will live in paradise and liberty." You may do so in spirit, but not in the mortal body as you pretend, till after the last judgement; for in paradise they have no corporal and mortal body – that originated with the fall and was called death and cannot be removed but by the last judgement; while we are in the world of mortality we must suffer.
>
> (VLJ. 92 – 5.E 564)

Central to this work is the idea that liberty and freedom is not material, but in the imaginative world, that it is an internal process, what might be seen as Bohm's infinite subject. This is the paradisiacal state lost in the fall to natural man and is restored only by coming to 'Jesus the Imagination'. In a 'last judgement' of the mortal man, before the light of eternal vision, this is the direct connection to all and everything. We can see from this work that it is an iterative process, a repeated fall and return. From a Kabbalistic view, this is a process of coming to know the mind of God; and from the East, coming to self-realisation beyond the notions of good and evil that are constrained to 'the world of Generation' (as Blake calls everyday manifestation). In its everyday form, this can be seen as the day to day struggle of living one's life in a resonant, participatory way.

Raine (1982) frames the revelatory and prophetic trajectory Blake offers us:

> This lifelong defence of the prophetic tradition of the Jews as against the rationalism of the Classical philosophers rests upon his realisation that the prophets speak for an all knowing mind that lies beyond natural reason.
>
> (p. 53)

Here Blake presages the work of Whitehead, (1978), where these ideas are reformulated and where a secular and creative 'God' is seen at work in the ongoing process of becoming. However, he shifts from a Platonic primacy to a being, to a continually co-creative process of becoming, an evolving search for novelty in a perpetually co-evolving universe. It is the creative appetite for novelty that calls to becoming, whether you place this in the context of a God or another symbol. I think it is a proximal choice, a choice of image, but the function is the same.

Plate 2
The Consideration of Satan
When the Almighty was yet with me,
When my children where about me

We can read this pate within a Kabbalistic and Neo-Platonic frame. For Blake, and indeed for Plato, there are four levels to the divine and personal experience. They are emanatory models, in that energy emanates from the divine down to the world of creation, that in which we perceive our life to be material. This Platonic model is expressed in Blake's universe as Eden, Beulah, Generation and Ulro (celestial, spiritual, natural and the spiritually blind). Raine (1982) describes them as:

> Eden (the mundus imaginalis in which the unfallen and still androgenous man is in the presence of God); Beulah, the state of marriage, which comes into being in the 'deep sleep', which fell upon Adam at the time when women became a separate being; the world of Generation (Swedenborg's world of uses); and the 'fixed and dead' world that Blake calls Ulro.
>
> (p. 44)

I have come to see this frame as Eden – the divine world, Beulah – a soul world, Generation – the world of material manifestation (in Blake's terms 'vegetative') and Ulro – that of a spiritual death brought about by rational materialism. I accept Raine's interpretation of Blake that '[he] attempted ... nothing less than the reversal of the premise of material science, which he saw ... as provincial, local and temporary deviation from the universal and normal tradition of spiritual knowledge'.

Blake's fourfold vision, which I repeat here, was:

> Now I a fourfold vision see,
> And a fourfold vision is given to me;
> 'Tis fourfold in my supreme delight
> And threefold in soft Beulah's night
> And twofold always. May God us keep
> From single vision and Newtons sleep!
> (1802 E 722)

In Plate 2, we see in the upper third of the central image God – Yahweh – in Eden, with the divine family or council representing 'the communion of saints, the aggregate of Christian thought' (FD, 2013, p. 105). It is noteworthy that he is referencing the book of the law, as we see Job, below, in the lower third. This is the mosaic (the law of Moses) given to order a society that could not find itself. Blake was concerned about this rational rigidity as we see throughout the whole of the Job narrative. The tablets of stone feature in Plate 11 also, whereas the truth of our becoming is often symbolised by scrolls.

In the world of Beulah, we see Satan – Blake's 'Satan of the Selfhood'. Here, they discuss the agreement that will give Job to Satan to be tested, in other words the whole psyche given up to narcissistic need. Also here we see the faint images of Job and his wife's spectre either side of Satan, their hindered selfhood about to fall and be altered in the unfolding process we are witnessing.

In the world of generation, in the bottom third of the image, we see Job, his wife, his family and the angels sent to question him. I would read the scrolls they carry as the true record of Job and his wife's life and their becoming, whilst he points to his righteous adherence to the letter of the law. They are sent to protect and are reminiscent of the recording angels we will meet in the margins, from Plate 5 to 16, when they are replaced by more participatory figures.

Here in this level of generation, we also meet Poetic Genius – the figure with the scroll behind Job, and a figure reminiscent of Urizen, the rational builder of worlds who carries the book of the law. I find it of note that they are so close together. Behind these figures there are three trees, reminiscent of the three pillars of the psyche represented in the Kabbalah. They carry Blake's vine, his symbol for interconnectedness. Note also the sleeping dog. This suggests to me that all are in slumberous darkness and separated from the divine inspiration of the 'True Man'. Here, Blake is consistent with Plato in seeing that souls fall into incarnation as they fall into slumber. Ultimately, for the unfaithful, this is the self-righteous slumber of spiritual death. As we will explore, like Blake I do not see faith here in the context of a dogma, but faith in the continuation of life. Through my work, particularly in addiction, I see the only thing there is left to have faith in is faith itself.

Spector's suggestion that Blake developed his vision through the Christian Kabbalism of Franciscus Mercurius van Helmont (1614–1699), rather than the more commonly held view, that Blake formed an entirely new myth of his own, argues that rather than the linear narrative of an exoteric Christian myth – birth, life, death and assent to heaven through the ransom of Christ – Blake explored an esoteric Kabbalistic cycle of exile and return, death and rebirth, through which one internalises the spirit of the divine light in order to reflect the eternal source. This is a perpetual process, as for instance expressed in the fall and rising up of his painting of 'The Vision of the Last Judgement' (1808).

Importantly, salvation by divine grace, as the ransom of Christ, is replaced by friendship, by moving from a model of divine intervention to one of relationship. I understand this as moving towards a consciousness of resonance and away from one of exploitation. We come to know the divine relationally, for Blake as an internal lived experience. Blake expresses this experience directly in the later plates, 15–21, and this is crucial to my reading of these images. I see this as resonant with Whitehead's (Mesle, pp. 72–78) approach to power as receptive and relational.

Within the Kabbalistic myth, good and evil are inclusive within God and therefore neither are ungodly. This is true for Blake's worlds of Eden and Beulah. 'In Beulah "The Contrarieties are equally True"' (M 30:1. J 48:14, FD, 2013, p. 66). Blake's view was that God believed the only sin to be that of hubris, of eating from the tree of knowledge, and knowing the difference between good and evil. Spector (2001b) suggests that the Christian Kabbalistic myth is rooted in the Lurianic myth, and that it is Adam's eating of the fruit of the tree of knowledge that causes the catastrophe that befell creation to be reified into the cycle of material existence. The fault is actually in God and the withdrawal that allows for creation but also the separation of the sefirot Din (judgement/rigour) from Rahmin (compassion/mercy). This breach accrues all energy to Din and shatters all others, breaking the structure as a whole and forming a drop into material reality. It is the responsibility of humans to clarify this error and reflect the divine light fully, thus collaboratively repairing the error with God. Therefore, in this imagination, humanity is a reflection of creation, 'as above so below' and its concomitant. This reflection is the intent of creation per se. In a private conversation, Brian Lancaster, the Kabbalist and cognitive neuroscientist described that the rules in Jewish culture are supposed to correspond to the laws of heaven, so by obeying them you follow the heavenly order, thereby altering something in your body, a relational correspondence right down into the corporeal experience.

For me, it is essential that the correspondent changes in our becoming are embedded into the experience of the body. I see this would map onto Bohm (1994, pp. 121–151; Bohm, 1996, pp. 73–82) idea of 'proprioception', the felt interrogation of experience in the body as to the antecedents of that experience, along with its associations and assumptions. A means of experientially attuning to Whitehead's (Cobb, 2008, p. 61; PR, 21) notion of 'concrescence', the coming together of events to form the novel event in hand; what I would see as the direct experience of the emergent process of creating, as a felt sense in the body. For Bohm, this process gives access to the subtle order of the implicate obscured beneath the noise of fragmentary thought.

As we progress through the later plates we will see how Blake experienced and understood this process from a visionary perspective, particularly from Plate 15, through to the end of Plate 21. The conflicts we feel between fragmentary, partial thoughts and the actual lived experience in the body can be sensed if we suspend the thought and propriocept. Putting the thought aside, neither denying it or completing it, but noting its existence, it is possible to find an apperception of the associative symbols, so we are able to access some of the 'tacit' feelings and assumptions that drive our fragmentary thinking. Bohm (1996, p. 84) would suggest that this proprioception leads to a participatory way of becoming, akin to a time before we perceived ourselves as separate from the world system as a whole, similar to that of the hunter-gatherers, but in a more aware state, with our current capacity for perception, thinking and abstract relations. This trajectory will unfold, but at this instant we are caught in a rigid moment, only able to perceive the proximal instance of what Bohm sees as literal thought. This is what Blake's letter of the law, Job, his wife and indeed Yahweh hold.

Blake directly challenges the rationalist and materialist hegemony from which we now benefit and suffer. He was concerned to follow his vision, a vision of restitution, the bringing of balance to the system within which he was living. Of course, this is also at the root of the Kabbalistic temporal and spiritual imagination of the world, one of restitution of a fallen order, generated through the will of the divine energy (God) to be known and reflected, not for its own joy but for the beings which inhabit the creation made for this reflection. This creation myth fits with Blake's vision and is a means of apprehending the relationship between us as individuals and the system of creation as a whole. This is accessed for Blake through his image of the True Man or Poetic genius.

For me, Blake's insight encourages one to bring more to the experience of the work of psychotherapy, individually and in groups, moving further from reason and theory the deeper you drill, contextualising reason as a component in our experience, but not its aim – much as Jung would argue 100 years later. In *Sapiens* (2014) and *Homo Deus* (2016), Harari points to these shifts in his grand sweep of history. He focuses upon the cognitive and farming revolutions that lead to the development of humanity in its current form and, the technological shifts that we are currently experiencing, the industrial and knowledge revolution. These are changes that we are bearing in our being and our social relations. Harari is a Buddhist, practicing in the Vipassana tradition, and brings that form of attention to his thinking. He makes specific note to the felt sense in the body during his meditation (2018, pp. 358–364).

Here, I would see a resonance to the Tibetan Buddhist practices of Reginald A. Ray. Ray (2016, 2020) cites modern neuroscientific literature, both the left and right brain work of McGilchrist (2009), and the top down and bottom up structure of Solms (2021). His conceit is that meditative practice reaches back to an embedded consciousness of a pre-Platonic (Bhuddist/Taoist) world, and towards the experience of the hunter-gatherer's oneness with their environment.

Reggie Ray discusses left and right brain functioning similarly to McGilchrist, but links the right brain more to embodiment or 'soma' (2020, pp. 14–19). In my experience, the changes that take place in psychotherapy take place in the body. They may accompany a thought, but something is known physically, there is a sense of something shifting, a newfound lightness, resilience or flexibility, when changes really take place in someone's experience of their life – known in their bones.

I have to say this is congruent with my experience when working in groups. It is the felt experience that indicates most. When working with addicted people it seemed as if processes in my liver were the important thing to notice, not my thoughts, nor my feelings, but my hepatic functioning – the digestion of the toxic suffering in the whole system. A patient of mine described his daughter first articulating shame as feeling hot, which we both experienced in the session, and felt for her. In both instances, a great deal of thought as to how this corporal experience could be understood and negotiated was expressed, but first they were directly felt and processed as experiences in the body, resonantly and shared between.

Ray discusses this perspective in the context of Tibetan Buddhist mediative practice, which has a bodily focus. He has augmented his studies of Buddhism to draw on many traditions, offering practices which foster understanding of the embodied mind. He makes the point I discovered in our communal practice at CORE that:

> We now know that the body itself is intelligent and aware, down to the cellular level. So there is no body that is in some sense not equally and at the same time

"mind." And the mind, rather than being a separate entity, is intimately connected with, if not reducible to, the collective awareness of the neurological network of the body; so there is no mind that is not, at the same time, the body.

(2016, p. 21)

Left brain functioning for Ray is the conceptualising, abstract, executive and conscious 'ego mind' (in the Buddhist context); the right is holistic, non-conceptual and linked to the awareness of the body. He also articulates this in the context that Solms does, as bottom up and top down. Bottom up is direct unmediated experience out of the body; top down is the cortical cooling consciousness. Solms structures this slightly differently, not seeing the bodily experience as unconscious, but the feeling experience that wakens brain activity in a homeostatic sense. This throws upside down Freud's theory of the Id being unconscious.

Ray makes interesting differentiations of endogenous and exogenous experience in that he frames endogenous within the purview of what is known consciously rather than the simplicity of external and internal input:

"Exogenous" means "arriving from the outside," and it points to "right brain" or bottom-up knowing, an experience of utter unfamiliarity: we feel as if information is arriving from outside of the domain of our familiar, conscious, ego world, coming as new and as yet unprocessed, undomesticated (by our ego). Exogenous refers to phenomena that arise naturally and spontaneously from the darkness and the unknown (i.e. subcortical and largely unconscious) regions of our body: feelings, sensations, intuitions, "felt-senses," visceral impressions, somatic memories – arriving in our awareness in a direct, fresh, immediate, and naked way. Neuroscientists speak of "exogenous stimulae." By contrast, "endogenous" means "coming from the inside," which refers to coming from within the already existing and known database of the "left brain," the self-conscious, self-referential ego. Endogenous thus points to what we recognize as familiar – experience mediated by and filtered through ideas, concepts, assumptions, judgments, conclusions that already exist in our consciousness, based on the past, through which we process our present experience in order to "know," manage, and control it. Endogenous involves top-down application of the familiar so that we can label, conceptualize, and pin down the unfamiliar and – to ego – potentially threatening and destabilizing influx of the unknown. Neuroscientists refer to "endogenous control".

(pp. 23–24)

His Intention is to link mental experience directly into the body, linking to Gendlin (1978, 1996) and the 'felt sense' to his practice. This is common in such models and I think a useful way to bear experience. He proposes that through the practice of meditation we are able to come into our body 'Soma' interoceptively – a felt sense through the actual body – then to the field of direct experience. I think this field is akin to what David Bohm is referring when he talks about proprioception.

Bohm expresses this particularly in the context of the group and the group's capacity for resonance and experience. My felt sense of hepatic disruption as I worked with addicts would be such an experience. I might then think or feel emotions or thoughts in this context also, but there is a resonance in the body.

Ray makes a perceptive point about soul and 'ensouling', which he would frame differently to the Platonic image, and see as the resonant experience of the co-creative process held in the body, down to the cells and the field of energetic relations – the field of direct experience. He develops his practice in the context of Vajrayana Buddhism and the Sidhars, 8th to 12th century Indian lay practitioners who rejected orthodox religion and focused upon embodiment as meditative practice. They are credited with developing Vajrayana, Dzogchen and Mahamudra practices. Ray's work is set in the tradition of Tibetan Buddhism focusing upon awareness as experienced as love. I see this experience of the creative whole as resonant with Whitehead's (PR, 348) experience of the love of God, the perceptual and valued appetite of the universe longing for the novel that brings existence into being.

Ray makes a call for a re-imagining or re-experiencing of the connectedness of the hunter-gatherer consciousness, as does Bohm (1996, pp. 84–90). Two sides of the coin are before us, material and spiritual, perhaps also the same coin we have struggled with for some time, of a separate selfhood in the context of a whole. I am suggesting that we need to re-imagine the symbols we form and remember they are generated in the context that we and they are set, but are participatorily embedded.

This is an imagination that Blake offers us – a template for individuation, psychological and spiritual, but as a group. He offers an archetypal dramatis personae, a group template, full of characters engaged in the myth of exile and return, death and re-birth, fall and redemption, a core experience of being human, particularly in Western culture. I think it is politically and culturally significant that we require the myths of the past to be altered, or at least recontextualised, before we can develop a space that recognises the context from which we come. This is reflected both on an exoteric materialist social model and an esoteric spiritual mystic level.

With the image divided into three parts – that of Eden, Beulah and the world of Generation (Ulro at this time is depicted in the following plate), we are being shown the internal world of Job. Both he and Yahweh are concerned with the book of law and although unconsciously, Yahweh is still available to him, he has not yet fallen into Ulro (spiritual blindness), cut off from the inner life of imagination and vision. This process takes place over the next four plates.

In the upper world of 'Eden', we see Yahweh and the six angels of the Elohim who we met in the frontispiece. They are the builders of creation, and Ein Sof, the source of divine emanation, is represented by the disc of light behind Yahweh. The angels appear to be examining a scroll which Raine (1982, p. 48) sees as the true record of Job's life. This is also reflected in the bottom part of the picture, the world of Generation, where the two angels are showing Job their scrolls as a record of the good and evil acts of his life. Scrolls appear throughout the plates, usually in the upper margins on the left and right, perhaps commenting on the process as it unfolds and the recording of Job's transformation. We see them here for the first time, as if questioning Job and his faith. The question though is not about Job's adherence to dogma, the letter of the law in his books, but his faith in the principle behind this, in the becoming and the creative ethic.

At this moment, there is communication between Job's internal worlds. The clouds, which Blake used to symbolise the opening and closing of spiritual consciousness, as well as access to the spiritual and divine realms of experience, are open to the heavens. The emanation is flowing down from the divine light through Yahweh, Eden and Beulah to the world of Generation, our differentiated evolutionary world of matter. However, Job is unconscious of these levels of his being; he is adherent to the 'law', to the dogma of his 'faith', but not connected to its internal, imaginative 'poetic genius'.

It is important to note here the similarity between Job and Yahweh. This is not accidental. In the margin above, the image is the phrase 'we shall awake up in thy likeness'. This is clearly a reference to the correspondence between Job and Yahweh, presaging the moment the divine life is realised as a coincident internal experience in Plate 17. This, I might argue, is the hermetic law of correspondence, and the relationship between God as an apperception of the whole, and humanity as the particular event; the reflection of the divine in the human, the mirror between heaven and earth, the all reflected in the one. Blake will have known of this Hermetic tradition and, as we know, sees God and humanity as one.

However, Job has his left leg forward and Yahweh his right. Again, Raine (1982, p. 49) takes this as a Kabbalistic reference and indicate the twin left and right pillars of the tree of life – Judgment and Mercy – that are synthesised in the central pillar of lived experience. This would indicate that Job interprets the law with due judgement, to the letter, and that Yahweh is merciful. Both Job and Yahweh present rigid faces; however, I read a certain despair and defeat in Job's face, as if there is an awareness of what is to come. This is something which one experiences when patients first begin their work. There is often a defeat in them which, although attached to a symptom – relationship difficulties, problems at work, anxiety, depression or sometimes more difficult symptoms – is recognition that the unseen order they have made for their lives no longer works.

For me, this is also reminiscent of Jung's approach to the Job narrative, which focuses upon the transformation of Yahweh in his encounter with Job; the transformation of the deep Self (in Jung's terms) upon its encounter with the ego. This is a process which brings into consciousness that which was not before, each drop of feeling resonating upward to a novel expression, building resonance through changing and adapting images; in other words, Jung's transcendent function, as we have seen in Chapter 1.

On the personal level, this is the narrative of the plates understood as a journey of individuation conducted in the visual language of imagination and symbol. However, I see that this is then embedded in the collective, both social and spiritual. Blake considered that imagination was the link between earth and heaven, between matter and spirit, as would be the case in many mystical traditions. One might imagine the figure with the glowing coronet seated behind Job (holding a scroll) to be Poetic Genius. He is unnoticed by Job, who self-righteously points to the letter of the law, justifying to the judging angels his pious actions. Poetic Genius, Jesus the Imagination, the True Man, is a crucial figure for Blake, as it is the manifestation of the divine within the being through the conduit of imagination. This is not reason, but the entirety of all being accessed through the life of imagination and symbol; or, as Churton (2014), the scholar of Western Esotericism, puts it:

> For Blake, Imagination was not simply a faculty, a kind of creative tool, a department of brain ... Imagination was divine life itself. Imagination retained the link between earth and heaven, matter and spirit. Its fruits: intuition, poetry, painting and music. Blake, with staggering idiosyncratic audacity, would refer to 'Jesus the Imagination' because traditionally Jesus had opened that link, descending and ascending with the angels, and in His being constituted that link ('I am the Way'), that 'golden string' Blake would come to celebrate in his epic *Jerusalem*.
> (Churton, Kindle location. 1347)

Having opened the heavens to man's vision, to simple folk, not just intellectuals, Blake could say 'the kingdom of heaven is within you'. Blake could say that Jesus was the offspring of God 'and so am I, and so are you', as he informed a perplexed Crabb Robinson in 1826.

Here, Yahweh is offering Job to Satan (the central figure in this image) to be tested. This idea is known from the Job story in the Bible and is clearly referenced with the words, 'Hast thou considered my Servant Job'. Cruelly, this is at the point that Job might be considered at the height of his capacity, 'When the Almighty was yet with me. When my Children were yet about me'. But, as we have understood, this situation is founded on hollow intellectual, pious and self-righteous, reasoned faith, devoid of actual spiritual inspiration. It is fundamental to the piece that Blake is equating Satan with an ideology of materialism rather than morality. He understood materialism to be denial of the spirit.

We see three other figures (possibly the three other Zoas) and, hidden in the tumult, the spectres of Job and his wife. According to Foster Damon (2013, pp. 380 & 382), Blake's spectre is 'the rational power of the divided man', what we see here as Satan of the Selfhood and what Tweedy links to the left brain functioning that McGilchrist (2009) describes. Tweedy (2013) explores this notion in depth through the Myth of Urizen (your reason). The key point is not that the left brain reasoning is wrong but that the mechanistic and out of control idealisation of reasoning during the Enlightenment is destructive and deadly, to which Blake reacts. "Though knowest that the Spectre is in Every Man insane, brutish, deform'd, that I [the Spectre] am thus a ravening devouring lust continually craving & devouring" (FZ vii:304)

However, although this selfish rationalising is the Satan of the Selfhood that we will pursue, Blake does not limit the spectre to one of the four Zoas. All have a spectre, a shadow, linked to the mechanistic rather than inspirational evocation of our becoming, as shown in the downfall of the first six plates. The spectre of the Zoa Tharmus, representing senses and the physical body, is sexual potency and avaricious desire; Luvah, the prince of love's spectre; is war; and the spectre of Urthorna (earth owner), the Zoa of creative imagination, is Los, when separate from Enitharmon, 'spiritual beauty and the twin, consort and inspiration of Los', as described by Damon. For Jungian thinkers, this may appear similar to the typological quaternary for the functions of the ego CW6 (1931/1971) or his archetypal notion of the shadow (Samuels, Shorter & Plaut, 1986, p. 138). I would not directly compare, other than to make a link to a notion of completeness felt in the four, which Jung points to, as it seems does Blake, and to note that given to Job in Plate 19 towards the end of his journey is a trinket (an earring, as mentioned in the Bible) representing this quaternary form.

Blake believed that Satan, the accuser, could take the form of any four Zoas,[3] that is the four eternal senses, the functions of our psyche akin to those described by Jung (CW6.1971) typologically, and the four means by which we engage with the world. Here, it is reason, or rather rationalisation, the shadow of reason, that is the criminal. Raine equates the four Zoas, which she sees as representative of the four animals of Ezekiel's chariot, to Jung's four functions: reason is Urizen, feeling is Luvah, sensation is Tharmas and intuition corresponds to Los (1982, p. 49).

Satan is a more complex figure than in the Bible because he is an agent of God. Blake would not question that everything is by divine permission, a part of the whole. Satan's kingdom is not outside the divine order. As Blake's discussions with Crabb Robbins (CRD) indicate,

> The devil is eternally created not by God, but by God's permission ... There is a constant falling off from God ... Angels becoming Devils ... Every man has a devil in himself and the conflict between this Self and God is perpetually carrying on.
> (Raine, 1982, pp. 52–53)

Raine suggests that he continues to avoid the trap of dualism, the split between good and evil, by insisting upon the illusory nature of Satan's world. This we might see as Bohm's (1994) fragmentary and contingent nature of thought.

Andrew Solomon (1993) references the ten figures surrounding Yahweh's throne as the ten sefirot of the Kabbalistic tree. I don't want to over-emphasise the mapping of differing models that Blake will have synthesised to form these images; Blake's imagination is also his, and a creation of his experience. Therefore I believe the work is better read poetically, as apprehension rather than in search of what is literally accurate. I would not insist upon conformation to a model as we might see it today, with far more access to the history, the dogma and the context of Kabbalistic thought, than would have been available to Blake. For me it is important to see this in the context of a lived life. We can make some attempt to understand what it is that Blake is alluding to, and what it is that we are experiencing, but it is the lived experience on both counts for me which is of value, not a fixed order of referent symbols. I believe Blake would have sympathy with this view, to quote him in the guise of Los, the Zoa of Divine imagination.

I must Create a System, or be enslav'd by another Mans
I will not Reason & Compare: my business is to Create.
(J, 1820, 10:20–21E 153)

For instance, it is not my thoughts about how I work with individuals or groups that is the most important, but how my experience of living informs theirs and, through the conversations we have, they can come to a renewed vision of their life. It is a lived and felt experience held in their and my mind imaginatively; it is the resonance between us, that generates the space for creative change. I might think about this in terms of a Winnicottian (1971) transitional or analytic space, but it is the actual fact of the existence of this creative and playful space that creates the possibility for change. If I were to look through a Bohmian lens, I might think of the relational field embedded in the implicate, the quantum relationality of the implicate where all matter is the relationship between differing energies. Or to think about Whitehead's 'appetite' (Cobb, 2008, p. 36; PR, 32), a loving for becoming. However, it remains the case that there are various imaginative instruments one might use, psychoanalytic, neurobiological or social. The key for me is not to be instrumentalist, but to be musical, and bear the poetic juxtaposition of experience. Winnicott appeals as his work is founded in play and imagination, the experiment and adventure in becoming together, for instance his use of the squiggle game (1968) to work with children each by turn adding to a squiggle that Winnicott started on a page to form a frame for the consultation (Abram, 1996, pp. 303–310). For the group, this is the playful space between its members, the resonant environment created as we meet which I would see maps both on the Winicottian, Jungian and Bohmian notions of participation.

I remember a group at CORE where we had a new member, someone who had fallen so far they had nothing. They came to the community and were supported by absent parents. They were new to addiction release, and indignant at finding themselves in this situation. They mounted a spirited defence of their behaviour. I would meet this kind of behaviour with a series of questions that would ultimately lead to the boundary of not using, and taking responsibility for that boundary, usually ending with my saying something like, 'Who is it that lifts the glass?'

We were some way through this process and my humour was wearing thin, as were many of the group she had engaged with before. Out of nowhere one of the community, also new but from an opposing end of the social spectrum, leant forward and said, 'You are being interviewed darling'. The conceit being that this was like an interview in a custody suite. I was surprised to see my actions in this light and the person acting in defence of their using remonstrated, but it shed light playfully upon the context and the need for a clear and negotiated boundary for the group. Although the two protagonists were acting out this process, it was in some way participated in by the whole group.

Participation in this context goes some way to thinking about how on various levels we might begin to understand our conscious experience as reflexive, internally and externally. With his mythic and archetypal dramatis personae, Hillman offer an image that can reflect the actions of the group as both an internal and external process. The archetypal structures inside are reflected in the group outside and also, if you are minded to draw the metaphor, the system of the planet. This is a way of perceiving the unfolding whole in a particular experience. In the vignette, above one can see protagonists taking on archetypal roles, particularly that of trickster, but puer and senex[4] was present in the dynamic as well as authoritative boundary negotiation.

Exile and Return

The Kabbalistic myth is one of alienation and return. In the context of Job's story, this is exile from and return to community, transformed and indeed redeemed through relationship. This maps successfully onto the psychodynamic vicissitudes of building and changing a psyche in a transpersonal context. We made great practical use of this in our community at CORE, receiving those exiled through addiction and naming the changes people made for themselves. This enabled both the changes made to be internalised and held in an individual psyche, but for that to be seen in a relational context. The Jungian individuation narrative can be seen in this frame as a progression to oneness again congruent with the whole. This also works in a group process when it is possible to simply suspend the capacity for individual rational understanding, to hear the development, I would say spiritually, of the interconnected context of the group's capacity, evidenced in the process of community ritual where change is addressed through the trope of exile, encounter with death and return.

VIGNETTE

Early in my career I used to work with groups of men where we would create rites of passage through which it would be possible to negotiate change. A typical example might be to do with grief or loss. We would discuss the context of that loss and the unresolved feelings that might be held by the person suffering, for instance a difficult father or the sudden death of a sibling. The person for whom the ritual was to be designed would be sent away from the group, and we would discuss what might be the most creative way their dilemma could be met. We would create a ritual on that basis. With a loss this might take the form of a graveside experience, where the unresolved grief and feelings associated with the loss could be expressed and witnessed.

Another example might be a symbolic confrontation with an oppressive figure, often an abusive father, where by the person is supported and held in the group to challenge this figure, working through some of the concomitant dynamics as they are projected on to the group members. This all occurred in a closed group, working over several days in a residential environment. People got to know each other and could provide both insight and relational containing to process the work. A great deal of thought and generosity needed to go into this ritual process, and a profound containing frame had to be built. I would describe this as forming a sudden community. However, real change and resolution was possible in the relational space we made together, in the dialogue we formed.

My experience in communities and particularly at the CORE Trust would bear this out. Whilst one could easily focus on any individual in the community, come to understand their needs and work with them to resolve internal conflicts, the community itself provided a frame for them to receive and express projections as a live and ongoing process. There would always be a mother and a father, good and bad, scapegoats, tricksters, puers, puellas and any of a myriad of 'archetypal' characters present at any one time in the building. Differing people at differing times would pick up these roles and act them out, expressing their personal and interpersonal relational narratives. People's internal narratives would weave into the external narrative of the project. Then so would the narratives of the project begin to work on them. By forming a home, or a place of refuge, we were able to bring to light difficulties that the patients could work with and re-imagine. This was done to some extent by the staff team but mostly it was process of community that the staff team steered and contained.

Here in Plate 2 we are meeting the major protagonists of the Job story, the theoretical protagonists that we are using to frame the Blake images. For the new event to arise, the perishing of the old has to occur. This process has begun here but is still consciously denied. With respect to addiction, the image then is of denial, the ignoring of the using problem as it grows to destroy life. This is using and not caring for, or even perceiving, the damage that it is wreaking upon self or the world around us. The drugs are still doing what they first did when we encountered them, but somehow not quite like they used to. The internal hurt, the trauma, is still contained, although using is diminishing our access to our internal experience.

72 Perishing

Plate 3
Denial
The fire of God is fallen from Heaven

Thy Sons and thy Daughters were eating & drinking Wine in their eldest Brothers house & behold there came a great wind from the Wilderness & smote upon the four faces of the house & it fell upon the young Men & they are Dead

In the last plate we met the first three levels of Blake's universe: Eden, Beulah and Generation. In this plate we meet Ulro, a hell of spiritual blindness. Up until *Jerusalem* (1820) Blake included the world of Generation in Ulro, but he altered his structure in this work, and does for the Job story also. This is the only plate in which Job does not appear. Satan, opaque, is impervious to the spiritual light and is destroying Job's house and possessions with fire. In the psychological reading of these images, this would be seen as a classic psychic crisis, a depressive or anxiety-related breakdown, at worst a psychotic event. From a transpersonal point of view this is the outbreak of a spiritual crisis, the crisis of faith that Blake is taking us through to reveal a deeper truth.

This kind of experience is perceived in a group when one member brings up conflict and difficulty that challenges the group as a whole and alters the underlying structure and consciousness. Often this is experienced with rage, or anger, expressed by one member or between members, which needs to be met and contained as individually and in group they negotiate their experience. Solomon (p. 21) links this image to rage. The work that follows unfolds through the group and, if contained, reveals the conflicts below the surface.

As an example I will bring a group where a man arrived full of rage. He had been in a possibly violent situation with his new girlfriend, a social engagement that he could not leave easily, where someone was causing trouble. He had a history of violence deep in his past and this event had brought it to the surface. His rage and terror was difficult to contain, not that it was expressed to other members of the group, but it was difficult to keep him in the room. The atmosphere was electric with the urgency of the situation and the tensions were palpable. However, the rage was held and discussed and over the hour and a half it shifted to grief and loss. Each of the men shared experiences of violence. The antecedents of violent behaviour began to come to the surface and were thought about. Violent parenting, violence at school, despair and no way to think about the experiences that had been endured. Of course there was no real resolution at this point, just the hurt, destruction and difficulty. This is where we are in this plate. By the end of the group, the man who had arrived in distress had calmed and was able to leave in a safe state. However, the dynamic of the group had changed, so that the fall out could be worked on over a much longer time frame.

To return to the plate, we might imagine at the centre of the image, Blake's Poetic Genius, the True Man, holding the infant, or Divine Imagination, away from the destruction. It would appear that they are the couple with child behind Job, in Plate 3. I believe this shows that some psychic integrity is maintained. We might also read this image as the ego's defences and assumptions being burnt off. Blake makes much of fires and the enjoyment of genius, as seen in 'The Marriage of Heaven and Hell' (1790). The Hell of energy is set in contrast to the Heaven of reason; the energy for life.

> as I was walking among the fires of hell, delighted with the enjoyments of genius; which to angels look like torment and insanity. I collected some of

the Proverbs ... The Proverbs of Hell, shew the nature of Infernal wisdom ... I came home; on the abyss of the five senses ... I saw a mighty devil folded in black clouds, hovering on the sides of a rock, with corroding fires he wrote now perceived by the minds of man, and read by them on Earth.

How'd you know but every bird that cuts the airy way is an immense world of delight, closed by your senses five?.

(Plates 6–7. E. p. 35)

Fire is one of Blake's quaternary of elements and comes from the east, from the rising sun. The other three are Earth (north), Water (west) and Air (south). Fire is the consuming fire of spiritual love and compassion; however, in its black form, as here, it is experienced as torment and destruction. It does nothing but burn away error. If we are identified with that error then it will be experienced as uncomfortable, as for the man in the vignette above. Foster Damon (2013) uses this quote from *The Marriage of Heaven and Hell*: (MHH14 E, p. 39).

The ancient tradition at the end of six thousand years is true; for when the cherub of prohibition leaves guarding the tree of life, 'the whole of creation will be consumed and appear infinite and holy, whereas it now appears as finite and corrupt'.

(2013, p. 138)

Here, he illustrates not only direct reference to Kabbalistic thinking, the six thousand years of material creation brought about by the eating of the fruit of knowledge, but also how fire is transformative for Blake in a spiritual sense, although this is not Job's current experience. For him, there is pain and loss and despair.

Blake did not believe that this was simply a tale of good and evil, but the interplay of dual energies, which are not split, and when resolved give a true infinite vision. I agree that the contraries are necessary and in dialogue. His principle disagreement with Swedenborg was this that Heaven and Hell are not split and separate, but contraries. To quote again from the poem:

Without Contraries is no progression. Attraction and Repulsion,
Reason and energy, Love and Hate are necessary to Human Existence.
From these contraries springs what the religious call Good & Evil. Good is the passive and obeys reason, Evil is the active and springs from energy.

(MHH3. E, p. 34.)

Energies that have been ignored are rushing up into consciousness to be known, the constellation in Jung's sense of the transcendent function. In terms of Solm's construction of the unconscious, I see this as life surfacing through the felt sense of the body in an attempt at homeostatic management. Insofar as the homeostasis goes out of balance, disturbance is felt.

Solomon (1993, p. 21) points to the slain muse at the bottom of the image, murdered in his mind, by the reason of the spectre – Satan of the Selfhood. Access to the creative is slain by literal thought, which is fragmentary and contingent. We begin to see scorpions and the reptilian skin of leviathan in the margins. The clouds have folded in on Job and he now has no direct contact with Yahweh until later, when Job in a new form is able to experience him, in Plate 13.

In terms of addiction, these are the first inklings of the 'using' not being of value. Chaotic using behaviour is beginning to surface, and life is beginning to be impacted in a visible way. The psychic state that was adopted to repress is acted out all around. Life begins to become unmanageable.

Early in my work at CORE it became clear that people would come in for a rest from using but with little intent to stop. Life would be chaotic and unmanageable, perhaps a health problem would have arisen, often there would be a sense of desperation, as the weight of the fall could begin to be imagined, but the momentum to stop was not there; an idea but not really a felt sense. One such person whom I clearly remember was able to parrot the necessary ideas and intentions, but as we sat with the despair and abuse at the root of the using, a fundamental sense of defeat arose, and we knew this was not the time for them to stop. They had been a victim of abuse at the hands of the Church, so trust was really at a minimum and there was a real confusion about good and evil. To sit with them was a strange mixture of peace and despair. Indeed, despite our best efforts, attendance waned and then stopped. I felt tragedy in their defeat, and to this day I wonder what happened to that particular person.

From a group perspective, I see this image as the beginnings of a change in the individual's relationship to the group, the integrity of the individual psychic boundary is shifting. The group will have appeared to shift in relation to that individual and they may not any longer feel either safe or a part of the group. There is a challenge to the ego structure of the individual's experience which itself is then a challenge to the integrity of the group. This can be difficult to experience and can result in scapegoating, flight or expulsion. It is important to my mind to try to hold these tensions and allow the structural breakdown to occur in a contained way, and perhaps point to the process, certainly to hold it as consciously as possible in mind and body; in other words, what is the body feeling, what is in resonance with the body of the community[5], which I can share with the group as a whole. The phrase, 'the body of the community' is how I came to understand the slightly ineffable component of community building that constituted not only the members, but its history and perhaps the physical context in which it was set, a building or a place.

At CORE, we did not use drug testing or have much in the way of rules at all to negotiate the boundaries. It has to be said that we were mostly experienced practitioners holding a community of experienced users. There we were three rules that we did set: (1) it was a project where we were engaged in stopping using, so people were not to come to the building drunk or stoned. If they did they would be sent home and asked to come back the following day. They would then need to detox and restart the programme; (2) you could not smoke inside the building; and (3) we would not accept any oppressive behaviour on grounds of race, creed, gender or sexual orientation. This last rule was of course a trick. Who was to define what was oppressive and how? The beauty of the trick was that it opened up all boundaries for negotiation right to the boundary which was the most important: how to choose to live in the face of death, how to let go of the using and live.

The most frequent criticism of the project was that we were too lax in our boundary setting and did not have rules. It used to cost us a lot in access to finance and the respect of the establishment. We cared little for the establishment, but a bit more cash would have been helpful. What we did care about was how people changed and how they chose to live. This choice always started with facing the moment depicted in this plate: the destruction of the old imagined order, accepting that and authentically choosing to live.

If someone came to the project and used, the group would begin to feel this. We may not know specifically who was using and how, but the community would shake and burn much as in this image on Plate 3. Eventually, the using would surface, and either stop or the user would self-exclude. Sometimes as a staff team we did have to set boundaries explicitly, an example of which we will meet later, but mostly the boundary would be set within and by the community. Through this uncomfortable holding we could come to a sense of agreement and explore the issues in hand. We could bear the fragmentation that is presented with using and work it through.

The Fragmentary Nature of Thought

David Bohm (1994; 1996) makes much of the fragmentary and representational nature of thought. That is thought which is in the past tense, and can be held on to as a truth, when in fact it is only a representation of a previous state; not only that, but it can only be a fragment of the whole in movement and therefore an incomplete representation. Thinking is different, it is in the present and part of the moving whole, set in a context. Reified thoughts, even bodies of knowledge, are seen as 'necessary', just as the world is, when perhaps they are contingent upon the context in which the thought originally sat. Necessary in this context means that it is something that cannot be other than it is, whereas contingent would be contingent upon conditions and would vary when those conditions changed.

Bohm uses the example of a table. A table is not a complete notion, it does not include the atoms or sub-atomic particles of which it consists, but it is a necessary symbol in the context of understanding its hardness and its being used to put things on. Internal psychic and social thought systems suffer from the same problem.

Our representations and the tacit meaning constructs they rely upon may not be coherent with the world as we are actually experiencing it. For instance, we can no longer exploit the planet as if it were an infinite resource, nor treat any system or component of it in isolation. We are too many and have too great a grasp of the complexity of the ecology of the planet to be able to continue with that exploitative idea, which it has to be said, was a reasonable construct until just over one hundred years ago when our population was much smaller. Our consciousness of exploitation is doomed in the current context. It no longer serves our needs and actively hinders enjoyment, and it seems to me that we are addicted to the processes that sustain this particular process.

Representational thought alters perception as it is projected back into the perceptual process, limiting it and altering the way we perceive. Bohm (1994) suggest this process is both intellectual and material, rooted in the bio-chemical, as new neuroscientific research is showing us. Bohm references synapses, Pavlovian reflexes and conditioning as the means by which this is deeply rooted within the body. It would appear that McGilchrist's (2009, pp. 421–462) model, with a left brain that is taking control, might also articulate the dilemma we face. The resistance to change then is for Bohm as much at the level of the synaptic and endocrine, the neurobiological, as cultural and psychological (Bohm, 1996, pp. 79–82). A representational structure can be held in the body, resonant with Ray (2008a,b,c, 2016, 2020) and McGilchrist (2009, 2021).

We can read this incoherence, as Bohm (1996, pp. 77–78) understands it, as symptomatic, in the way Hillman (1975a; Hillman & Moore, 1989, pp. 143–148) describes symptom as a sickness of soul pointing forward to a new becoming, to create space for a symbol that better describes our experience in the context we find ourselves. In this way, Plate 3 points to the horrors we are now experiencing, as our old thought structures decay, and the self-righteous Satan of our collective selfhood, the tacit assumptions behind our exploitative (and it has to be said patriarchal) consciousness begin to collapse.

> at no stage can we properly say that the overall process of thought begins or ends. Rather, it has to be seen as one unbroken totality of movement, not belonging to any particular person, place, time, or group of people.
> (Bohm, 1980, p. 75)

Blake's formation of the Job narrative can be read as the breakdown of a fragmentary, contingent 'symbol', an image that has outlived its usefulness, and the 'perception of a new order of necessity' (Bohm, 1994, pp. 218–219). This is what I express as the poetic moment, the instant of apprehended and novel experience.

Suspension and Proprioception of Thought

Bohm (1996, pp. 83–95) suggests proprioception of thought as the means of deconstructing representational assumptions, addressing in the body the moment of experience, rather than an abstraction into recursive thought structures. This is very similar to the practice of meditation as conceptualised by Ray (2020, 2008a) in 'somatic descent'. Proprioception is the process within the body that links us to our experience of the body, for instance feeling the movement in one's arm and knowing where it is in space. Bohm suggests if one suspends a thought that this does not repress it or allow it to be completed or expressed. One can look to what one feels in the body. Here, it becomes possible if one allows sufficient clarity to begin to experience the tacit assumptions that form the fragmentary thought. I would read this much like McGilchrist (2009, pp. 198–208) describes the referring back to the right brain for contextualisation.

Bohm articulates a difference between the subjective 'I', which is infinite – 'unlimited', and the objective 'me', which is operated upon the paradox of the observer and the observed actually being one thing (1996, pp. 80–82). This construction too can be seen to map onto McGilchrist's thinking. As we pass though this Job narrative we are at the point in the process Blake is articulating that the dissonance between these differing perceptions of the world is coming to light. Unfortunately, there is quite some difficulty to be endured before we come to any synthesis. Job will persist in his attachment to his spectre, or to his understanding of his righteous behaviour.

This shift beyond subject and object leads to a perception of a participatory experience, an experience which includes the context in which it is being experienced, not only internally but also in relation to others. This participation is framed, by Bohm, in the context of the participatory experience of hunter-gatherers, as it is for Ray (2008b), but the context we now inhabit is different, because of the action of the symbols we have formed in the meantime. Their meaning is implicit in the whole system, because they have been thought. We will need to find a new context that offers such participation.

In the passage of the plates, we are not at this stage yet of suspension and proprioception, we are simply experiencing the upwelling of the thought that it will be necessary to suspend, a dissonance between internal experience and perceived event. The realisation that what we had perceived as necessary is in fact contingent. There are four more plates until we can really begin to address that process, which is the period when we are subject to breakdown or defences of the ego (dissociation, splitting, denial or de-personalisation); or in the context of the larger group, falling into the basic assumptions (Bion, 1961): pairing, fight or flight, dependence or aggregation and massification, as Hopper (2009) has described.

There are a myriad of technologies to address this process, the bearing and containing of the rawness of life. In the end, it is the group experience, what is simply human relation within the community that provides containment, the capacity to receive experience and bear it. In the Job narrative, there is a wide community, there is internal and external experience, divine and human, that contain Job. This is why Whitehead's idea that we receive into life rather than act upon it is so powerful. The question is not, what can I do to make this safe? in the group example used, but, how can I receive this experience so the creation of meaning is possible? This is also true for the ritual work described above. How can one receive the grief of a father who has lost a child, or a son who has lost a mother, to enable that loss to be mourned.

My experience of containing the meetings and groups that constellated around the bombings in central London during July 2005 was of defeat and despair, as was much of the tone of my work there. I described the moment when the group clearly appealed to the staff team to make it safe, as they were perhaps experiencing the very same explosions I felt in my chest. I could not make this experience safe and felt afraid of my closeness to the dangerous events. One of the underground carriages blown up outside Russell Square was a carriage I habitually use, and still do, to travel to work. The likelihood that I would have been in it was small, however, no less real. Structurally and personally, it was necessary to bear the experience for and with the group and continue to provide psychological capacity that allowed movement, not the rigid holding on to thought, as had become a habit for Job, but the suspension of the fixity of an idea.

One might frame this in the context of Bion's (1961) basic assumption, dependence, where the group seeks a leader to provide answers or a direction. I felt that I must resist this dynamic, and not collapse into the idea that 'I must sort this out', which was the demand made to the staff team, but wait and allow for something new to arise. My colleague's interpretation provided an idea that allowed for something not to be 'sorted out', but allowed for, the acknowledgement of the danger we were all in, especially in the context of using. This intervention both stated the social fact of life, that it is not safe, but can be made 'safe enough', and grounded in the work of the practice.

The fantasies of violence and sexual competition one might frame in the context of 'pairing', and the desire to expel and persecute the transgressor of an agreed boundary in 'fight or flight', but the more profound and complicated question might have been who to fight and where to fly? We were thrown up against the fact of our participation in a *whole world narrative*, in which we were component. There is no other, no object, only the illusion of such as an operational convenience.

All of these primitive (early life) experiences were ignited in that group in a felt sense, and needed to be contained, thought about and borne communally. It was my responsibility to lead this with the staff team. It was indeed uncomfortable, as this plate is uncomfortable. Unfortunately for Job, it is not going to get more comfortable for some time. Of course, as we passaged through the torment and struggle of the group, and its following experience, we began to process what had happened, to find a new accommodation for what had felt intolerable, and the realisation that we had formed a safe-enough context for these experiences to be processed. This would allow for the symbols that had been thrown up to become relationally negotiable. The person who threatened violence, and was made a scapegoat, was not thrown out. Boundaries were set and negotiated. Draconian, impossible rules were not formed, and the discomfort of change and becoming was negotiated.

As De Mare et al. (1991) describe, the group forms its own culture to articulate an experience. There are things that can be done, particularly in the context of trauma work, that will substantially shift the weak foundations of our psychological structures, giving an underpinning to our constructed frailties, but I believe we have to remember that we are a component of, and a reflection of, a continually evolving process which is creative. It can be useful to remember that the process will unfold when these primitive defences erupt, and so the eruption is also useful. These processes in that context are homeostatic, both personally and socially.

Plate 4
Lost Perspective
And I only am escaped alone to tell thee

Plate 4 illustrates the reporting to Job of the loss and destruction of his property. There is a distorted perspective showing the distortion in Job's world. Satan is abroad, as you see from his image in the upper margin. He has command over Job and his whole world. Job is fully cut off from his spiritual truth, and his understanding of the world is insufficient to encompass what is happening to him. The mercy needed to temper judgement is not available to him, so he must fall. He is being judged and found wanting. He has not the inner resources to meet Satan as the accuser.

As we have seen in the Lurianic myth, it is the excess of judgement, accruing all to itself, that breaks the sefirotic vessels of the tree of life and collapses the connection between humanity and the divine. This disrupts the relation between God and creation, causing what was a spiritual experiment to fall into material manifestation. It then becomes humanity's cooperative responsibility to repair the connection. Job is hanging onto the letter of the law because he has no understanding of its deeper truth, and no means to understand that this is the problem, so the pain and loss is experienced as persecution, Blake's wrathful, torturous black fire.

Perspective is distorted in the megalithic architecture behind Job and his wife. They appear unaware of the cause of their disruption, and pray hollowly to a God that would appear not to listen. Job is cut off from his children. Either they are dead or they are dead to him, in the confusion of his unrelatedness. In the Bible, his wife is lost to him too, but here she continues with him throughout Blake's interpretation of the piece. I consider this to be a reflection of Blake and his wife Catherine's relationship, where they were connected and deeply involved in the work together. She was the only person he let help him with his alchemical printing process, and she believed fully in his visionary experiences, as recounted by Crabb Robins in his 'Reminiscences' (1852).

'It is quite certain that she [Blake's Wife] believed in all his visions'. And on one occasion not this day speaking of his Visions she said – 'You know, dear the first time you saw God when you were four years old, and he put his head to the window and set you screaming'

In the plate, I see Blake expressing disorder through the rationalisation of the Enlightenment. The quotation below, from 'The Mental Traveller' (1801–1803) shows how he viewed the rigidity of the rational and abstract, obscuring the imaginal and perceived, relational and participatory.

> The Eye altering alters all;
> The senses roll themselves in fear,
> And the flat earth becomes a Ball
>
> The stars, sun, moon, all shrink away,
> A desert vast without bound,
> And nothing left to eat or drink
> And dark desert all around.
> (62–69 E, p. 485)

I don't think that it is a perception that is as simple as either, but that both exist. The differing perspectives are necessary contraries, the spiritual and the material between which life emerges.

Solomon (1993, p. 23) sees this attack taking place in the realm of authority, where Job's self-righteous view of himself is challenged. Job assumes and is complacent about God and himself being good. He is still of the mindset that God is a good God and therefore is in shock at what is happening to him. He is good and God is good, but bad things are happening, how can this happen? He is stuck with a dogmatic understanding of the discrete duality of good and evil and thereby a victim.

In the context of the addiction process, I would say that this is the first inkling that something is going wrong, that our using is causing a problem, but we are not able to understand that it is the using that is the problem. We repress and deny. We locate the issue externally, not wanting to face what underlies our desire to use. The hangovers are difficult, and we are not really able to function. This is the point where things begin to become 'unmanageable', as those in the Twelve Step movement describe it.

Often people would present to CORE with the use of multiple substances and work their way back through them, heroin, to methadone, to alcohol, to cigarettes, indeed to sugar, revealing under each the layers of their struggle with life. All point to the same thing, using a substance, or for that matter a compulsive behaviour, to alter the way one feels rather than accept the feelings that are arising in the body at the moment of experience. I remember a client who could not let go of the last two milligrams of methadone; for some time they stayed stable and then gradually and finally not so gradually fell back into using. I never got to find out what was the trigger for them falling back into using, as they left the project. What was not understood or accepted was the principle that the feelings arising would be borne and allowed to alter. This of course is more possible in group than individually, which is why the Twelve Step movement has such success.

The ego, in Jung's (1916/1958; CW8 1969; Miller, 2004), formulation of the 'transcendent function' cannot accommodate the dissonance between external reality and internal experience. A new symbol that will be able to accommodate both is required. This symbol forms in the unconscious. In Bohm's (1996, pp. 73–76) terms, I see this as the need for the suspension of the fragmentary. Representational thought is required and proprioception of that thought to formulate a new symbol.

Blake is presenting an idea of good and evil in itself being wrongly constructed; the contraries are necessary. Now is not the time for some pious God to save Job. Only a full and thorough examination of the context in which he finds himself will help him find a means of recognising his distorted and undoubtedly rigid perspective. This is clearly expressed in the stones that seem to hem his distorted view and resonate with Plate 7, where he enters Ulro, spiritual death.

Plate 5
Hypocrisy
Then went Satan forth from the presence of the Lord

According to Solomon (1993, p. 27), the central theme of Plate 5 is unknowing self-righteous hypocrisy. Job blindly continues to do as he believes he should. He has no capacity to understand that there is a deeper understanding that he needs to reach. He continues to offer alms as a literalised ritual of gift, based on his limited view of his plight. This is not a truthful, generous gift but one based on the desire for receipt – the utilitarian gift. This is a gift of the cold charity of the Deist religion, devoid of visionary truth, with a rational utilitarian bent; a Benthamite measure of value so beloved of the Enlightenment capitalists and the Victorians. In my view, this represents the mechanistic operation of recursive representational thoughts or feelings, which are habitual, dead, untruthful and incoherent to the process of the wider whole, as Blake bemoans in *Jerusalem* (1820). The Gothic is gone from the imagery and the druidic primitive murderous religion is in its place. The Druidic[6] religion represents the cruelty and deadness of the 'Deist religion' that Blake so vehemently fought. Rocks are reminiscent to him of the mind of Ratio acting on fallen humanity, 'condensing them into solid rocks with cruelty and abhorrence' (J, 19–25 – E p. 164). Here, we see a clear enough image of the Stonehenge which interested him, representing the religion of human sacrifice. The landscape is bare and barren. His conception of the druid is in keeping with his time and much based on the work of Stukeley (1740), although we have since learnt more and come to form a different opinion of druidic culture.

In Eden, the twelve figures of the divine family look down in dismay, unable to connect with Job. The divine family, or the Council of God, is the communion of saints, the aggregate of Christian thought, the body of Christ, consisting of the elect, dead or alive (FD, pp. 105–106; Raine, 1982, p. 67). The aggregate sense of human experience is a central idea for Blake. In this context, the sum of Christian experience is put together as the Council of God, the Council of for me the whole. The recording angels look on in the margin quite understandably in despair as they witness Job's inevitable fall and the suffering he will endure.

To listen truly, and to receive what is said, is hard. To allow oneself to be open to feeling vulnerable, to let our assumptions about identity and self be challenged in this reception, requires a strength of faith that Job is about to find but does not yet understand. Job is unable to hear what is being asked of him; if he were he could save himself considerable discomfort and jump forward to the restitution at the end of the piece.[7] Of course, it is the understanding that is learnt through the discomfort that enables us to bear our vulnerability.

Working with addiction there are many examples of Job's attitude. I had a friend who when something went well would buy a bottle of champagne in the pub and pour it into the street. This was his ritual sacrifice, but he did not think that perhaps he should fixate less on alcohol, drink less, and life might be more easy. Or more tragically, there is the client who turns up having used, sweating and gouching out,[8] thinking that they are doing something for themselves with the work, but repeating only the unconscious actions of despair and defeat that using tries to hide.

The group context offers a means by which this can be addressed more directly. Users can spot users. A room full of users who are trying to stop using will become agitated by someone who has used. If held in the right way the using can be challenged, and an understanding as why it is not a useful way to address one's difficulties can be found, but one has to have trust in the group, the humans within it and the process the group will follow.

Clinical Example: Pepe

At CORE, a man came to work in the project and stayed for some time. He engaged fully in the community and was a figure of some romance and charisma. He was beautiful and tragic with a long and beguiling history. He worked through much of his chaotic using history and was all but totally drug free. He had quite an impact on the community. However, he did not want to give up cannabis use, which was a boundary for a project based on abstinence. We worked with him on this, as we did with any drug which was not the identified drug of choice on arrival, but ultimately he was challenged by the group and the boundary was set. It was the agreement in the project that unless he stopped using cannabis he should leave. This was likely to be deadly, and indeed he did die of what we understood to be an overdose soon thereafter. It would have been hypocritical to let him remain part of the community, as much as we would have wished for him to stay. He was unable to hear the hypocrisy of his position, and we could not collude with that or behave hypocritically ourselves, and not keep the boundary we had negotiated as a community. The tragedy in the room was palpable. This moment is still referred to between people who were there some twenty years later.

However, it represented the need for the group, and the capacity of the group, to hold in mind the process that was being negotiated collectively – the release from addiction. Pepe remained attached to his idealised dead object, the group struggled with real relating to living people, not dead, and of course far from ideal. Although deadly to him he was perhaps right to recognise that the group held something that he could not bear, which was the difficulty and vulnerability of relating, and he realised therefore that he must leave. For the group of course, it was a profoundly moving and conflicting experience, hope mingled with despair and fear, that there but for luck, or some semblance of resolve, go I; as well as relief and the fruitful experience that it is possible for a community to maintain its boundary and work with the suffering ending using had engendered – ordinary human feelings. Notwithstanding the grief felt at the loss of a friend.

Yahweh at first would appear drowsy, which Raine (1982, p. 67) links to the Platonic sleep of incarnation and forgetfulness as the soul descends to the earth, to Generation.[9] The book is closed and the scroll of Job's life is abandoned, dangling from Yahweh's left hand. Job is cast out to his fate on the sea of time and space. Satan is acting here as the forces of destiny. However, if you look more closely, the whole scene has a sense of tragedy and compassion. Yahweh would appear to be in fact full of grief, as if knowing of the process that must unfold and his part in it, which, as omniscient, we would expect that he should. This whole narrative will inevitably play itself out with each actor taking their role in an almost deterministic way. Even Satan seems to question God's intention with an expression which seems to say, 'do you really want me to do this?'

Blake considered material experience as loss, the loss of vision and disconnection from the spiritual world as true death. Literal death, he saw as the loss of a body that that was grown in this life to protect the soul. The Platonic notion of incarnation as sleep, innocence can see eternity as it 'exists really and unchangeably' (Raine, 1982, p. 69). Experience 'is the deadly dreams the soul falls into when it leaves Paradise following the serpent', to the world of Generation. We have seen the scales of the serpent appear in the margins of Plate 3, but the serpent is now alive and fully present in the foot of this plate, and its tail replaces the web of religion seen in Plate 2. The vision of eternity is now lost. Job is closed off to his inner spiritual world and abandoned to his fate. The angels within the image represent the care from Yahweh but Job does not notice them. He weakens and despairs. Satan pours poisonous fire into Job's ear considered by Blake to be the spiritual organ.

This is not an entirely involuntary process. In *Jerusalem* (1820), Blake's final great epic poem, in which he expounds his myth, it is essential that Los, the hero of the tale, engages voluntarily with the process of change, but it is an inevitable process once it has been entered, as the 'Last judgement has been passed', the realisation of 'error' has been made and cannot be turned back from. This judgement comes with every out breath and is redeeming, made anew, each time we breathe it in. However, it is entirely possible that the choice is not made, and the encounter, as with Pepe, heads towards a literal death. The figure of Stonehenge I have found referred to as the door of death, as it appears in Blake's illustrations of Blair's poem 'The Grave' (1808), as it is the frontispiece for *Jerusalem*. The megalith sits behind Job and his wife as they enter. I am suggesting this death would be the death of the old self-image, the identity as addict for users, Blake sees it as the death of spiritual blindness of Ulro, that is about to come the loss of the vision of the infinite.

From a Jungian point of view, the connection between ego and Self is disturbed (Edinger, 1986). A new symbol is forming in the unconscious but being expressed in tormenting images, nightmares and psychic symptoms defended against with hollow and tired practice. The unconscious symbolic components of the transcendent function, that is hidden from the ego, may erupt into consciousness in fragments (as in Plate 9) but the symptom calling the new into life is essentially still repressed at this point, repressed and being acted out, performed rather than consciously understood, as in the hypocritical giving of alms. Job would do better to be generous to himself and think more deeply about his context, but that would be too frightening and challenging of his identity.

With reference to the group narrative, the felt sense is not yet fully with us, we are perhaps not ready to be aware of the uprushing experience and its proprioception. We need the old, fragmented contingency to hold together, lest the psychic energy breaks us. Too much unmediated psychic energy will fragment the ego. As Elliot alludes, the human capacity for reality is very weak. The defences are still in operation and the event collapses into its habitual order of externalised or internalised aggression. Yahweh's knee is contracted in judgements along the Kabbalistic pillar of severity. Satan pours poison into Job's ear, and the serpent arises to consume him from the margins – for Blake the ear was the spiritual organ. Given this context, there are no means to renegotiate one's psychic perspective with the assault from within and without, from heaven and earth. It is no wonder that the continuance of the fall is so inevitable.

Blake offers relief through the two angels, left and right, in the world of Generation, an indication that Job's plight is held in mind, however absent, drowsy or disturbed Yahweh might seem to be. For me, this is the function of the group. Whatever struggle the individual is engaged in, there is the possibility that some members can hold in mind the process that is being experienced. From a psychotherapeutic point of view, the facilitator then holds the frame for the group to work in, is mindful of the process and may steer or call attention to its unfolding.

As with the vignette above regarding Pepe, the group was able to hold in mind the needs of the individual members. In the context of the whole project, the service users that had been with us for a long time were able to bear and hold something for those who were newly arrived. The staff team held the boundaries within which this process unfolded. The appeal was beyond the individual psyche to the group and the whole. In the context of CORE, this was the old users, as the divine council, the guardians of the group's history. For the individual, there is some component of the psyche that witnesses and holds together, so that the falling apart is not a disintegration, where the psyche fragments and flies apart, as in psychosis. There may be splitting, denial and depersonalisation, but the parts are held and can be rebuilt with new insight and perhaps greater strength.

In the profound and eternal round of suffering and ignorance that is the human condition, and that I have seen in my work, it is difficult to shorten or alleviate the struggles my clients/patients have. Once, they enter the process of change, we fall together, but that falling together offers a relational opportunity for something to be different, as illustrated in the progression of these plates. For now, one more insult before we are fully fallen.

88   Perishing

Plate 6
Agony and Ecstasy
And Smote Job with sore Boils from the sole of his foot to the crown of his head

Satan now has full possession of Job and attacks his body directly. Job has not only lost his material wealth, he has lost his vision and connection to God. Here, we see arrows from the four corners of Blake's image of the psyche, the four Zoas – Luvah, Urizen, Tharmas and Uthorna, 'The four eternal senses of Man' (J. 36.E, p. 182)

Raine (1982, p. 76) sees the attack in this plate as particularly orientated to Luvah (love), sexual guilt, represented by the scales of the phallic serpent worn by Satan. The fire from the vial poured on Job she sees as the Urizenic fire of the troubled mind and the boils of physical illness. He is disconnected from Yahweh, who has left the images now, returning once in a dream and then fully, after Job's fall, which takes place in Plate 13. With his head thrown back and his arms outstretched Job seems to be ecstatic. He is experiencing a connection to something, all be it through the great suffering in his body. Here is a sense of the proprioception Bohm refers to, albeit in an unpleasant and overwhelming form. We feel it in and through the body, not in abstraction. This is the opposite of the fallacy of misplaced concreteness. It is the actual event, with no abstraction to distance us form it. The incoherence is agony.

The clients mentioned in the last three vignettes all had serious health problems, sores and scaring and abscesses caused by injecting, lost limbs and failing livers. During their time with us some repair took place, but the physical damage and the suffering in the body were substantial. Pepe reported that he had only once felt clean in his life, and the dynamic of abuse and shame at root in the other two was palpable. As yet they had not found the resources or resolve to surrender the using and appeal to human relation.

In this image, the status quo is broken down. The sun is disappearing and is nearly out of the picture, night is nearly upon us, the dark night of the soul which will be endured for the next five plates. Blake has devoted half of this work to the fall, to the disintegration of the psyche. The falling apart is fully half of the story of change, whether we would like it to be or not. In relation to this image, Solomon (1993, p. 29) emphasises despoiled and betrayed love, that feels both an internal and external betrayal, so like the despair of self-abandonment and hurt that is so destructive in addiction.

It is notable that Satan is standing on Job's knees. The knees for Blake represent the form of contraction, as opposed to expansion, which we will meet in Plate 18, the crushing and breaking down. Satan's other foot is on the solar plexus. The universal image for the centre of energy is located behind the naval, the lower 'Dantiene' or 'Hara' in Chinese or Indian philosophy (Hoxun, 2004, pp. 115–120; Ray, 2020, p. 34). This is clearly the breaking point, where the old self structure Job inhabits has been broken down, the agony that would be ecstasy if it were to be perceived from a different context, but that is not possible, as we are not past or even near the nadir. Job has not let go. In the margins, we see demons and spiders spinning the threads of fate, and the locust or grasshopper, the bringer of pestilence and destruction. Even the two angels of record are turned for the moment to demons. The crook, the symbol of safety, is broken, as is the clay jug. Containment is lost.

All this is lost to Job, and he is left to despair in his fate. He is unaware that it is his self-righteousness and his hypocritical, material fixation that, according to Blake, causes all this hurt. Job is accepting of his fate. He will still keep his faith. This is important in the move that I see in Blake's Job (as opposed to the Job of the Bible); this is about the internalisation of the divine, the face of God inside.

In terms of the narrative of addiction, we are entering the nadir of use. The old using life is dead, but the using has not stopped and the new life is not anywhere to be seen. We are no longer able to move forward or back. Unfortunately, this dead place of recurrent using can be inhabited for years, for as long as the body will sustain the abuse, and indeed often beyond. We are at the deepest despair, in Blake's terms, the place of spiritual death, with no hope of an enantiodromea, a volteface, a sudden turn to the opposite, that the pendulum will return to the resonant, and a recognition of the value of the relational over the material.

Notes

1 Kathleen Raine describes how 'on plate 32 of *Jerusalem*' we see Jerusalem, the soul of Albion, "the lamb's wife", with a Gothic church in the background, while Vala, the cruel 'Goddess nature', is given the symbol of St Paul's, Wren's Temple of the enlightenment and reason.
2 The mosaic law is the law of Moses, the ten commandments, needed because it is not possible to discern truth through theory alone.
3 Blake saw the four Zoas as the fundamental aspects of man: the body, Tharmas – west; his reason, Urizen – south; his emotions, Luvah – south; and his imagination (Damon, 2013, p. 458). In *Jerusalem,* they are described as the four eternal senses. They are often mapped on to the four functions of Jung's typology. However, there are problems with this.
4 It is often that archetypal images come in pairs, this is such a situation where the puer, the young man, often flying boy such as Icarus, is matched by the old man who may be more wise, the senex.
5 The body of the community is how I came to understand the sense of community formed over time. It was not the physical environment nor just the people that made it up, but the resonant and historic sense of community formed by the members and the context over time. It resided in no one person, but had a sense of its own solidity.
6 Foster Damon (2013, p. 109): 'to Blake, Druidism, far from being the pure faith of Abraham, symbolised Deism … it was the religion of the patriarchs from Adam until Abraham shrank from sacrificing his first born'.
7 Gouching out is when one has used sufficient heroin to make one drowsy but not completely unconscious, so one slips in and out of a state of slumber.
8 Gouching out is when one has used sufficient heroin to make one drowsy but not completely unconscious, so one slips in and out of a state of slumber.
9 This motif is seen in the Arlington Tempura, where Blake depicts the Porphyry's De Antro Nympharum (1821), a description of the descent and return of souls.

Chapter 3

Ulro
Spiritual Blindness

To the Queen

The Door of Death is made of Gold,
That Mortal Eyes cannot behold;
But, when the Mortal Eyes are clos'd,
And cold and pale the Limbs repos'd,
The Soul awakes; and, wond'ring, sees
In her mild Hand the golden Key
The Grave is Heaven's golden Gate,
And rich and poor around it wait;
O Shepherdess of England's Fold,
Behold this Gate of Pearl and Gold!
                    Dedication to Blake's illustrations of Blair's Grave (1808)

The Second Coming

Turning and turning in the widening gyre
The falcon cannot hear the falconer;
Things fall apart; the centre cannot hold;
Mere anarchy is loosed upon the world,
The blood-dimmed tide is loosed, and everywhere
The ceremony of innocence is drowned;
The best lack all conviction, while the worst
Are full of passionate intensity.
                                        W.B. Yeats (1919)

Ulro – Spiritual Blindness

Now we reach the point of spiritual blindness, or the fallen state. This is Job's alienation from the divine, his total desolation. It was only towards the end of his myth making that Blake differentiated between Ulro and the world of Generation.

However, this is clearly a different and important condition, as opposed to the downfall we have just witnessed. He has devoted four plates to this component of the story, so it is important that the nadir is endured over some time, whether temporal or psychic.

Raine (1982, p. 44) refers to Ulro as a fixed and dead world akin to how Blake sees experience. Bound by the five senses, error was brought into existence in a space and time external to consciousness, but within the mind of the natural frame, so the naturalisation of the self as separate from the divine equated to death. Blake follows a Platonic line to incarnation, seeing the soul descend into sleep. Ulro is the nadir point of this fall, from oneness with the whole, with God, to the dead rational world of Locke and Newton, with only material engineering, as we live our lives devoid of a spiritual vision. This would be an example of McGilchrist's left brain only view.

Spector (2001a, p. 134) suggests that Ulro is a macaronic composition different to others, such as Urizen, who is a composite of notions of reason. There is no ready English cognate upon which the composition Ulro is formed. She suggests that it refers both to the negation of vision and the negation of evil, the second promoting a vision of God. This view in the context of my work with addiction would ring true. How in the face of death can we chose life? This sets Ulro as eternal death and God as eternal life. My experience with most of my therapeutic work is this: we have to face what is deadly and chose to live. We need the faith to live until of course this life comes to an end. This, of course, is stark with addicted people. Death is readily acted out through the using and the likely outcome of continued use. Several patients have said to me heroin is no use 'unless it makes me go to sleep'. However, there is hope in this that through the using, although half dead, some experience is a little digestible, and this experience can be used to build symbols by which to live.

This was the work of CORE, to allow for the relation to a dead object, the heroin or alcohol, or for that matter cannabis or tobacco, to move to actual human beings with which the user can reciprocally relate: true self to true self, as we see in Winnicott's (Abraham, pp. 277–282) model, or infinite subject to infinite subject, as in Bohm's. This relational reciprocity, as we know, breeds life, both literally and metaphorically. It is the held in mind, the loving that creates the space for life to begin. If there is no one actual mind available, then the border group, the collective, the social, the archetypal, can be used to provide containment. An example might be using parents who are not available to the child as they are caught in the using and not relating.

When at CORE we used myth and poetry and ritual, or for that matter acupuncture or craniosacral therapy; there was always a person or people whom one was relating with, and with whom this experience was felt. Actual loving beings receiving and reflecting a lived engagement. By framing this shared experience in the context of homeliness and away from the theoretical roots of the work, we made it more accessible, but not less rigorous. We emphasised the compassion not the judgement; however, in some way a judgement was always there as a boundary. The using had to stop. So instead of the void of a dead object – no relating with no boundary – there was actual relating to actual living people with agreed and clear but negotiable boundaries, and the capacity to bear the responsibilities that went with them.

Here in the next four plates, we explore the various faces of Blake's eternal death as we head towards the choice to live or indeed, as in Pepe's case, not. More often than not when trying to give up the using wins. I think it is important to recognise that to live is always a choice and one that will increasingly be volitional; again, as I see it, driven by the success we have of prolonging life, and the numbers there are of us on the planet, where we are a product of social structures or of resource allocation, desire and faith.

94 Ulro

Plate 7
Despair
*What! Shall we receive Good from the hand of God and
we shall also not receive Evil*

In this plate, we enter the state of Ulro, the total withdrawal of energy from life. The clouds in the margin obscure any contact with Yahweh, with the divine or spiritual life. Job has lost everything, and, as you can see from the image, he is in despair. The sun has almost gone from the image and we are fully in the Druidic world that for Blake centred on human sacrifice. It is representative of the sacrifice Deism made, a natural religion, with a god as divine engineer rather than spiritual becoming. Note that the recording angels are also holding their heads in their hands. The human sacrificial alters are prominent. The comforters appear. As in the original story, the comforters come to help Job but they come with the old structures of reason and righteousness, so are no comfort at all.

The arrival of the comforters is important from a group context. They have the same mindset as Job – they know that God as all good can't behave in the way he is. They are, it would appear, both fearful for themselves and in despair as to what has happened. Most importantly they are able to bear the experience with Job, to help carry his suffering, as is the case in group sessions. Although they are not able to bring new insight, they will represent Job's dilemma to him in its old form. No doubt they are caught in the old dogma that God is desirous of the righteous man, or at least three of them are. The fourth will act in Plate 12.

So often, in the midst of the darkest time, even when there is conflict between group members, and something is arising that will need to be worked through, I have experienced how the holding of the group can allow something to open, for something new to arise. An example comes to mind involving a group of men, some of whom had suffered with difficult fathers, and some who had suffered with being difficult fathers, feeling they were unable to find the inner resource to meet their children. One might imagine that this would create a polarised situation, where the hate between the two sides of this difficult tension, those who were abusive and those who were abused, was re-enacted. This could have been entirely possible had it not been for the containment of the group and the good will that had built up over the years. A place was found for the despair and difficulty of both experiences, and something of a dialogue between the two was possible, a humanisation of both contexts. No immediate solution was found, but a compassionate bond was formed, allowing communication across the gap between the differing experiences. Each person in their own time was able to find something that helped the particular narrative they were holding onto. In the space, between the two conflicting positions there was something new, something that could alter the fixed states, and some sense of trauma could shift in this relational context. Through goodwill there was a suspension of the old thoughts and the beginnings of a new perception. Both sides could perceive something in the other and shift their own stuckness; indeed, they could alter their relationships outside the group to accommodate this new insight. Over time this was and is returned to as a theme, much as the sequence of this image can be seen as part of an iterative process.

In this plate, Job is not yet in that position. He is not able to change. He is broken and unseeing because of the loss of his previous identity and his blindness to the cause. The comforters are stuck with him, adhering to the dogma of the previous life. He is bereft and despairing, and they are confused.

At the top of the plate we read:

> What! Shall we receive Good from the hand of God & shall we not also receive Evil?

This is a reorientation of the faith that God is all good, which was the case in Plate 2. Blake is transcending the binary of good and evil, as one might transcend the binary of God and Self, which we will come to later. Remember Blake points to this, that the only sin is that of the hubris of knowing the difference between the two.

In Plate 7, Job is destroyed. He has the measure of the problem, through continued faith in the process, not the dogma, nor his literal thought, but the process. Here, we see the seeds of Jung's (CW11, 1952/1969) interpretation of the mythic structure that God is redeemed in humanity, as much as humanity might be redeemed by God. Rather than a split system, it is a perpetual co-creative process in a systemic context. The illusion of separateness is that of perception and the apparatus of perception. We will return to this theme later, but in this moment of contraction is implicit the beginnings of a release to expansion. We begin here the move from ransom and dependence on God's grace to relationship and responsibility, from a fixed and unilateral perception of constant being to the relational fluid becoming. Whitehead (Mesle, 2008, pp. 42–56) articulates the idea that to step beyond, involves a wider reconnection to the co-creative process as participatory. One could call this a re-enchantment with the world.

The comforters appearing at this point resonate with the group and the old order, but they also introduce a wider relatedness as the process of the group will be the resolution to Job's suffering. However, here they can only see that Job has somehow brought this on himself. How can a righteous man be treated in this way by a good God? The wicked in the end are destroyed by their own wickedness. Raine (1982, p. 83) points to this, linking it with the law of Karma that assumes the interconnectedness of the world. That there is an equal re-action to any action; actions are seen to be born of thought, which itself is born of desire. If we give in to desire in a self-willed way, we act out of selfishness and we will meet the products of this selfishness further down the line; not through magic, but through the simple repetition of the desire and thought, like the simple repetition of desire and using. The reverse is true. If we resist selfish desire and act for the good of all, for the whole in context, we will meet, further down the line, the fruits of this action. If we take this in the context of Ulro, to which Spector points, and I believe Blake does too, it is inevitable that this contraction leads to expansion.

Blake puts this quote in the margin: 'Ye have heard of the patience of Job and have seen the end of the Lord'. This quote is from the *Epistle of James* (5:11) and Raine (1982, p. 82) recognises in it the suffering humanity endures before enlightenment. There is a process beyond the binary relationship between God and

Job which we have explored through Whitehead and Bohm. It seems part of the process, understandably denied in general, that we experience to the limit of our being before true wisdom is found. Where have we to go when faith is outside of us, in dogma? In the personal, we have to search within. In the group, we have to do the same, but recognise its resonance with that of others. This is a difficult thing to achieve, as it offends our narcissistic sense of being and what we have to do to withstand and accommodate our own experiences.

Bohm (1996) approaches this through 'dialogue'.

> dialogue is a multi-faceted process, looking well beyond typical notions of conversational parlance and exchange. It is a process which explores an unusually wide range of human experience: our closely-held values; the nature and intensity of emotions; the patterns of our thought processes; the function of memory; the import of inherited cultural myths; and the manner in which our neurophysiology structures moment-to-moment experience. Perhaps most importantly, dialogue explores the manner in which thought [...] an inherently limited medium, rather than an objective representation of reality – is generated and sustained at the collective level. Such an inquiry necessarily calls into question deeply-held assumptions regarding culture, meaning, and identity. In its deepest sense, then, dialogue is an invitation to test the viability of traditional definitions of what it means to be human, and collectively to explore the prospect of an enhanced humanity.
>
> (p. 50)

I see a bridge between the visionary experiences of Blake, who would imagine conversations with Plato, and Bohm's understanding of the implicate. Through his visionary imagination Blake was able to penetrate the implicate order beneath the explicate of the everyday. As Churton (2014) asserts, it is clearly a function of Blake's imaginal perception that the visions manifest; it is the form that the imaginal perspective and the co-creative process is seen through. Higgs discusses this in terms of synaesthesia (2021).

In his introduction to *On Dialogue* (1996), Nichol discusses Bohm's means of dialogue in the group:

> As a means of enquiry in a group, Bohm suggests that we engage in suspension of thought and pay attention to the body's response to that. He argues that it is possible to suspend assumption. For example if you think someone is a fool, you suspend your words: (A) refrain from saying so outwardly; and (B) refrain from telling yourself you should not think such things. In this way the effects of the thought, 'you are a fool' (agitation, anger, resentment, for example) are free to run their course but crucially, this is in a way that allows them to simply be seen or experienced, rather than fully identified with. So the principle is a process of suspension of any identification with the fragment – thought – and to explore the context in which that thought sits, the predicates upon which it is founded. This can be seen to be reflected in many meditation practices: notice

the thought, felt, image, but do not attach to it, allow it to arise and fall, then the tacit process beyond that thought comes into view. With meditation comes in many forms and has many end goals, but this process which has to some extent a similar quality has the goal of an apperception of the unfolding of the co-creative process as a whole, which is being experienced, and then inhabiting and witnessing that process.

(pp. xv–xvi)

As a practitioner one does this all the time. One bears the experience in hand and tries to imagine both what this might mean for the other participant, or participants in the process, and indeed what hidden unconscious contexts might be brought to the surface. As an example I would often experience the work at CORE as a hepatic process; it felt that what was going on in the room was going on in my liver. The thinking was not in my head.

Bohm (1996, pp. 83–95) argues, in the activity of suspension, that the role of the body is of central importance. If a strong impulse is suspended, it will manifest physically, and a spectrum of emotions will emerge. This is his meaning for proprioception – to feel into the workings of the body. Being given immediate sensory feedback about what is happening inside the body and inside the psyche offers the opportunity for the recontextualisation of that thought and the perception of its predicates. This is highly reminiscent of what Ray (2016, 2020) might see as the right brain process appealing to and being embedded in the body (soma), or McGilchrist's understanding of right brain activity after the processing of the left. We might call this listening to the felt experience.

In Plate 7, Job is overwhelmed by this upwelling of experience, as the fragmentary thought is no longer able to contain his experience.

Bohm (1996) writes:

> Literal thought aims at being a reflection of reality as it is … we are giving them too high a value they can cover some reality, but don't cover all.
>
> (p. 85)

He makes a link to a previous, more participatory, mode of thinking.

> Half a million years ago people didn't really need much literal thought. They lived in small groups of hunter-gatherers … But then came the agricultural revolution, and larger societies developed. These societies needed much more organisation and order and technology, and they had to use much more literal thought. They organised society by saying, "you belong here, you do this, you do that." They began, therefore, to treat everything as a separate object, including other people.
>
> (p. 87)

So Bohm is pursuing a method of group enquiry that exposes what he sees as the implicate underneath the literal exposition of the explicate – the frame through which we have dogmatically perceived the world for much of our experience, since the advent of farming and the formation of large cultural groups that generate a fragmented and conditioned 'left brain' view of the unfolding of our life.

Bohm makes an interesting point in the context of our conditioned view of experience – our assumptions of subject and object are socially determined, not participatory. Our experience of the world is conditioned by this objectification. He argues that it is possible to re-imagine or re-perceive a participatory experience through dialogue. Blake is pointing to this also, in saying, as he does in Plate 1: 'it is spiritually determined'. The spirit he points to, I would argue, following Spector (2001b), is Ein Sof, the source of all becoming, the source of all creation, the great nothingness. For Blake, this was the divine human imagination.

For Bohm, the whole process of fragmentation is supported by culture (1994, pp. 22 & 47). Culture is the means by which an idea spreads and functions (Ibid., pp. 185–186 & 188–189). I see that ideas live in us as we live in the medium of the world. This may be mythic or it may be philosophic; indeed it may be scientific, but it is culturally informed. Cultures may live and die, like empires, but they exist in the moment, like a 'me'. 'I', the subject, on the other hand, is a component in the whole, born with and an expression of it. As with Blake's Job, we are coincident with the whole and in this context we are infinite subjects. However, this is not knowable in the limited frame of sign (Jungian),[1] but imaginable in the frame of symbol (Jungian), which crucially contains the numenous and implicate context of the unknowable and ineffable whole, the subtle implicate beneath the explicate.

> Such perception is a flash of very penetrating insight, which is basically poetic. Indeed, the root of the word 'poetry' is the Greek 'poiein', meaning 'to make' or 'to create'. Thus, in its most original aspects, science takes on a quality of poetic communication, of creative perception of new order.
> (Bohm, 1980, p. 145)

The interesting point that Bohm makes is that freedom in this context is not the choosing of one event over another, but the change of necessity; what is necessarily so, not freedom from an oppressive fragment, a thought, but a freedom to, an opening to, a co-creative apperception of becoming.

In this plate, Job has come to that point of experiencing, the limit of the thought frame that he has inhabited, the idea of an all good God, who will benefit the all good devotee, is broken. So a self-image is not fixed, but perceptual and forever shifting in the frame of the context in which it sits. I am reminded of the Alexander technique,[2] as an example of this process. You break the habit in the body and allow experience to change from the bottom-up, not top-down. The instruction comes from a cortical level, an abstract idea. A top-down instruction exists, but to inhibit habit rather than actively cause action. The result is both physically and psychologically transformative. The body chooses what is the best posture, and the feelings attached to physical habits are more readily available to conscious experience. The processing of these can be felt more readily in the body. Meditation is an example of how these habits of thought and imagination can be broken, opening more freely to the perception and experience of the unfolding process of becoming as it is experienced. If we follow back, the way Bohm does, the cultural roots of this process, it can be seen as communal and social in its deepest context. From a psychological point of view, it is easy to see how components of my psychological narrative might be used by a 'me' or others as an imagined and transitional object, i.e. the projective work of therapy.

As we have seen Bohm (1996) argues that creative imagination and insight is brought about through dialogue (Dia = through, logos = meaning). He understands this as the deconstruction of relational and internal meaning to imagine a new necessity in context (personal, social and whole) with the capacity to suspend thought, the dogma that comes with it, and deconstruct assumptions, both personal and contextual, which are hidden underneath. This involves both vision, frustration and good will, as does any creative act, artistic or scientific. This for me is the process in the rehearsal room, in group, as well as in life and, I believe, exactly the process articulated by Blake in these plates.

For me this plate describes the point of addiction where we are bumping along the bottom. The quiet drunks you have seen in the pub with their lonely pint; the 'Waitrose' drinkers who, alone at home, drink in solitary despair; the addict, in their room, caught in the cycle of scoring and using; or, more mundanely, the worker trapped in the office fourteen hours a day, neck-deep in files and over-eating.

As a rule of thumb, it used to be said that it took six attempts to stop 'using'. Since I worked at CORE, I met people who have said that they gained from the experience there, but did not actually stop then. It was part of a cumulative effect of different approaches. For me, this is part of the sadness of what has happened in the addiction field over the last twenty years. In the search, for a rationalised and I would say commodified, means of treating addicted people, the state brought about a homogenisation of the services, breaking down a diversity of opportunities to stop. People are not efficient. They are diverse. What works for some will not work for others. To lose this diversity defeats the joy of relation across difference and the opportunity for healing and the new.

In this plate, we see Job at the point of realising his brokenness in the context of his community, and indeed Yahweh and the divine order. Now, the work of dialogue between him, his community, and his internal world, has to reveal a new vision.

Plate 8
I Wish I Were Dead
Let the Day perish wherein I was Born

Lo let that night be solitary
& let no joyful voice come therein

Let the Day perish wherein I was Born

And they sat down with him upon the ground seven days & seven nights & none spake a word unto him for they saw that his grief was very great

After seven days and seven nights of grief, Job begins to curse his fate and wish that he had not been born. The margin around the image is corrupted by fungus. The counsel of Yahweh is withheld. All is in darkness. There is bitter weeping and lamentation. This is the point of contraction represented in the knees being drawn up. This contraction is the view of the material world as merely matter, bereft of its spiritual greatness and divine resonance. Raine (1982, p. 86) mentions that constriction as the expression of spiritual struggle is particularly characteristic of Blake, and he expresses this tension clearly in *Jerusalem* (1820): 'The Circumference is within, Without is formed the selfish Center' (J.71.7 E, p. 224)

He sees as dead the naturalised[3] world, devoid of the spiritual life that is
'selfish', that which is perceived as illusory, in Buddhism 'maya', or in Platonism, for instance, the myth of the Cave, where as the outer world is illusion:

... in your own Bosom you bear your Heaven
And earth & all you behold; tho' it appears Without, It is Within,
In your imagination, of which the World of Mortality is but a Shadow
(J71.17.E, p. 225)

Blake's wish for Job – and others, following his own experience – is the internalisation of the divine. Seen in crisis, the darkest point of the descent contains the seeds of a new vision. In her commentary, Raine (1982, p. 86) refers to Bachelard's (1943) description of human imagination, discovering in the natural world, a language of symbols to express states of mind.

This interplay between humanity and the world as a participatory 're-enchantment' refers to the neo-animism I am seeing in Hillman's work (and those that follow it), and the accrual of feeling/experience in Whitehead's pan-experiential philosophy, who gives primacy to feeling over matter, an expression of Bohm's infinite subject falsely separated from an illusory objective reality.

Job is in the world of 'Newton's Ratio', the ordered known and, to his mind, dead, disconnected from the limitless view of eternity and our context in it. This is the left brain only view shared by Urizen and Satan, not contextualised by the right and its overall appreciation of the whole. To return to the symptom of addiction, this is the despair of using. The loop is almost endless, with each glass or each sip, hating oneself for the action and wishing for a death. The death of course wished for is the old and useless life that for a time served well but now simple destroys us. Hillman discusses in 'Suicide and the Soul' (1964) that the suicide generates a particular problem for psychoanalysis. All too easily it is possible to rob someone of their soul by removing the symptom that expresses it. He links the wish for death by suicide to death that needs to take place in the personality for the psyche to shift and to move on. A part of the personality is identified with, so the death that is imagined is that of the whole being. The job for the analyst is to shift the identification and help the patient know what part of them needs to be let go of. With addiction, this can often present in the context of the inner child. The damaged child needs something, and until it can receive it, it will not let go. Job must suffer more before this shift is possible, and it will nearly kill him.

Plate 9
Eliphaz's Dream
Then a Spirit passed before my face the hair of my flesh stood up

Eliphaz is one of Job's principle comforters. He kneels and points above to the image of his dream, the first presentation of the return of the internal and the imaginative, the life of the soul and its divine connections. Job's family are currently inaccessible, not connected to the process. They are to return to the narrative, but at this time it is still as if they are dead. This is a fragment of new life; it is not yet known and not yet knowable.

For me this is a dream, not a personal dream but a dream from deep in the collective. It is in the group and for the group, not just for Job or Eliphaz as individuals. Job may well be carrying the narrative in a personal sense, but he is embedded in the matrix of the group, and the echoes of change and new vision is within the group, to be brought to light. This is an echo of Bohm's thesis that the life of the group is interconnected (1996) and through the loosening of boundaries of self we can recognise resonance in the system. As with the group of fathers, or the group struggling with the London bombings, they are set in a context beyond the individual members. Symbols reflect in the context of the whole and may appear anywhere in the group.

In this image, the sense that something is breaking through is palpable; a constellation of thoughts or images from the unconscious which will manifest in the conscious mind. Through the lens of the transcendent function, we would see this as a new symbol forming but not presenting in a form the ego can digest. It is still perceived in the old context. There is further change to come and trials to face for the ego to be able to assimilate the new and as yet unconscious symbols. The old established order is too strong and too rigid to see in anything other than in its own terms. Thus, the comforters see it as proof that Job is at fault, not God.

Raine (1982) is particularly impressed with this image.

> The psychological truth is astonishing. Here the as yet unrevealed Presence passes across the stage of another's dream as a figure of awe and terror. Job is not yet himself open to receive such a communication of wisdom; but the apparition of Eliphaz stirs a response in Job's soul ... Job understands, while the others merely listen.
>
> (p. 89)

The synthesis of a new group symbol is yet to be made. Between Job's questioning and Eliphaz's image the new can begin to emerge. There are three plates to go before a dialogue can be formed that will bring a new vision for the group. The literal representations are not yet truly challenged. Note in the margin we are still surrounded by the Forest of Error.

Although Job has not yet grasped what is happening, he appears to understand or to wonder. Note the questioning on his face, rather than fear or despair. He sees something, but not clearly. Eliphaz is locked into the previous narrative, but something awakens in Job. Eliphaz' left hand is raised, perhaps linking to the right brain, to a deeper context that is arising. The playful balance between group and individual expresses here the emergent and resonant context I am trying to articulate. It is within and between that this resonance is taking place; not just for Job alone, but for the whole system.

So in terms of Bohm's (1996, pp. 23–25) imagination of the group, this is an experience of the proprioceptive process, the appealing inward to the felt sense of what is experienced, the exploration of suspended thought or feeling that, although tense and difficult, is beginning to offer some new possibility for insight. The literal thought is not yet fully seen, yet Job's quizzical expression holds an attitude that can begin to see where the thought's representational antecedents come from, and the possible reaction which can now be processed and re-imagined, or re-perceived.

Plate 10
Scorn
The Just Upright Man is laughed to scorn

Many have thought that Plate 10 relates Blake's feelings about his own life. Although clear in his faith, Job is hurt by the accusations of his friends and comforters. It must have been agony for Blake to have such clear convictions, and yet not be able to convince others, to be ignored and dismissed. What a relief towards the end of his life that he was accepted by the small group of artists, 'The Ancients', and John Linnell.

At this point, Job experiences his plight not as the group's. We are still in the position where he is 'Laughed to scorn'. The bat wings in the margin are reminiscent of Satan, and the chains pull the recording angels into mortality. The raven[4] and the owl at the foot of the image in the 'Forest of Error' are birds of death. These birds have both captured creatures – the serpent and mouse/toad (Raine 1982, p. 93), highlighting images of mortality and death. Raine sees these images representing the death of the vegetative body, but not of the True Man. From a using point of view, I see this as the need to resist acting out, to feel shame and blame, and the horror of manifest hurt, and to choose not to act out, so the using self perishes rather than attempts to defend itself through using again. The next living moment will, of course, come, but Job is not ready.

Solomon (p. 37) may have an interesting view here, linking the eagle to the sun, the owl to the night, and the false wisdom of the generated soul, both showing the emphasis on mortality. Of course the mortality that we are approaching is the death of the old self-image, which is about to happen over the next two plates, but here Job hangs on, deepening the polarisation between him and the comforters – between the individual and the group.

The Druidic landscape is utterly barren. However, the barely sketched Gothic arch in the upper margin holds the language of Job's faith, knowing he will come through this, whilst he despairs of the faithlessness of his accusing comforters. The two figures supporting the arch look as if they are being pulled by chains of time and matter into the pit of the underworld, clinging on by their fingernails. The tension is reaching its peak, prefiguring the final confrontation with the old ideology, a rigid and self-righteous state of being.

Notes

1 In a Jungian context, a sign is like a road sign which points to something. A symbol has beneath it the ineffable link to the collective unconscious.
2 Alexander Technique is a postural training treatment that uses the body's innate sense of what it needs to find its right posture. It was invented by F. M. Alexander, an actor who became unable to perform through tensions held in his body. By undoing, this habitual tension and allowing the body to assume its natural balance he was able to speak clearly. The benefits of this are both a better posture but also access to the thoughts, feelings and assumptions that underlie that tension.
3 Naturalised in this context refers to the natural sciences and the outfall of rational materialism
4 Foster Damon (2013) sees this as a cuckoo, Solomon (1993) as a bird of prey.

Chapter 4

Turning Point

Ode to Salt

And then on every table
on this earth,
salt,
your nimble
body
pouring out
the vigorous light
over
our foods.
Preserver
of the stores
of the ancient ships,
you were
an explorer
in the ocean,
substance
going first
over the unknown, barely open
routes of the sea-foam.
Dust of the sea, the tongue
receives a kiss
of the night sea from you:
taste recognizes
the ocean in each salted morsel,
and therefore the smallest,
the tiniest
wave of the shaker
brings home to us
not only your domestic whiteness
but the inward flavor of the infinite.

Neruda (1954, Trans Bly et al., 1993)

DOI: 10.4324/9781003354642-5

Fulcrum

We are at the fulcrum point now,
That space between evidenced
By zero or infinity - all reflections.
I mean here the single event.
After the breath - we fear, we love,
We rejoice just for an instant
Before the corpus drags the
Involuntary I to becoming.
Beyond you, beyond me
In the space between living
And dying all is possible.
Just for that instant death
Holds out hope for eternity.
Yet is it true it is sound.
For sure it is all fear and all joy
The one moment where
We imagine our souls could fly,
Before the next foot fall, next step
In the solid path of this practical day
Reflecting the infinite that loves us so.
                        Wright (2020)

110 Turning Point

Plate 11
Nadir
With Dreams upon my bed thou scarcest me & affrightest me with Visions

This plate is the nadir point and the beginnings of the move beyond the self-sufficient rationalising mind. Job's self-righteousness meets its apotheosis, its nemesis: Satan as the image of Yahweh. This is the 'reasoning spectre', who appears as the demiurge, the Platonic and Gnostic creator of the world. Job still clings to self-righteous ideas of the law, unmediated by compassion or mercy, as referred to in Plate 2. Here we meet, as did Dante (1265–1321), the devil in the pit of Hell.

For Blake, this figure is the manifestation of materialist reason, the Urizenic figure pointing to the tablets of stone, the Ten Commandments at the top of the image, the rigid Mosaic law: 'Thou shalt not...' Blake had no doubt that the Mosaic law was the law of the demiurge, the artisan builder of creation, or in his view, Newton's dead materialist engineer, here in his evil form. Of course, as has been the case throughout the piece, Job is also meeting himself in this demonic form. Job and Yahweh appear as reflections of each other; God is inside. I envisage this figure much more like the archetypal defence of the true self, as outlined in the Jungian analyst, Donald Kalsched's (1996) synthesis of object relations and Jungian thinking. In this model, a false self continues to re-abuse the true self, keeping it isolated from contact with others, from the environment and the context. To follow Kalsched's model, there is an archetypal internal jailor keeping the true self from connecting with the outside world. Here, it is represented as Satan of the Selfhood, the materialist, humanist God of the Enlightenment. For Blake, this was the Deists. To follow Kalsched's idea, this figure protects the individual from the pain of previous unbearable hurt, but often is itself experienced as re-traumatising.

An example of someone in this position might be a 'dry drunk'. In terms of the Twelve Steps, this is someone who toes the dogmatic line, rigidly pursuing the often persecutory dogma of the steps, full of self-hate. However, they never surrender to the psychological and spiritual challenge that those steps offer. They never relinquish the defences of the ego that lead to using or opening to the greater life this lies beyond that surrender. They can be forever trapped with a persecuting inner life, attached to the theory of addiction release, not the letting go of an identity first as a user then as an addict. This is the little death that is actually needed to release from using and open into something new.

It is not without irony that's Blake's artisanal skills, which kept him an outcast due to class conceptions of art of the time, are the means by which he expressed his genius. I had the opportunity to look at the copper plates in the British Museum. This revealed so much more than the prints we mostly see. His work with the graving tool is of course outstanding, but conveyed in the detail is such a clarity of experience, it evoked a visceral response. He brings his vision into the body, as would any great artist, but with such transcendental vigour. It was as if something happened in the space between the lines, that which he gouged out of the copper to leave the becoming life, as happens to Job in this dream, gouging out a space for the new to emerge.

Below, we see the serpent-scaled demons, seeking to drag Job into hell with chains, the recurrent symbols of Satan's matter. These are the 'mind forged manacles' of Urizen (1794), of the materialist that will only recognise the five senses as a means of apprehending the world. The serpent is above, variously, according to Foster Damon (2013): 'the symbol of evil since it seduced Eve: hypocrisy, worship of nature, the priest, and nature itself' (p. 365). 'The serpent's coils represent its dull rounds and repetitions' (MHH 20). 'The vast form of nature' is 'like a serpent' (FZ I I I: 97–101; J 29:76, 80). I read this today as matter devoid of its lived component, dead and inert, something I believe we are reimagining.

In Blake's time, industrial change and increased materialism were not only a source of social injustice, but the injustice of the 'boy ripped from his soul', which he speaks to in Songs of Innocence (1794). Like Raine I see Blake fighting against the Puritans – 'the certitude and anxiety of the Calvinist soul'. Today, we find this in the nihilistic philosophy of capitalist markets, which have separated themselves from an ordering principle, other than the idealisation and rationalisation of a means of exchange. The alternative would be to explore a true relational exchange. Psychotherapy might be such an instance. There is often a financial exchange between parties, around which there is a material agreement; however, more fundamental to this there is an exchange between parties which is an exploration of what it is to be human in which all participate, whether a traditional dyad or a group.

Raine (1982, p. 201) suggests 'Satan's cruelty wears the guise of virtue: he pursues his war against the "kingdom of the world" by establishing a code of Virtues in whose light Imagination stands condemned' …

Pointing to this quote from Milton

[The] four iron pillars of Satan's throne'
(Temperance, Prudence, Justice, Fortitude, the four pillars of tyranny)
(M.29.48. E p 128)

We see not only the dogma that 'God is good' being challenged, but also that unswerving adherence to the letter of the divine law has broken down. The need to turn towards something other than a transcendent didactic God is apparent. For Blake, this is the internal world of the divine in which we participate and will meet in Plate 17, not an objectified material world of matter. In his terms, this is error or creation.

Today, we meet the same hypocrisy in the puritan war on addiction as 'the war on drugs'. The rigid and regulatory persecution of the suffering, who use ultimately because of the struggle they have to live a broken and difficult life. Using becomes a bore and one gives it up unless there is an underlying struggle that the using is masking. As I see it, people give up when the pain of using is as great as the pain it masks. In the penultimate, vignette of this plate a colleague of mine articulates this experience at their point of change. Our job as practitioners is to help bring about this realisation. They would describe this as bringing up rock bottom. Drugs are a commodity like any other and they trade in suffering, the same suffering I see Blake pointing to.

There is an aphorism that 'Drugs fill a God shaped hole'; by this I would not specify a Christian God, although I think this phrase comes from the Twelve Step movement, founded in that frame. I would point to something more syncretic, as we did at CORE. We recognised that there was a longing for the sacred in using, a longing for relatedness in the context of the whole. Through analytic models this could be reduced to mother. God fills a mother and indeed Father shaped hole, but that is more reductionist than I would like to make it. Mother and father in this context would represent the unfolding whole and viewed developmentally as the figures we negotiate a self from, in that undifferentiated context – quantum parents.

We use because we suffer, and we suffer in our relationships to each other, and the context in which we live. We could call this incoherence, in Bohm's (1996, pp. 88–89) terms, being out of kilter with the moving and unbroken whole. This separation is a social construct formed out of the fog of fragmentation which can be interrogated and deconstructed, revealing its contingencies and errors of literalisation. Whilst we use this 'Satan' is real; when we stop all is revealed and life opens its possibilities. This process of opening will form the second half of the Job narrative.

In terms of Jung's trajectory for a life, this moment can be perceived as a mid-life crisis, whereby the turn away from the ego and to the path of the second half of life's individuation takes place. Satan is pretending to be true depth, the depth of spiritual vision, but in fact his is the confines of a rigid and unseeing literal structure, wearing the clothes of the divine without the content of mercy, of compassion, of 'Jesus the Imagination', and his creative vision who we meet in the following plates. This is the turn, if you remember, from the Frontispiece that upends the horror of creation and reconnects us to the divine. For Blake, the imagination is the divine connection. Rigid, rational approaches to understanding, centred on unpoetic knowing is, as Blake would say, 'error'.

By remaining faithful, Job counters this assault and is able to bear and know somehow that the cruelty is not true to the everlasting. However, he is not yet able to find this in 'the imagination'; to perceive the true divine within. He is still constrained by his belief in the laws and his righteousness bestowed by them, the stone tablets central to the image. The unfolding of this is a process of revelation, and the resulting expansion of consciousness is the narrative for the remaining ten plates.

Blake makes some alterations to the Biblical version of Job, changing worms to fire, emphasising the nature of spiritual transformation, as Blake experienced it. This is represented by the black fire of torture and torment rather than the fire of divine compassion – 'the genius of hell', which is the energy for life that Blake sees in the fires of hell.

Blake focuses on first two and last four chapters of the biblical story of Job. Plates 1–6 follow Chapter 1 and the first half of Chapter 2. Plates 13–21 reference the last four chapters. The final plates, 19, 20 and 21 only indirectly reference the final verses of Chapter 42 (Hiles, 2001). Plate 11 is the lowest point of the journey.

The vision of God appearing out of the whirlwind that will arrive in Plate 13 does not occur until Chapter 38 in the biblical text.

From the foot of the plate, we see two quotes that show the meaning of the image as an exposition of the self/ego's hegemony over our experience:

> Why do you persecute me as God & are not satisfied with my flesh. Oh that my words were printed in the Book that they were graven with an iron pen & lead in the rock for ever
>
> For I know that my Redeemer liveth & that he shall stand in the latter days upon the Earth & after my skin destroy thou This body yet in my flesh shall I see God whom I shall see for Myself and mine eyes shall behold & not Another tho consumed be my wrought Image
>
> Who opposeth & exalteth himself above all that is called God or is worshipped.

I read these passages as the interplay of novel symbolic meaning as it comes into consciousness. There is a struggle between a new, third position, developing in a concrescence, a becoming, in Job's near unconscious. This is reflected in the tension between the ego and the Self, in Jung's model, and is expressed as the transcendent function. From that viewpoint, this is the point that the tension reaches its peak. The boiling symbolic shifts that are taking place in the unconscious are as yet unbearable to consciousness and are experienced as anxiety, dreams and images.

An example of the new symbol forming that comes to mind is a dream that a client of mine brought. It was a nightmare from a complex time, and they had experienced considerable and repeated trouble both at work, where they felt compelled to drive forward, and in their personal life, which was turbulent and in flux. The dream echoed both experience of trauma in the womb and of how that had affected a creative but anxious life. For me, it also illustrates the beginnings of the new symbol emerging into consciousness and the terror attached to that moment.

The dream content is of being pressed in a coffee machine as coffee grounds. Hot tar breaks out of the grounds, having been used. This is then mixed with meconium and worked into an iridescent dark green paste that the client smears with a pallet knife onto a canvas as an art work or car body work to repair it. The effect is breath taking in its beauty.

There is so much overlayed in this dream it is impossible to go into great detail here but I would like to point to the reception of value and creativity and the bearing of the terror as relevant to this plate. Whitehead's primordial valuing and creative universe is frightening to the small objective me as it emerges, yet also beautiful. We held this dream very gently and allowed it to speak for itself, much as one would hold an infant in the first moments of life. It appeared to me that a deep internal struggle was being borne and a new living symbol was emerging from that, a deeper connection to what Blake would call the True Man, beyond a powerful and traumatic early wound.

I see this thinking as relevant to Bohm's notion of proprioception. It is in the body that the experience is had and, if it is possible to suspend literal thought, then it is possible to perceive the assumptions of that thought and see the experience in a new way to perceive a new order of necessity. In group, this is more achievable than in the simple individual dyad. More dialogic positions are possible that counter polarisation and entrenched contingent thought. But this is only possible when the incoherence of contingent, fragmentary thinking is perceived, as until that point the old dynamic will repeat. Job is not yet able to perceive in a new way, but he is not departing from his faith either. He is still open and available to change. The symbol has not yet formed; the penny has not yet dropped.

Example from CORE

I have discussed earlier that we approached rules at CORE as communally negotiable. We would define the boundaries of the community together. As one might imagine, this involved a lot of discussion, but inevitably we came to the fundamental boundary of the project, which was using and not using, and behind that the choice to live. This process of perpetual group negotiation focused on exactly this choice, and a typical trajectory through the project would come to this point shown in this plate, each client having to face their own Satan and realise that they had stopped, that they had let go of the identity they had as an addict, and would begin to form a new one.

It was always a profound moment when the last vestiges of clinging to the possibility that using could happen was let go. It is felt as a final betrayal, but also as a release. At the end of a lengthy habit, the new place one finds is cold and alone and utterly bereft. Dignity has gone long ago, in servicing the habit, and betrayal has become such a currency that there is nothing to trust, especially the self. It is a profound and bare moment of humanity in which death is a real choice. The joy of the group negotiations in CORE was that this was known by everybody. It was simply a fact of life, that had to be continually chosen, and of course often couldn't be. Relapse being a natural part of the process.

Through the trickery of relapse, we find the corners of our soul which need our attention. I remember a client I met some years after my work with them at CORE, who talked of caring for a lost inner child they had neglected, and that this neglect would in the end lead them to relapse, if not addressed. I presumed their discussing it with me was part-confession, part acknowledgement of the defeat of living with damaged internal objects, and part pride that they had the insight to bear this hurt and change. It was a moment of compassion in the gratitude for the space and the gift to self. I remember a matching moment with them after a group, during which they had railed at the difficulty of their life, and the horror of not using and the worse horror of continuing. We were sat in the sun at the end of the courtyard where CORE was housed, both staring at our feet. I waited a moment and then said, "But we both know you just have to stop". To which they replied, with a shudder of defeat, "Yes. I know". The sun shone and the day moved on. I doubt this was the last time they used, but a cadence had happened, and the defeat had been admitted. In the admitting of that defeat, life became possible and the choice to live became real. It was a moment held in group, in community, where enough relational possibilities had become alive that the choice could be made.

This cadential shift had to be experienced by everyone in the building and everyone knew it. I think in fact it is a human truth that we all have to choose to live, all the time. Mostly, our body takes care of this for us; for instance, try not breathing in by choice. However, we have to decide how we are to understand the purpose of that life and its engagement with becoming, to find a coherence with the becoming world in which we are a part, to form symbols through which we live together. This is what I would see as a spiritual question and the choice we face perpetually, the choice Pepe could not make, but others in the room could. It was their reception of each other's struggle and indeed Pepe's that was the antidote to the half death of using.

I see that we face profound changes to the co-evolving structure of the group and the individual, the relationship between the individual and the context in which they sit, from the particular social, personal and cultural environment, to the wider context of the planet. We have the capacity now to connect on a planetary scale, one whole system, with eddies and pools and divisions, but connected up.

In practical terms, I have worked with people on almost every continent. I have not visited them, but I have been able to communicate directly either by telephone or internet. I have friends on most continents with whom I am often in touch. This is not yet open to everyone, but presents a wider perspective than we have previously experienced. Communities are forming in new and diverse ways. It could be seen that the life of the community is becoming far more fluid, less based in the matter of the ground in which one is embedded, and is now a matter of allegiance to a symbol: we are offered meagre symbols of nation, industry, commodity or faith. Yet, we have no clear over-arching narrative for this deep and changing process; we are in search of something new through the diversity of our symbol making, but not yet near. This must produce two effects – the personal resonance of the material environment inhabited, the earth that we actually inhabit, and the need to understand better the nature of the fluidity of symbol formation, and its importance to our connectedness. The less we are defined by place the more we are defined by symbolic allegiance. So less an objective component in a mechanical system and more a reflexive and participatory resonant event within a moving and experienced whole.

A symbol that I am suggesting is one of being embedded in the coherent whole; not merely as a function of a self-state, although I would see that it is a symbol thrown up by the process of self-orientation. This happens in a particular body that has experienced particular experiences, but also happens in a context wider than the body. The tragic vignette of Pepe offered above was set in the context of London as a diverse city. They happened not to be from London but nonetheless felt at home there, and at home at CORE. Also the bombings I used earlier as a vignette were driven by an international narrative and at the time I saw them as one of the opening salvos in a war of narratives which seems to have developed over the last two decades. However, they exploded in actual streets and tunnels and affected actual buildings and people, they resounded in actual bodies, including mine and those I related to, carrying symbolic meaning from and to the whole planet.

Symbol, Self and Group

It might be useful to think about 'symbol' and self in the context of group analysis and the social and collective unconscious. In the psychoanalytic cannon, there are two main frames for an understanding of the transpersonal unconscious, or the unconscious that is at root in the group or community – the social unconscious and the collective unconscious. The first is drawn from the psychoanalytic roots of group analysis, is socially reflected and would, to my mind, take a materialist point of view, as articulated by writers such as Earl Hopper (2003; Hopper & Weinberg, 2018). The second is the Jungian notion that the underlying root of the personal unconscious formed phylogenetically into a priori archetypal structures embedded for Jung in the alchemical notion of the Unus Mundus, and for archetypal theorists in the Platonic notion of the 'Anima Mundi'[1] – the world soul in which our individual souls are component and from which they are informed. The archetypal is a shared collective consciousness that can be seen in myth, religion and the spiritual frames that we use to organise our cultures and experiences (Samuels, Shorter & Plaut,1986, pp. 26–28).

However, Colman (2016) has put forward a case for the negotiation of archetype, and therefore, the collective unconscious, as socially and historically constructed, an emergent property out of the relationships of the group. This would fit well with the Whiteheadian notion of becoming that we explore in this book. Segall (2013) argues that Whitehead's philosophy of organism can be seen as a science of the world soul linking his work to archetypal thinking.

Whitehead was interested in the mathematics of new physics in relation to an organic evolutionary process. He wanted to include post-Newtonian physics, as he saw it; the quantum and the relative, which Bohm (1982) takes forward. Both suggest a creative ethic at the root of experience, which we will address in the next plate. This presents us with two problems. The first, which is the relative, that says the spatio-temporal environment as we experience it cannot be taken for granted; the second, the quantum, which says that solid matter can only be understood as the interrelation of coincident energies collapsing into a definite value. Whitehead inserts experience (feeling) at this point in a similar frame. He sees feeling accrue up through the evolutionary and organic process to experience, as matter does to organisms. Organisms in this Whiteheadian context are more complex interrelational forms, a 'society' of events. This replaces Newtonian solids with occasions, relationships in the flux of change, that congress into actual events, requiring duration in a Bergsonian (1910) sense, forever unfolding. Whitehead warns of the abstract, a 'misplaced concreteness', which is the abstract attempt to 'conceive the full reality of nature at an instant' (1938, p. 145) rather than continually referencing back to the ground of experience as it accrues to event.

The construction of self that I am putting forward, an emergent property formed relationally out of the conditions surrounding it, not fixed but congruent both with Whitehead and Bohm's models of the accrual of relational experiences and meanings. However, self in this context is forever changing, a resonant structure informed internally and externally, collectively and socially; a hallucinatory product of the organism's homeostasis, a structure of interrelated systems auto-poetically[2] created, set in the context of other external auto-poetic systems – social, material and cosmic, the nested self, creating and evolving systems of Whitehead's thinking.

To identify with any one material and experienced event, the 'actual occasion', and to reify it into an existing object that has substance over time, is a fallacy of misplaced concreteness. In so far as, we are able to draw a flexible narrative in the process of becoming and perishing, we are able to have a consistent sense of self; however, the more rigidly we hang onto these structures against the vicissitudes of experience, the more tension builds up internally with the dissonance – or incoherence – between the abstraction and the perception. Here in Plate 11, the tension reaches its peak before breaking down, or for that matter, through.

Incoherence and incompleteness is at root in the nature of the physical, and for Whitehead, felt in the body. In an everyday sense, we perceive a narrative and consistency over time. However, upon examination, it is illusory and fragile. This is not an everyday attention to tasks and living in the world which requires a shared narrative between organisms, but another persistent and participatory experience that disregards to some extent the processes of time; more a perceptual and contextual shift, which might be understood psychologically, spiritually or intuitively, and is in the area of the right brain functioning. I see it as a mirror to reality, the real behind the hallucinatory process we symbolically create to order our experience. Whitehead's perception in the mode of causal efficacy (1927, pp. 30–49). Here then, Blake points to the shattering of the old narrative and its terrifying redundancy.

Sloan Wilson (2015) suggests that our evolutionary struggle caused a shift from blind biological competitiveness to symbol formation, a Darwinian model. He has also suggested that this capacity for shared symbol formation heads towards altruism. Organisms are understood in the Whiteheadian universe as co-creators of their own environments, pointing to synergistic interaction as the primary mode of advantage, not competition. It is the relational nature of organisms in ecosystems whether atomic, biotic or anthropic which produces successful evolution, not the honing of competition. Not a competitive model but one of symbiotic relation driven by creativity and value, and felt as value, which he articulates as the spiritual love of God. In this sense, it is a secular God of creativity itself, both principle of creativity and ordering being through the value of that creation, a God whose primordial nature is value, which has the consequence of an actual event (Segall, 2013, p. 44).

The shifting of the root metaphor from mechanism to organism is a profound change and of course the change Blake is pushing. To reflect the whole universe as a fecund and creative organic process is to move away from the projection of a divine creator, demiurge or engineer, and to put more centrally the principle (as Whitehead does) of creative process, the 'life principle' (Segall, 2013, pp. 34–35) or Bohm's creative ethic (1998, p. 7). It is also to counter the mechanistic and mathematical thinking of the 17th century, to move away from a projection onto our own imagined creation to apperceive the creative process beneath. This is a fundamental recontextualisation, underway in this plate. The mechanistic left brain is at the end of its confabulation and about to be recontextualised by an encounter with the right.

Myth and Ritual

Joseph Campbell (1949), the mythographer and scholar, has suggested that we have been on an 800 year journey from a certain kind of embeddedness in the group or community to the idea of the individual psyche as separate from the group. He proposes the 'hero myth' as that of the archetype of the ego, and the hero's journey as the process by which this structure is developed. Moments in this process are marked by rites of passage involving the exile from community, an encounter with death and a return to the community, where one is recognised as changed. At the point of the encounter with death, some old identity is let go and replaced with a new image. However, there is a need for a renegotiation with the context in which that individual sits; the return to the community that is the second half of the journey of individual freedom. We are not only individual, we are in this together; our individuality is a product of the communal. We must return to that communal frame to be recognised as new or different, to have a more developed sense of separateness. Freedom in this is not a freedom from, but a freedom to; to express individually and in relation the exact resonance of our emergent becoming. We used exactly this model at the CORE Trust. We would take people who had reached this place in their life and provide a communal context for them to be received into a new becoming, so they had a new sense of identity; and were, indeed, not an addict.

This is a colleague's example of the moment in community, in rehab, of Plate 11, as it leads us into Plate 12. It has the flavour and structure of ritual, and a mythic sense to it, but it is a personal event and the point they stopped using. It is set in the community from which he is exiled (by himself). There is an encounter with death in the symbol of a friend and then a return as a new day; as it happened a new life dawned.

Sunrise

What a beautiful day, I was thinking. But hang on, I've never had a thought like this. What the hell is going on? And then I remembered.

   I hadn't slept for weeks; talking, talking, round and round in endless circles, confined to an old mental institution under the threat of being sectioned if I left. Yesterday was ok. Spent the day making sandwiches and drinks for the evening's gathering of relatives and friends, the weekly social that we were all expected to be part of. The thought of inviting anyone I knew to such an event was abhorrent. As if anyone of my acquaintance would enjoy such a time. How could I expose them to such a possibility?

Anyway, the evening came and I huddled in a corner with likeminded cronies, being somewhat surprised that some of those that came were actually laughing. Indeed some were dancing under the glare of the institutional lighting. How could they? It was pathetic.

As soon as I could, I left for the safety of the ward, with the same bunch who had stayed apart and tossed a coin for partners on the snooker table. A cry went up. When I turned around I saw my buddy lying on the floor, foaming at the mouth whilst banging his head on the solid carved table leg. His body contorted as the alcoholic fit went on. Not much the nurses could do except prevent him from biting through his tongue.

As he came out of the seizure it dawned on me that I was looking at how I had been on many occasions before waking up in hospital beds. Is that what I have put myself through? I thought. Is that what other people had seen on the pavements of London? Is that what my mother has seen her son like? I began to shake.

A nurse who I was close to came up and said that my wife and daughter were visiting the next day. "Don't let them in," were the first words out of my mouth. I was terrified that they should see me under these circumstances. The shaking increased as I tottered to my bed, sinking to my knees. I heard myself say, "If there is anyone out there I just want you to know I'm fucked." I crawled into bed.

Waking up the next morning, I crossed the ward to the window, where a beautiful day was ready to greet me.

The human capacity for symbol is the capacity for the aggregation of perceptual experience and its resonant exchange between societies of events – in other words, transmission. This for me is what Blake is getting at when he sees everything inside the felt experience. His visionary experience is a resonance with the whole, his imaginal capacity for symbol directly accesses the infinite subject.

Our proximal construction of self is reflective of the community we inhabit and is processed by the members of the community, themselves infinite subjects. The community informs the formation and experience of self, and vice versa, they are not separate entities. The histories that we bring to the table are component in this process. So the community experience affects the personal and provides a frame for the processing of experience. I would argue that it is the personal capacity to process experience and make it available to consciousness, insight and dialogic negotiation that enables change. This is expressed in the vignette above, the dialogic renegotiation of symbols to allow for the new to arise in relation.

Addiction provides an example of how this process might play out through the unintended consequences of our identifications. Addiction is the search, as I see it, for something alive and relational in the dead but certain object of drugs or alcohol. This plate is the point where that search has come to its end, and we can choose to stop. Vulnerable and bereft in the face of utter self-betrayal, habitual self-destruction and humiliation, death is staring us in the face, daring us to choose it. Satan, in a heavenly form (note here the image of Yahweh has cloven hooves; this is Satan the accuser), pointing to the tablet of the law: dogmatic mechanical error.

Sloan Wilson (2015) offers us a clear and optimistic model for a way forward, a communitarian and altruistic one based in group, not the proximal adaptation to altruism but the context of altruism in the group as the most effective organization. This is recognised in Whitehead's (Segall, 2013, pp. 57–59) assertion that nested organic structures that make up process are symbiotic. I have faith in this from my work with addicted people, and from working with groups. It takes a group to contain an addict as they let go of the using. The relational negotiation has to be open, honest and profound, but this is not such a difficult choice, when there is nowhere else to go except death. Everything else is stripped away, as is the dreamt process in this plate and as is shown to us in the next.

Some of the people I worked with individually came into my private practice after leaving CORE, one such is an illustration of this need for the group. This person had an interest in spiritual practice but was at that stage in their life unable to bear, individually, the experiences this practice gave them and had developed a habit against the difficulty of the transpersonal events engendered. They spent some time at CORE, eighteen months, perhaps two years, during which they developed strong communal relationships with the other members of the community. When they came to finish, they worked through the final three months of the programme diligently and came to the final ritual group that marked their ending quite high, not from using, but in what might be seen as a semi-transcendent state. Indeed, they articulated this as feeling in and out of oneness. From a psychological point of view, I was somewhat anxious that this was slightly manic spell and was expecting a crash. The group contained and related to him and each other, both in the context of the event of their leaving but also on a broader communal scale.

Fortunately, this event came in the middle of term, I was available individually after their leaving and we could negotiate the descent to a more ordinary state of consciousness. This was also supported with the social relationships he had formed with his cohort of the community. It was the group that contained their psychospiritual change in the project and continued to contain them after leaving. They went on to lead a full life, free from using and indeed communally orientated, at one point returning to CORE to lead some group work as they moved towards working in the psychological professions.

Now we turn to Plate 12, where Job begins to experience the new, and the penny begins to drop.

Plate 12
The Advent of the New
I am Young & ye are very Old where fore I was afraid

Elihu as one of Job's comforters is the crucial figure in Plate 12, and in some sense for the whole story in terms of his closeness to God. He stands to the left pointing both to the sky and forward. He is the young one in the group of comforters, who has been sitting quietly away from the struggle between Job and the others. Raine (1982, p. 207) links Elihu with Enoch, the prophet of the Old Testament who was so close to God that he never knew death. We then could see him as a manifestation of the mind of God, perhaps also the transpersonal witness that we experience outside of our personal self, or a manifestation of the whole. I would also link this notion to awareness in Buddhist thought as Ray (2016, 2021) and Lancaster (2005) do, an openness to the co-creative whole. This is the right brain perspective, which Ray draws down into the body – the right brain for him is the body, not just the material fact of the body but its resonant experience of becoming.

At this point in the story, Elihu steps forward and says that Job is mistaken, that this is not about him, it is about God. This is the essential shift in perspective that is necessary to move Job away from his locked position with Satan of the Selfhood – his spectre – and allow something new to surface. We might look at this in the context of McGilchrist's (2009, pp. 198–208) model, the moment of reference back to the right brain, to recontextualise in the light of reasoned and abstracted experience.

Something has died, as shown in the image of Job at the bottom of the margin. I would suggest that this is the old self structure. However, Job has not yet come to this realisation. Between here and Plate 17, Job's encounter with God (and the image of God) is internalised. The perception of the divine moves inside. Job is given visions of God and his creation as part of his transformation into new life. To begin the process of individuation, in Jungian terms, and the liberation[3] of self, as I see it in Eastern traditions. In the context of Blake's world, this is a visionary process and a teleological calling of us into life, becoming not fixed and backward looking to the antecedents of our arrival, but moving towards creativity, towards novelty, as Whitehead (PR, 21–22) suggests; the opening out of a contracted past to an expanding future, from the crushing despair of Plate 8 towards the resonant opening and expansion of Plate 18. We are now interested in where we are going rather than where we have been. Not freedom from what we have become, but freedom to what we might become. It was the facing of this moment which was always the release needed in addiction. As we saw with the two examples in the last image.

For me, the key to this image is its 'poetic beauty', as Raine (pp. 203 & 206) sees it, after the violence and horror of the last image and the despair that preceded it. This is the instant of apperception, the resonant moment of balance, the calm at the eye of the storm. A new perception is burgeoning, but not with us yet. We might compare this to the CORE service user on the bench, noticing for the first time that life free from addiction is possible. I doubt this optimistic thought was hung onto – doubt and horror would follow, and then remembrance – but this event, when someone chooses life, is always beautiful, and felt in the body, a right hemisphere experience, not a left hemisphere abstraction into social construct.

Job is in contraction, as can be seen in the central image. However, I read a peace in his despair, as opposed to the terror of Ulro. Something has settled, his faith has borne fruit, some insight, if though through exhaustion and horror, is at hand. It is easy to read this as the letting go of narcissistic defences to allow for an altered sense of self, or a connection to the true self, in Winnicottian terms, the shift to recognise that what is being held in self is not just for self, but the co-creative process of becoming, the shift towards the participatory. However that is yet to be fully perceived (this new perception comes in Plate 15 and then is incorporated in plates 16 to 21). Elihu's arms point both transcendently and immanently, for me expressing the overarching co-creative whole held in the process of material becoming. This demonstrates Blake's understanding that we are coincident with God. The figures floating up to heaven can be seen as a connection to the divine, perhaps dreams or the reconnection of experience to the whole. Adishanti[4] (the non-dual teacher) describes this moment after five years of Zen practice, faced with the frustration of not transcending the duality of subject and object – he thought that he might as well let go and die if that is what it took – at that moment something shifted and opened to him and he awoke. For Blake, this is the opening to the immortal, the 'True Man' who cannot die, which takes place when error is cast out, as in the shift from the last plate to this and the process that will follow it.

The two figures in the bottom left hand corner are seen as both recording and guardian angels for Job, pointing the way heavenward. The scroll can be read as the record of his life so far. He is now in a sense dead, as he is ready for new life to begin. Clearly, the Job of this narrative is unaware of what has happened to him, but there is acceptance and the capacity to hear. Job is clinging to the belief that he has done no wrong. He does not know why he has undergone this change. We know from the biblical story that Job does know he has done nothing wrong and there is no conscious cause for his pain. He has kept the faith through his trials. Elihu plays the role of revealing to him the synthesis that will offer a new life.

Here, we can see the process of the transcendent function offering a third space which is not with subject or object, nor a solid new synthesis, but a fluid dialogic frame in which the 'new' can 'become'. The new synthesis is forming in the unconscious to be unfolded over the next few plates. I would also point to the group frame as explicitly suggested in the image. This process is not for Job alone but for and with his whole community. As Job makes changes in his psyche the general group shifts.

After the pit of hell caused by hanging onto old habits, 'using' is burned out. We are left with the real; the choice to live or die. Job chooses life. Elihu, who can be seen as the embodiment of poetic genius, and as young, the new, points to the realm of dreams and imagination. As Hillman would see it, this is the window onto our unconscious life, the means by which the poetic imagination, 'the poetic basis of mind' (Hillman & Moore 1989, pp. 16–17) opens us to a more engaged connection to life (in his terms to the soul, an 'ensouling'); or, a re-enchantment, in the Platonic sense of a fixed soul being held relationally in community. In pointing across to heaven, Elihu synthesizes an imminent and transcendental relatedness. This is an actual relatedness to the world as well as the heavens, the cosmic.

The internalisation of the divine that Job is going through is relational, embodied, dynamic, connected to the experience of the world, not separate from it. At this point, we should leave Job to gather himself, crushed as he is by coming face to face with the hypocrisy of his previously dogmatic and self-righteous state.

Clearly inspired to speak out, Elihu points to Job's self-righteousness and asks him to remember the true nature of God, of the everlasting beyond our reasoned knowing, which is Whitehead's (Cobb, 2015, pp. 71–75; PR, 343–351) potentiating God; Bohm's creative cosmic, McGilchrist's (2009) embodied right brain, Ray's (2016, 2022) soma. In doing so, Elihu makes accessible the mercy of Job's faithfulness, a faith not in any dogma, but faith that the next moment will happen. This is the moment of the shift in perspective. It is not about me.

I read this as the beginnings of transcendence, the death of the ego, of the little self that dies eternally in Blake's endlessly repeated day of judgement. The beginnings of the process towards the 'trans-egoic', as the transpersonal theorist John Wilbur (1980)[5] would put it. Bereft and alone, one has to find the faith to move towards life, towards other, towards community; undoubtedly a life of suffering, but with experience enough now to relate reciprocally. This will be repetitive; an iterative experience of growth, but there comes a fulcrum point in 'using' when the pain of use is worse than the pain of becoming. At that point we change, and this is the moment we can hear when someone points out what to do and where to go. There are myriad stories which illustrate this change; for instance, the vignette from rehab in the last plate.

A Dream

Life is infinitely beautiful, but knowing of it is a finite agony

Early in the writing of this piece I dreamt I was working with my partner on a Commedia dell' Arte production in the desert. We had erected a large stage in a Viennese square with trussing and a lighting rig. We were coming back in the evening to the square and the hotel, a large belle epoque confection, and as we rounded the corner in the late evening there were the characters Pulcinella, Harlequin, Peirot and Colombine rehearsing a scene. My supervisor for most of CORE was walking up and down in the pit (in front of the stage), placing a box at various positions on the front of the stage, trying to decide where it was right. Finally, he decided on a slightly left of the centre line (the side of compassion), then he opened it. We looked up and the heavens opened before us in a wondrous vista of stars, as if a layer of unclarity, of the atmosphere, had been removed. It took our breath away.

The perception I had of my partner and I were as two figures pointing heavenward as in the bottom left hand corner of this image. I also associated that in this stage of a production everything is pretty much set. It has yet to go before an audience and come to its own life, but what you as director and designer (my partner) had brought, was now to be let go, so the production could have its own dialogic and relational life. The hope is that enough resource has been found for the production to live with each audience that comes to it.

Earlier I described a group where Pepe was unable to accept that his using had to stop. When it didn't this choice led to his death. I directly named this for the group. The group too knew this, but through their engaging with the project and continuing to choose to live they reaffirmed their intent and created the space to imagine a new life. This moment too had a terrifying beauty. The feeling was of profound grief that such a magical person could not let go of their need to use, but there was an uplift, and sense of triumph, in that so many could, at least for the time being. I was left with ambivalence and many of the opposing feelings of guilt and shame that I could not help Pepe. I felt anger at the stupidity of his choices, and a resignation that this is so often the case. As with all therapy, it is well to be aware of one's omnipotence. It is not by one's own effort that change takes place, one only tires to create the space into which a new life can be received, as in this image and the ones to follow, but it is not your choice.

Bohm and Whitehead on Creativity

Whitehead's (PR, 348) concept of God challenges a purely materialist view of our existence but raises the question of what it is that provides the unifying and ordering factor behind the process of our becoming. For Whitehead, God is creativity, a 'fellow sufferer' that poetically bears with, as the most creative possible event emerges. Blake would certainly refer us to a frame beyond the five senses, or what Whitehead (1927) would call 'presentational immediacy'. Blake's God as Whitehead's is not one that is separate from our experience, something other than self, but something internal.

Bohm (1998) links mind to the natural ongoing process of the world, suggesting like Whitehead that creativity is not a function of the human mind, but something intrinsic to the nature of the universe in general: the universe in its wholeness is founded in creativity. For Whitehead, the centrality of experience is not solid being but perpetual creative becoming and perishing. Bohm believes we are capable of being aware of the process of becoming as it unfolds, and realising the context – our consciousness – in which that perception takes place. We participate in universal creativity: a co-creative process, both of the world itself, and our perception of it.

Bohm would see that the sense of wholeness and beauty we may feel in, for example, an artwork, an elegant theory, or a beautiful landscape, is underpinned in a process of orders manifesting both in mind and nature. This ordering process is ongoing, not fixed or rigid. Beauty in this perceptual context is the result of a dynamic evolving process that consists of order, structure and harmonious totality. He argues, as with the fragmentary nature of thought, that this co-created process would flow dynamically if it weren't for cultural hindrances sustained through history and habit.

> To the extent that our perceptions of the world [are] 'reality'... we have a corresponding responsibility to attempt to bring into being a coherent relationship between our thought process and the world they emerge from and interpret.
>
> (Bohm, 1998, p. 7)

In this wider, cultural context he refers to 'self-sustaining confusion'. 'When the mind is trying to escape the awareness of conflict ... In which one's deep intention is really to avoid perceiving the fact, rather than to sort it out and make it clear' (p. 10). He argues that this creates a reflexive state of dullness.

> We should thereby give sustained attention to this confusion. Originality and creativity begin to emerge, not something that is the result of an effort to achieve a planned and formulated goal, but rather, as the product of a mind that is coming to a nearly normal order of operation.
>
> (1998, p. 127)

So here, he is describing the attention that is required to dis-ambiguate cultural and historical, personal confusions that we experience from the perception of the ongoing process of becoming, that we experience and are participating in. The self-sustaining confusion is that which Blake addresses in his expression of the Job myth and is the struggle today that we see with the disintegration of and dialogue between the narratives that we have formed and cling to, in order that we understand our world. This is the self-righteousness that Blake sees as spiritual blindness and the state Job is in as we start the piece.

Bohm grounds this literalised thought and dullness in the nature of experience, suggesting that even scientific theorisation does not reflect a certifiable objectivity. 'Each theory in each instrument selects certain aspects of the world that is infinite, both qualitatively and quantitatively in its totality' (1980, p. 11). He is addressing the inseparability of the observer and the observed as perceived at the quantum level. So we are component in the system, not separable from it. There is a deep intersubjectivity. It is impossible in this context to have anything that is truly objective.

Bohm argues that science cannot provide 'simple reflections of the world as it is' (Ibid.). However, it can provide paradigms: 'simplified but typical examples, the abstract from the actual world suggesting the essential relationships that are significant for observation and experiment' (Ibid.). Here, Bohm suggests that the paradigms and structures we create are phenomenological processes, the result of dynamic internal activity that occurs prior to the threshold of conscious experience, not only the data that we collect and the consensual interpretation of that, but the context – personal, cultural and collective – in which that sits.

> Paradigm formation can be seen as an individual, moment to moment construction – and therefore not necessarily determined by prevailing orthodoxy. To engage in a 'paradigm shift' then, is sensorial and immediate, as well as epistemological and historical.
>
> (1998, p. 154)

In Bohm's terms, this is the risk of a fragmentary thought structure – the mechanical, reactive process of thought to thought, locked within its own misplaced necessity without impingement of the wider context, without the capacity to re-imagine a metaphysics within which that thought frame sits.

Whitehead and indeed Bohm's perception of creativity and folding or unfolding processes offer a way to perceive beyond the necessity of the content of experience to the function of the process, but this requires an opening of consciousness, a preparedness to feel beyond the proximal content of experience to its predicates and its creative intent. One must accept, as Bohm describes, that this process is essentially unknowable in its complexity, which is only contained through ideas of truth and faith. It requires a certain kind of listening, a faithfulness, in his terms, to the function and truth of content. For me, this is reminiscent of McGilchrist's (2009) left and right brain lateralization and referencing.

> The left hemisphere seems to play a crucial role in determining what comes in to being; it is part of the process of creation. Applying linear, sequential analysis forces the implicit into the explicitness, and brings clarity; this is crucial in helping bring about what is there. But, in doing so, the whole is lost […] The right hemisphere needs not to know what the left hemisphere knows, for that would destroy its ability to understand the whole […] The left hemisphere cannot deliver anything new […] but it can unfold, or 'unpack' […] its great strength […] lies in the fact that it can render explicit what the right hemisphere has to leave implicit, leave folded in. […] This is also its weakness; to make literal for the moment is good, but the moment passes and the context reforms.
>
> (pp. 207–208)

So an objective 'me'-self, as it is constituted, would need to be attentive to this moment or experience, reflected in 'I' – subjective awareness – that generates this experience from a perspective of not knowing, but perceiving. The need to bear the letting go of previous imagination of pattern and order can and does involve suffering. The new that becomes is likely to be much the same as the last, but it may not be. To perceive in this way is to try to put aside all the conditioning, social and personal, that brings us to this moment. Something that can be conflictful and frightening. Here in this plate that moment is upon Job. He is reorienting himself.

Bohm (1998) see the moral neutrality of science and art as a function of the fragmentary nature of thought. He eschews the view that we are in the position of not fitting into a chaotic and entropic universe; rather it is the other way round, what does not fit requires the special explanation. So the universe is in motion entirely from the very fast to the very slow, all interlinked, except in the constructions applied by the recursive limiting and fragmentary structures of representational thought. Truth then is a fitting in, which beauty and felt perception is a means of apprehending; providing not only correspondence between facts, but the congruent fitting together in experience. It is clear here that language and reason are insufficient to this task in the left brain manner of differentiation and delineation. A certain poetics is necessary to begin to approach such an idea.

As we know from the consulting room, to consider and experience only from the standpoint of conceptualising thought hinders the process. There are many factors: conceptual, analytical, physical, intuitive and contextual, which come together to form a perception of the experience, the synthesis of which might indeed be challenging to a previously held idea in the patient or practitioner, or indeed both. We saw this with Job, Pepe, and the service user on the bench outside CORE.

It is possible through intention and goodwill to begin to apprehend a more complex and open perception of experience, which has a resonance of truth. Beauty then, to follow Bohm, (1998, p. 55), involves us in this resonance as a felt sense. There is something truthful and beautiful about the emergent process of the work when it is flowing elegantly. Of course, this is often not the case and disruption and hindrance can be creative, but there is an elegance to these processes when viewed in the wider context. This beauty can be difficult, as with Pepe, and aligned, as in the moment on the bench, but it expresses a coherence.

In my experience, particularly when writing poetry, there is a beauty in the relationship between the words that brings something alive, so the experience is of an aesthetic synthesis; meaning, if any, is only revealed much later. I am particularly moved by Plate 12, and its resonance in the wider current context, that I am trying to articulate as a change in consciousness. Fulcrum at the top of the chapter was my poetic response.

This is also true for the consulting room and the group room. There is a beauty to the experience when there is a resonant and open flow. This is not to preclude the necessity for the other experience, of discord and difficulty, but to bring attention to this difficulty, to allow it to reveal its antecedents and incoherencies, and to allow the unfolding in the moment of the incongruent thoughts to perceive a new necessity. This for me is a spiritual experience, one of alignment with the unfolding whole.

I suggest we can return to a more transpersonal and poetic notion of our resonant experience that is congruent with Blake's conception of the 'True Man', 'Poetic Genius' or 'Jesus the Imagination'. His visionary experiences were the perception of a new necessity that incorporated old and concealed traditions. We reach this place of synthesis, and a co-created expression, by Plate 21, which can then be returned to at the beginning, much as a Hegelian model might perceive the interactive process of the dialectic forming a new thesis/antithesis process after synthesis. Blake reveals to us in the next plates how he perceives this process.

For Job, the heavens are about to open and the indication for the dream at this point is that through the suffering and break down we hope that enough resource is available to choose to live, as with my colleague and their sunrise.

Notes

1 *Anima mundi* is a Greek idea picked up again in the Renaissance and followed by Hillman and other archetypal figures (Hillman; Moore, 1989). Jung refers to the *unus*

mundus following the alchemical tradition (Samuels et al., 1986, pp. 157–158). This idea has links to the quantum theories of Bohm as the interplay of the wider context and the individual experience.

2 Auto poesis is self-creation or self-organization. The term was introduced by the evolutionary biologists Humberto Maturana and Francisco Varela in their groundbreaking book, *Autopoiesis and Cognition: The Realization of the Living* (1972). The autopoietic system is one that produces itself. It is perhaps best understood in contrast to an allopoietic system, such as a factory, which takes in materials and uses them to produce something other than itself.

3 Both McGilchrist and Spector refer to the annihilated self in mystical practices. My understanding is not that anything is annihilated, but there is a process of release of an unneeded frame, a kind of self-liberation. Not an active act of destruction but more like in this picture the release of a constraining image to a more open and free perception.

4 Adishanti Practiced Zen Buddhism and then began teaching. However, his teaching is not constrained to a particular religious frame so is more generically non dual. "The Truth I point to is not confined within any religious point of view, belief system, or doctrine, but is open to all and found within all" (https://adyashanti.opengatesangha.org/about-adya (accessed 20/10/22)).

5 Wilbur offers a hierarchical structure for the development of human consciousness and the formation of individuality; the ego foregoes individuality in the context of the whole. He formulates this through the synthesis of many religions relying heavily on the work of Jean Gebser (1905–1973). He speaks of the shift from a consciousness led by a sense of self, founded in ego, to that which is more apperceptive of the whole as the trans-egoic.

Chapter 5
New Vision

Plate 13
The Tremendum
Then the Lord answered Job out of the Whirlwind

DOI: 10.4324/9781003354642-6

In a Dark Time

In a dark time, the eye begins to see,
I meet my shadow in the deepening shade;
I hear my echo in the echoing wood—
A lord of nature weeping to a tree.
I live between the heron and the wren,
Beasts of the hill and serpents of the den.
What's madness but nobility of soul
At odds with circumstance? The day's on fire!
I know the purity of pure despair,
My shadow pinned against a sweating wall.
That place among the rocks—is it a cave,
Or winding path? The edge is what I have.
A steady storm of correspondences!
A night flowing with birds, a ragged moon,
And in broad day the midnight come again!
A man goes far to find out what he is—
Death of the self in a long, tearless night,
All natural shapes blazing unnatural light.
Dark, dark my light, and darker my desire.
My soul, like some heat-maddened summer fly,
Keeps buzzing at the sill. Which I is *I*?
A fallen man, I climb out of my fear.
The mind enters itself, and God the mind,
And one is One, free in the tearing wind.

(Roethke, 1966)

For all are Men in Eternity. Rivers Mountains Cities Villages.
All are Human & when you enter into the Bosoms you walk
In Heavens & Earths; as in your own Bosom you bear your Heaven
And earth, & all you behold: tho' it Appears Without it is Within,
In your Imagination of which this World of Mortality is but a Shadow

(J.71.15.E p225)

I have quoted the Roethke for the line, 'What is madness but nobility of soul at odds with circumstance', a poetic truth in the experience of my work, I assume Roethke to be taking a generally Platonic sense of soul and its vicissitudes with incarnation, I would follow more closely Hillman's ideas and see this as the becoming experience as symptom challenging the context in which it forms. As a famous aphorism could be seen as a description of Blake's reception. However, I have quoted the poem in full as it expresses and contextualises the journey so far and the last line expresses the moment we are about to enter. The quote from Jerusalem points to where we are going – all is resonantly alive and felt in the body.

In Plate 13, a renegotiation of the relationship between self and context begins and a new image begins to reveal itself. The crisis of the last twelve plates is over. This is the direct revelation of 'the human face of God', as Raine (1982) entitles her book on the Blake plates. In the Christian canon it might be seen as a direct experience of the holy spirit. Its return has an awesome feel, an overwhelming sense of the collective. A new perception is arising as attention is paid after suspending thought. Jung would have called this a moment of 'tremendum', using the Lutheran theologian and philosopher, Rudolf Otto's (1869–1937) term for the frightening awesome nature of divine experience.

This sudden rush of energy might be seen as a spiritual crisis, or spiritual emergency, as referenced in DSM IV. The horror and defeat is gone. The false dawns of the emerging symbol are over, and now it arrives, often manic, sometimes terrifying or awful. This moment can be confused with an emerging psychotic event. Indeed, if it is not containable by the ego, it may become that. There is a contrast here between Plates 11 and 13. Both are difficult experiences – one the confrontation between the ego in its old fragmentary order and in this plate there is a confrontation with a new experience of the numinous, here expressed in the figure of God. The man who had a manic experience at the end of his time in CORE was bearing an awakening such as this. I remember also a colleague who's therapist ascended into a hypomanic state seemingly becoming more excited by the beauty of life and omnipotent about the role they could take working with people. Unfortunately this then descended into a severe depression and they had to be hospitalised. The containment of this particular change for me is the key allowing a grounded change to a new consciousness.

In *Peaks and Vales* (1979) Hillman argues that in 787 AD, during one of the great clashes between the iconoclasts and image makers that have occurred through history, there was a decision made by 300 assembled bishops to accept imagery, but only in a sanctioned form. This, he argues in this foundation piece on archetypal psychology, was the moment the soul was sidelined, and we were left with a dualist split between spirit and body. This was later developed in Cartesian (1641) and Newtonian (1687) thought, the naturalisation of the enlightenment that Blake was fighting, through to the positivism and scientism of today, what I see as the all too easy idealisation of mechanism into a reified but fragmentary truth, rather than recognising it within a sceptical context that is true to science.

Through his psychology of soul, Hillman suggests how we might reframe our experience in an interconnected way, participating imaginally in the process of becoming as it manifests in the living imagination, as a participatory and mythic experience. I see this as neo-animism, a return to the participatory continuity with nature and enchantment, but chosen, so it is a volitional re-enchantment.

In Plate 12, there is a sense of the immanent and the transcendent participating in experience, as Blake was able to inhabit, a synthetic whole. The polytheistic world that his imagery enables, of figures and angels, is a view as differentiated as any pagan pantheon, for instance, the Greeks or the Norse, and as imaginally immersed as any of Hillman's vales. In the upper margin, where the angels of the Elohim (the seven eyes of God), the creators, are seen, we might imagine they are re-making the world, but now we begin to realise the re-making is perpetual and cyclical. Yahweh provides the image for Whitehead's (PR, 347) appetite for becoming in the moment. Yahweh is loving Job back to life. For Blake he is the 7th creator, 'Jesus the forgiver', the compassionate redeemer who turns on its head the wrathful production of his predecessors, of the Elohim as set out in the Frontispiece. They are turning the letter of the law into a path for becoming; Job and Yahweh are now collaborating.

Here the context is shifted from the left brain as the master, to the left brain as the actioner of intent. Left brain literality is being transformed by the recontextualisation of reference back to the right brain. In the lower margin, the 'Forest of Error' is laid low, which is the hubris of Job, in other words our small, self-righteous view of the world. Satan, who represents the left brain only view, is set aside. Job's life up until now has been lifeless and dead. Elihu has pointed to the shift that needs to take place. Making clear that it is not about Job but about God that this struggle is taking place. The renewed spiritual life begins to connect us to Job.

Raine (1982, p. 215) sees this as spirit re-entering the work, as an immanent presence. She argues that the appearance of the Elohim points to the transfiguration of nature into an internal human experience (countering the subject-object split). This is God distributed through nature, or the universe being revealed internally through Jesus the imagination. Blake's Swedenborgian view that the universe is reflexive of human form in all its parts would see that this is an internal process, and the experience of the natural world is illusory. I see this as a focus on experience as real, the process of arising and inter-connecting to the living universe.

Blake expressed it thus to Thomas Butts

In Particles bright
The Jewls of Light
Distinct shone clear
Amas'd & in fear
I each particle gazed
Astonished, Amazed;
For each was a Man
Human-form'd. Swift I ran,
For they becon'd to me
Remote by the Sea,
Saying: Each grain of Sand,
Every stone in the Land,
Each rock & each hill,
Each Fountain & rill,
Each herb & each tree,
Mountain, hill, earth & sea,
Cloud, meteor & Star,
Are Men Seen Afar.

(2 Oct. 1800.E 712)

Bohm (1980) described how the implicate order reflects beneath each explicate event, so that the whole is implied in a particle of light. Mesle (2008, pp. 100–101) also describes from a Whiteheadian perspective that droplets of experience, concress or come together, eventually breaching a threshold where the complexity generates consciousness in a self-reflexive form. So from this context self-reflexive consciousness is an emergent property of the complexity of the system; that of homeostatically sustaining an organism in the context that it sits, within its ecosystem; not a split off part, but a fragment. It must follow as I argue that the increased complexity of that system increases the capacity for consciousness. As we form evermore complex systems for relating our consciousness must become broader and our attention has to turn from simple selfhood to that selfhood in context, in group. Here in this image is the eruption into life of a novel event, a new perception beginning to be made. This is the shift in perspective that I am trying to articulate in the context of the group, away from self as a solid function over time, to a labile and complex, fluid and emergent reflection of the system it is both a component and reflection of.

Experience, feeling and emotion are among the words Whitehead alters to re-imagine our life. In his 1997 paper, linking Blake and Chan & Zen Buddhism, Ferrara points to the correspondence between experience and intent common in both the Buddhist tradition and Blake's poetic expression of the universe as co-creative. He emphasises how both traditions see that over-intellectual emphasis upon abstraction clouds the capacity to experience.

> The Divine Vision, Blake maintains, is the natural prelapsarian state of the integrated psyche in which all the zoas are harmoniously balanced. The Divine Vision is obscured from our everyday consciousness because the renegade intellect (Urizen) can see only the ratio, and not the infinity that lies just beneath it.
> (p. 62)

He then compares this to 'Buddha Nature',[1] which is:

> Reality is all-inclusive, there is nothing that can be outside of it. Because it is all inclusive, it is the fullness of things, not a content free abstraction, as the intellect is too frequently apt to make it. It is not a mere aggregate of individual objects, nor is it something other than the objects. It is not something that is imposed upon things stringing them together and holding them together from the outside. It is the principle of integration residing inside things and identical with them
> (Suzuki, 1991, p. 99)

This is a world that is not conceived by a dreamer like God but composed of an infinite number of individual drops of feeling all woven together by the experience of each other into a resonate whole. The whole in appetite for novel creativity pulls us into becoming. So, in this plate, Job receives the experience of becoming, no longer preoccupied with rules-based materialism, and feels its impact as an awe-inspiring expanse. Compare this to Plate 11, where we saw the black fire of torment. This is the compassionate redemption of an all loving and valuing whole. The difference between the two is the destructive and obsessive constriction of reason alone rather than reason set in context.

Clinical Example

Most of the people at CORE who managed to stop using, particularly after a long habit, would report that, to some extent, the word seemed brighter, as if oversaturated with colour. Emotions were loud, everything seemed more intense. This lasted for some weeks, not only the euphoria of having, at last stopped, but as if the contrast had been turned up. After a while this dimmed and life became more normal, and the everyday trudge through the vicissitudes of the soul would commence, what I saw then as the long walk back to a more normal life.

The vignette at the end of Plate 11 where the client leaving CORE became manic lasted for a few weeks but settled into a new life, brighter, wiser and more spiritually grounded, as we will see happens in the next plate.

New Vision 137

Plate 14
The Divine Order
When the morning Stars sang together, & all the Sons of God shouted for joy

In this plate, Blake is presenting us with an image of the divine order as he imagined and perceived it, the apperception of the 'poetic moment', but not yet inhabited, as it is still separate from Job. The previous image is one of its awe inspiring and inchoate arrival into consciousness. This is its full glorious manifestation.

Raine (1982, p. 222) describes how 'Blake has represented the living universe of the imagination, the universe as a phenomenon not of matter, but of consciousness'. Although it appears without, Blake perceives it within. Plate 14 is an expression of the expansion of the consciousness Job is experiencing coming into focus. The death of the old order in Plates 11 and 12 creates the space for the re-perception in Plate 13, and the clarification in this plate. Blake understands this as a poetic experience, beyond the material constraint of the body and an experience of consciousness, which similarly to the neo-Platonists he would see as matter and subject to death (Raine, 1982, p. 226). However, I would differ from Blake and see it as a function of the body, as Ray (2016, 2020) might articulate. It is through body and imagination that it is held and perceived. This is Whitehead's (1927) perception in the mode of 'causal efficacy', rooted in his pan-experiential perspective, that consciousness interpenetrates matter, in fact precedes it.

A new symbol becomes clear, a new sense of the becoming whole is emerging, but here it is still reminiscent of its old form. God is showing Job creation before its internalisation. Whitehead looks at symbol in the light of perception (1927). He sees that we perceive in two modes: that of presentational immediacy and causal efficacy, the former being the world of the senses, the latter being the experienced sense making of that, what we make of the world because we remember experiencing it. The relationship between the two he describes as a symbolic reference. In so far as there is a mismatch between presentational immediacy and the symbol as it is received in the mode of causal efficacy there is room for imagination (p. 19). It is here that the apperceptive new can form. Roy (2017) sees this mapping on to McGilchrist's model.

Now we enter a world where consciousness is visible beyond and within the material. Job has passed beyond the bounds of the limited material world of 'Ratio' and is able to see the internal limitless world of 'Jesus the Imagination'. However, he has not yet let go of his self-narrative, a 'me' in Bohm's terms, to inhabit the 'I' of infinite subjective experience. That is to come in Plates 18–21.

I see in this plate echoes of the Kabbalistic and Platonic universe, but of course it is uniquely Blakeian. In the upper part of the image is Eden, where the morning stars sang together and sons of God shout for joy, and the souls gather before incantation. In the level of Beulah Yahweh constellates, where there are images of Sol and Luna, light and dark; then we see the world of Generation, where Job and living humanity exist enshrouded in cloud. Ulro is represented as the serpent in the lower margin, but is now asleep and still, in Blake's terms in its rightful place. The cave-like structure is perhaps a reference to the Platonic cave, as Raine (p. 225) suggests, but also the limitations of hindered consciousness and our material universe, the consciousness of a rigid and fixed self. Here Job has not let go of self totally, not yet internalised the divine, become or realised the 'True Man' within, but is becoming aware and open to that experience.

Job and Yahweh's poses mirror each other. Their legs are arranged, as in image two, symbolising judgement and mercy. However, in this image Job is able to connect directly to Yahweh and receive from him. A mutual reception. All the protagonists seem to be in a pose of prayer, as a means to engage with the infinite, the whole. This is the direct apperception of the divine human imagination, the appeal to the unending or everlasting in its wisdom to penetrate the finite, resonant experience of the universal context. In this central world of Beulah, we see the sun and the moon, alchemical symbols of opposites and transformation, of male and female. Above we see the 'sons of Eden', each a human spirit ready to fall to the world of Generation, then to be lifted back to Eden. They are androgynous. It is an idea from Jacob Bohme (1575–1624) that the androgynous spirit is divided into gender, with the fall into incarnation, a conceit of unity becoming diverse in matter.

Yahweh is now becoming present or imminent, no longer the transcendent distant God. The divine halo I see as Ein Sof, the direct and unnameable experience of the divine in Kabbalistic terms. This now begins to manifest in this plate, in Job's soul. This image of an external divinity is still evidently necessary (until Plate 18), but the relationship between and across is becoming both clearer and more felt, the beginnings of the re-enchantment and altering of perception that will lead to a participatory experience.

With reference to using, this is the experience of the world after stopping. What is depicted in Plate 13 comes first, being overwhelmed by the brightness in the world, and the relational context you will begin to become aware of and inhabit. Plate 14 has a sense of the brilliance of the order that is there to be experienced, but as yet is somewhat out of reach.

Plate 15
The Past Order
Behold now Behemoth which I made with thee

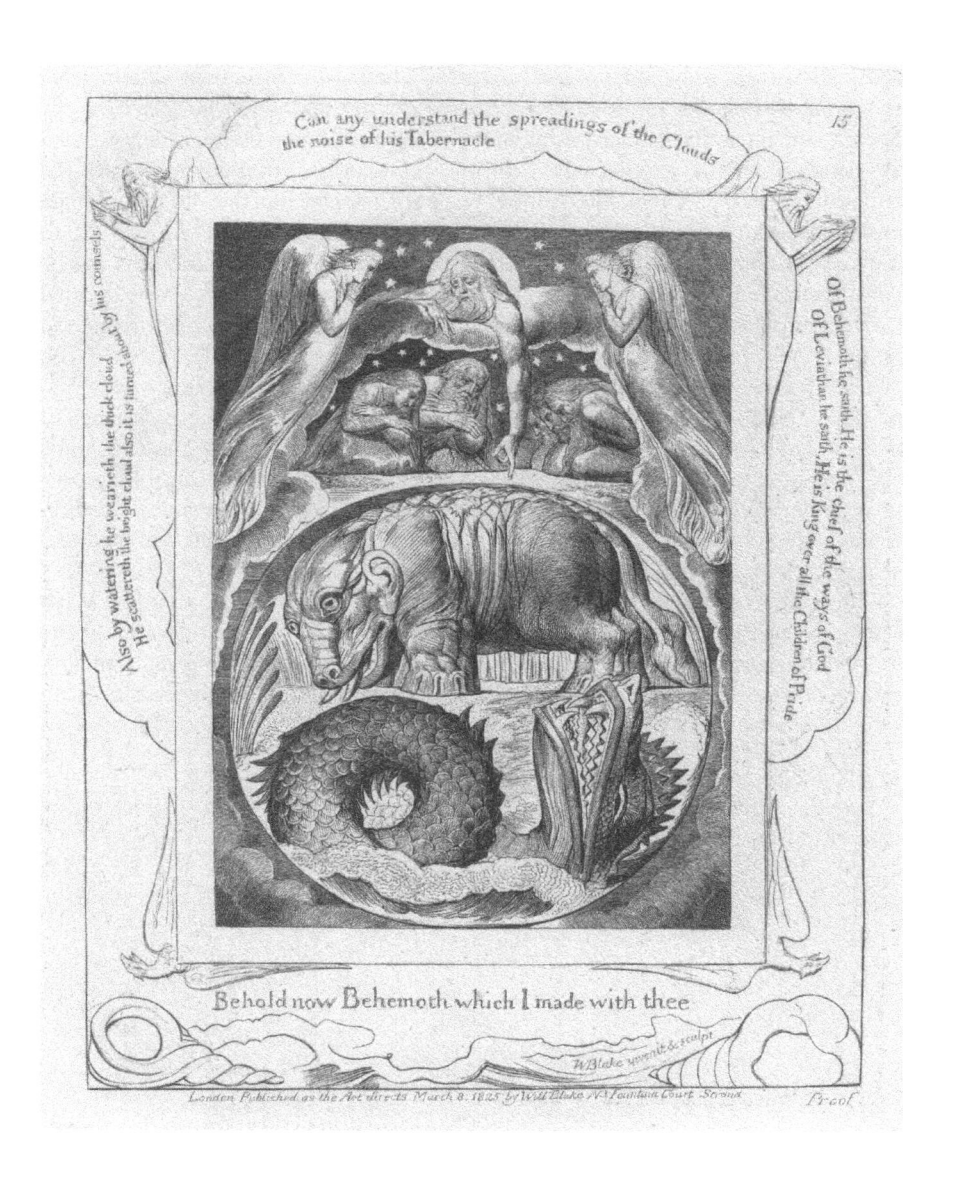

This book proposes that something from within us could be re-incorporated to the psyche, consciously and participatorily. As we crowd the planet our relationships with each other cannot easily follow their old paths, our relationship with the planet suffers in the same way, our connections and methods of communication are changing as we build new technologies to share and manage knowledge. I see the emergent experience of becoming witnessed more widely en masse; there is a new apperception in tension with old reified orders of power that we try to cling to.

I see this as precipitating a need to move from a consciousness of exploitation to a consciousness of resonance, to recognise ourselves in context receiving into life, rather than acting on a dead world that we exploit. As we do this there is a general cultural reorientation and renegotiation, both individually and in group. I see this involves a volitional sacrifice of a fixed identity, a breaking down of old power structures internally, as well as externally, as we try to organise new ways of imagining and participating in our collective life. Of course as this process unfolds we become confused and afraid. The old structures are not let go of lightly. As with addiction, it is a persistent and difficult struggle to move to a new order of necessity. That necessity erupts partially and seemingly incoherently with patients. The grief cycle, for instance, would appear in its theoretical form to have a structure, but if you have worked with anyone who is mourning, the process is repetitive. All components of anger, grief, denial and acceptance seem to erupt by turn and at once. The same is true as we let go of our old imaginings and grieve their loss. Bohm (2008d) felt there was no likelihood that we would see these behavioural patterns change, which is why he proposed dialogue as a means of framing this activity, through which one can work past turbulent fragmentary thought.

I am proposing that Blake had access to the collective consciousness that had been repressed by the dominant hierarchy of the enlightenment, and that he articulated an emergent process of becoming. He was clearly ahead of his time and, as a result, often misunderstood, not accepted or seen as mad. This plate is the point where he begins to embark on the part of the narrative where we change towards a more participatory becoming, as opposed to valuing a reified order of power relations, as we have seen articulated in Whitehead's (Mesle, 2008, pp. 72–78) and Bohm's (1996) thought. Blake experienced this as a personal internal process. I am suggesting that now we are beginning to experience it in a more collective form, in the context of the group.

I read this plate as a presentation of the participatory order of the hunter-gatherers; the world of incarnation and, according to Mulhern (2015) and Solomon (1993, pp. 55–63), the deep unconscious. Mulhern sees Leviathan and Behemoth as great dragon figures, symbolic of the Mother Goddess and the nature Gods of the pre-patriarchal cultures. These are still not clear to Job; he is not yet fully participatory in the process of his becoming, but separate from it and merely a witness to it. This full participation will come in Plate 18. Yahweh shows Job the joy of his creation, and Job is now equipped with the capacity for new insight. Yahweh points with his left arm through the pillar of mercy, of compassion, from Eden and Ein Sof (the halo behind him), through to Beulah and the world of Generation.

With Job, his wife and the comforters, to a transformed Ulro, to the possibility of creative redemption. The angels from Plates 2 as questioners, and 5 as guardians, ascend back to Eden. The final records are made, seeming to take on some likeness of Job and Yahweh.

In the margin of the plate, Blake writes, 'Of Behemoth he says he is the Chief of the ways of God. Of Leviathan he sayeth, He is King over all the Children of Pride'. Yahweh is making clear to Job that the whole of creation is the great oeuvre, not just the human perception of the divine and our capacity to symbolise. This would seem to echo the right brain perspective of the whole in context, however, much use the left brain's linear processing is required to make things happen. Experience is all of a piece, not separated by the splitting, for instance, of good from evil, or any of the manifest binary interpretations of becoming that bring about fragmentation. The interdependent and relational nature of the process of becoming can be seen to be the core of Blake's interpretation of the Book of Job. So here begins the process of experiencing the whole, of experiencing Bohm's new necessity, by perceiving its contingency and the implicate context that lies behind it.

Before Job is the process of reorientation and revisioning that takes place in the remaining plates. To this point Job has suffered and been subject to the tensions between his self-righteous abstract and dogmatic concept of becoming and the actual emergent process that is unfolding through and with him. This trial takes place in the context of his whole community. In Plate 12, we recognised the defeat of this old representational perception of the order of things, the letting go of an old fiction for self. In Plates 13 and 14, we saw differing perspectives of the new general order and perception as it begins to unfold into his life. Here he begins to recognise the new context. This image of Yahweh as contextualiser will itself disappear in two plates, but at this point it is a necessary imagination to reframe Job's perception, which is still in the form of a rigid self as being. He has not yet transcended self.

This is the last time the recording angels appear, the last time the concrete self is inhabited. Here begins the letting go of an external divine experience as a separate object, and the beginnings of an opening to a participatory and inhabited creativity. In its fullest sense this is the beginnings of the transcendence of self, of ego. There will be a further letting go of an old self-structure and recognition of the divine as internal, coherent and participatory.

'Behold now Behemoth, which I made with thee' is inclusive. Creation and humanity are not separate, but of a piece, becoming together. It is abstraction and meaning that has generated this separation, the reification of our understanding that in Bohm's terms is only a fragment of a perpetually unfolding whole. Blake's words in the margin of Plate 15: "Can any understand the spreading of the clouds and the noise of the tabernacle" point in this direction of perceptual experience, away from abstraction and the limitation of representational thought to that of direct participatory perception through imagination.

In Plate 15, by looking back we enter an unfolding that opens to a future participation which is articulated in the next six plates. I am not proposing the idea of a regressive return to an old way of becoming but a new participation, contextualised differently through the experience we have now had. Not a forward and back but an across, a dialogue. I see this as akin to the brain processing dialogue McGilchrist describes, but at a communal level.

The Jungian and Buddhist frames offer a passage through life, from merger to ego formation and separateness, then a return to oneness through either individuation or the 'enlightenment' journey. It is in this frame that place, a return to a participatory experience of becoming. I do not propose to discuss here the differentiation between the Jungian idea of individuation or the Buddhist view of enlightenment, or for that matter the Kabbalistic notion of knowing the mind of God, which would be more close to Blake's perception. There is insufficient space and I suggest we are moving to a syncretic and more nuanced perception of this differentiation.

It would seem we are looking to an inclusive paradigm shift that is able to recognise the contextual shift of today's post-self experience. Implicit in this moment is the death of the proximal self as anything other than a perceptual tool for the broader context in which it sits, as a resonant perceptive experience revealed, not as separate from the whole, but embedded in the co-creating and emerging process. Self's permanence shatters in the face of this experience, hence the end of the record. From that shift a new paradigm unfolds, a new perception of a new necessity, what we will see in the following plates.

VIGNETTES

An individual example of this participatory and implicate felt experience might be when a patient is at beginning of their work. We see the narrative ahead in the initial session, as if a glimpse of the whole process is reflected in that session. This perception is, for me at least, mostly intuitive, and often felt, but is usually there. It is not a bad rule of thumb that, reflected in the initial session, is the whole course of the analysis, both seen and unseen. The key is to be able to listen for this. I have a colleague who for their training was asked to record sessions. When they were played back they said it was possible to see the whole process implied in each event. This is an example for me of perception outside of time and space, however, it takes some skill and practice to learn the right way to listen.

One of the questions I ask myself in each initial session, and throughout the work, is *at which place is this person in the arc of their life?* Near the beginning? Near the end? Forming or ending significant relationships? This provides a place of orientation, not in gross time, but in the context of their passage through a lived life, a context in sequence. Personal experience gives something of an idea of what to expect, but wonder is the therapist's best friend. How is this to unfold for them out of their previous experience? What story will they make of their lives given the stories they bring? Beneath any presentation will be a whole social and cultural context that will gradually unfold into the work that has been dialogically interpreted between the individual and their context, and in turn will become negotiated between as we look for a new way of imagining. For me this is an intersubjective and receptive process. In this context it is not what I do but what we can receive into the moment and find that has the highest value, as Whitehead suggests.

I had a patient who was struggling with a sense of identity, both as a performer and with their place in the world. The initial session was challenging, with a sense of falling, of self-loathing and tragedy. The emptiness was palpable and dissolution filled the air; however, there was also a feeling of unrealised potential, a creativity pointing to a future. Their history of inflated and cultish parenting only served to exacerbate both disconnection from experience and suspicion of the concept of the future altogether. The entire journey was an unfolding of this process, an opening to and from; from the constrained and dogmatic history of being part of a cult and growing up in a state of dependence; to an open appreciation of their own becoming. Indeed, this was a return to faith, but perhaps a Blakean faith in humanity and imagination rather than in any dogma. In my patient's narrative a fall did indeed come in the form of betrayal, both by self and other, particularly in a relationship, and then a letting go of the identity that they had formed, a shift in that identity that both reframed the experiences of hurt and loss, experience of their previous history and experiences to come. All of this was contained in the experience of the first session, although not all of it was visible at that point.

The life that emerged was one of freedom from the previous condition and movement to a new identity, which made useful the hurts and disruptions of the past, opening fully to a creative life as it manifested. The process involved not only a deconstruction of the habits of living, but the metaphysical structures that had come to form the meaning frames and their repercussions. We had to deconstruct the structures they had faith in, and replace them with the faith to continue to live in circumstances of real fluid change. This involved digging into the social and contextual dogma presented through their parenting, to a faith in becoming. Digging beneath what Sloan Wilson (2015) would call the proximal adaptation to the functional adaptation. Not the dogma of the cult they had experienced but the faith that the next event will arise out of the decaying ashes, or this perishing moment. To present this in Whitehead's rubric, we were bearing the value that is guaranteed by the whole to allow the coming form to concress. This was done through a process of dialogue: receipt and exchange between them and I, and indeed faith in the process.

The particularly interesting part of this narrative was not the individual one that I have set out above, but how this unfolded collectively. With each step of their shifting understanding, they moved to an external and communal sense of self, using the internal narrative shifts, and the experiences that had injured them, to develop a community in a creative context, between them and I and their community: familial, social and professional. At the point they were able to take this on and develop the process beyond the need for us to work together, they left our shared process. I believe they came to be able to do what we did together alone. My component in this dialogue was no longer needed.

This change we have made to our consciousness cannot be undone. We cannot return to previous organisations of our experience, but we can remember them and bring them into focus in a way that is relevant to now. We function predominantly in a subject and object model, born out of our process of development, but we can re-synthesise this model in the context of our new experience, and a new understanding of that experience. Metaphysics, as Bohm (1998, p. 20) understands it, is a form of art that helps us make sense of the world around us. We are using this sequence of images by Blake as a model for a new way of being. This plate is the moment that the beginnings of that revelation, that new perception, begin. Up to this point, the old has been deconstructed, and then the reconnection with the whole has been made. Now we move forward towards something novel and full, letting go of the old imagination, the old self.

The Job story is a means not only of challenging the proximal situation, Job's experience, but the system in which that sits. This is the key to the reciprocal and relational nature between Job and Yahweh, God and humanity, between everything and the event, the particular and the whole. It could be framed in the more divine aspects of Whitehead, as the primordial nature of God, the valuing and receiving aspect of the whole, the consequence of which is the actual occasion, the event. But, better here to focus upon the happenstance of event and the flow of the process as it reflects and unfolds within and between us. What we see in the light of symbol is the recursive nature of meaning informing event. It is the re-introduction into the process of the meaning event, felt and resonant across a whole, the interaction of matter and meaning, and thereby mind and soul as a perceptual frame for becoming.

Blake's work offers us this direct connection to becoming. We will come to discuss this later, in Plate 20, but he was able to frame the experience in many ways, particularly in the context of the political shifts and burgeoning freedoms of his time: the Industrial Revolution, the French Revolution and the American Revolution. The noumenal world beyond the phenomenal of material experience was open to him and he has left his image for it here, difficult as it is to deconstruct. This plate shows us how participation is possible. He now goes on to offer the change that this reorientation generates for us as individuals, but more importantly I think, at this time, as groups.

Raine argues towards the end of *The Human Face of God* (1982) that both Blake and Jung point to the second coming being a process experienced in the masses. I happen to think that this is likely to be the case and it is the time we are living through. I see this imagined in the final Plate 21 and expressed in our thinking about our species and its relation to the context it now finds itself in. The struggle with our power, in the mode of exploitation, the omnipotence with which we have killed the nature Gods and nature following that, all for a transcendent God, to become the chosen ones, which leads us to finding him dead and to feeling the responsibility we gave up to him. In fact, we have done none of this, just imagined a separation from that which we are a component in and coherent with; we have the capacity of awareness, some of which is expressed individually and some of which is expressed in the group. It is a relational and resonant event, an awareness of the unfolding process of the whole. This separation and return to participation is the capacity that has given us our perspective of the planet and is the capacity that will allow us to occupy this space creatively. However, it is also the capacity that, when reified, can destroy everything as the context changes around us. This is the event of self that is the symbolic relation between events, recontextualised in the frame of the whole.

The fluidity of the process as it unfolds within and between us is suffering. Self in this context is important only in so far as it can listen and be able to bear the unfolding experience, and not define it but express it, to allow experience creatively into consciousness. For me this is a poetic process of reception and valuation. We receive the moment into life and orientate ourselves towards it. This will come to the fore in Plate 19, but is implicit before the fall of the proximal self-image as Satan.

Yahweh points to the womb-contained Beasts of Leviathan and Behemoth, and to the rough, broken cloud of revelation. This is a vision in Jungian terms into the collective unconscious. It is the link to the next part of the process which he is undergoing, a recognition of his more divine capacity. Previously we might conclude that Job has been struggling with his personal unconscious complexes which, at their archetypal root, are driven by Satan of the Selfhood. Here, there is a revelation of the shadow of creation, the broken and loved aspects of God. Jung makes much of this struggle in 'The Answer to Job' (CW 11, 1952, para 648) where he argues that it is man's redemption of God that is the theme to the biblical Job story, and that it pre-figures the Christian myth. Blake turns this into a Christian myth, but from a Kabbalistic perspective. Here, there is the struggle of the contraries of good and evil – evil Leviathan and good Behemoth. As Blake puts it in *The Marriage of Heaven and Hell* (1790), 'Attraction and repulsion, Reason and energy, Love and Hate, are necessary to human existence' (l. 149). However, as Raine tells us he resolves this duality transcendently in Jesus the imagination the complete non-dual image (1982, pp. 287–293).

Blake does not see that the contraries are at war, but in a dance of creativity. Negations are bent on each other's destruction, not the contraries, not the refusal between the left and right brain, but the 'yes but' of recontextualisation. Plate 15 is part of the transformation that has to take place when we consider the whole to include the contraries. This is important if we are to synthesise the two opposites, as in Jung's transcendent function, where the constellation of opposites is able, through symbol formation, to find a new order. Through the contemplation and bearing of these struggles, this process is developed, integrating the products of the psyche. In the context of this piece, here the new symbol is forming that can be brought to consciousness for a synthesis between old and new.

I do not see this as an entirely binary process, particularly in the context of the individual experience in the group. It is easiest to present things in this form – self and other, good and evil, tribe and out group. However, as is expressed in this sequence of images, although the binary level exists within human experience, there is more often a polyvalent experience of togetherness and otherness, a diversity of possibilities of self and other. In this image, Job's comforters and Job's family represent the human experience. There are many of them, and indeed in the divine realm there is the divine council and the angels, and Satan with his hoards, as Blake did not split heaven and hell. A truly polyvalent company. This is a crucial point Bohm makes about his understanding of dialogue. When there is more than one or two positions in the room it is possible that a negotiation between polarities can be formed, if the psychic tension can be borne. This then opens to the possibility of a wider apperception of the context in which that polarity might sit.

Whilst working on this book, I have come to believe that Blake pre-figures the work that we are currently undertaking in our collective life, the evolutionary development that Sloan Wilson (2015) points to of finding better imaginative solutions to the functional need for altruism in groups. Implicit in this model, moving evolution from biology to symbol, contains the perception that, reflected in our experience, is the mechanism for the change of the whole system. To identify that as a personal responsibility omnipotently separate from the whole would be terrifying, but to see it as a collective responsibility offends our individual narcissism and the agency needed to keep this one organism going. A dilemma of knowledge if ever there was one and the dilemma Job faces with his rigid adherence to self-righteous dogma. I would imagine that this work has not gone unnoticed, but has been sustained in the esoteric traditions of the world and our major religions, which Sloan Wilson describes as solutions to the altruism problem. We are now gaining access in a more direct way to this experience and its context as we develop sophisticated and dialogic notions of selfhood, which point towards the greater experience of the whole as it unfolds in our finite personal experience.

Here in this plate we see that Yahweh reveals himself as, at core, the earth deity we used to love, naming Leviathan and Behemoth, greater than any human creation, here before us and being here long after. This is a vision of oneness prior to the human order and prior certainly to the advent of the transcendence of God. In the Bible there is no doubt as to the level of humanity in the face of this terrifying image of the completeness of creation. Job has to accept the actions of God, good or evil. Blake has chosen to alter the narrative structure and add more components. These components not only Christianise the Jewish narrative but also feminise the Christian narrative, as the later plates reveal. For instance, he keeps Job's wife alive as a figure and an important protagonist throughout the piece. He includes a figure in Plate 17 that can be interpreted either as the Shekinah or a Sophia figure, and he references Jesus as the final figure of the Elohim, who turns a dark story light. Of course this is taken further than a Christian myth. I would say Blake's *Job* points to the development of consciousness going forward, making him 200 years ahead of his time, revealing an internal divine which we are participant in and transcending the subject-object split; that process is to unfold over the next few plates.

A year into the pandemic and some way through the writing of this work I was faced with the question of what is the source. Bohm talks of an imaginary flow into life from the source to event, Whitehead (PR, 21) talks of the creative as the universal of universals, (God as creativity), both presenting the valuing context and the material outcome. I felt I needed to experience what this was, rather than gather an abstract understanding from reading. I have practiced qui gong for many years and try to think of this in that frame i.e. the force from above and the force from below meeting in the human body. This is also the root metaphor to acupuncture central to the work at CORE. The imaginal frame I was trying to engage the ineffable with takes something from this frame. I resolved to address this through ritual with a colleague at CORE who was extending and developing 'men's work'. This was founded in the archetypal Hillmanesque frame of metaphor. If nothing else I thought it would be an opportunity for us to be together, and think and moan about the world going to hell in a hand basket, which is an age appropriate pastime of choice.

I arrived and stayed overnight to prep the work, and then perform the ritual the next day. I described my thinking. He had devised the ritual for his Japanese garden. We ate together with his partner, had a lovely evening, and I went to bed. I awoke in the night, as I was expecting to, with ideas of what it was I needed to bear and let go, the principle image for which was soul; soul perhaps in the Platonic frame and soul in the frame of Hillman's (1964, 1975a, Hillman & Moore 1989) work. I was unsure and slightly uneasy. There were other more narcissistic hindrances, but I think they were incidental to the central frame of soul as a reified object.

In the morning we came to work through the process. I walked down the hill and could feel a descent into the earth, as the qui gong and associative meditative practices would expect, even before we had started. He described both what we were doing and the context that he had devised, what each image and architectural feature was for and represented, and how I might chose to use them. As we processed through the journey the descent got deeper, and the felt sense of the earth as a living, ringing, joyous ferrous being became stronger; shining at the centre of the earth, radiating upwards in an infinite stream of light and life that opens through us to the upper worlds. An orange ball of creativity.

Wales had other intentions. It had already started to rain as we came out to the garden. This was strengthening, and as I came to let go, bearing the perishing in the moment, I slid and slithered down the hill to a millstone in which I was to leave the paper where I had noted in the night my intentions. I lifted it up to remind myself and speak, and the now heavy rain washed away the words. The Gods had laid on a panto. I could not but laugh.

I struggled back up the hill to my friend. We closed the frame and walked further up to the entrance of the garden. He commented that "usually here I send people back to finish what they might have shirked, might have finessed, but", as the rain fell more heavily, "I get the sense we are done". Of course I agreed, soaked as I was to the skin, damp as I was with the letting go and the ferrous glow still with me.

The upward journey was to come later and I will share it in Plate 18, but the abiding image of this was the ferrous and fecund life of the earth, as a living being which resonates with us and the universal whole.

Notes

1 Buddha-nature is the capacity for enlightenment and freedom present in every being, a fundamental core of goodness, wisdom, and compassion that is hidden by clouds of ignorance. It is like the sun that continues to shine regardless of the clouds that may cover it. By clearing away those clouds of greed, anger, and selfishness we uncover a state of perfection that is, and always has been, our own true nature.

Although it may be difficult to completely overcome all our limitations and clear away those clouds, the fact that our nature is fundamentally the same as a buddha's makes the whole path to enlightenment possible. …Everyone has buddha-nature. The only difference between us and an enlightened being such as a Buddha is that a Buddha recognizes this nature and the rest of us do not. (www.buddhanature.tsadra.org accesses 21 Oct 2022)

One can understand Buddha Nature, either as the potentiality in each person to become awakened, or the presence of the already fully awakened mind that is merely covered over. Buddha-nature is the unity of emptiness and clarity that is experienced as open compassion beyond being and non-being, existence or non-existence accommodating everything (Wellings N Private Conversation, 2023).

Chapter 6
New Context

Just as the winged energy of delight

(translated by Robert Bly)

Just as the winged energy of delight
carried you over many chasms early on,
now raise the daringly imagined arch
holding up the astounding bridges.
Miracle doesn't lie only in the amazing
living through and defeat of danger;
miracles become miracles in the clear
achievement that is earned.
To work with things is not hubris
when building the association beyond words;
denser and denser the pattern becomes—
being carried along is not enough.
Take your well-disciplined strengths
and stretch them between two
opposing poles. Because inside human beings
is where God learns.

Rilke (1924, trans. Bly. 1981)

The Lamb

Little Lamb who made thee
Dost thou know who made thee
Gave thee life & bid thee feed.
By the stream & o'er the mead;
Gave thee clothing of delight,
Softest clothing wooly bright;
Gave thee such a tender voice,

Making all the vales rejoice!
Little Lamb who made thee
Dost thou know who made thee
Little Lamb I'll tell thee,
Little Lamb I'll tell thee!
He is called by thy name,
For he calls himself a Lamb:
He is meek & he is mild,
He became a little child:
I a child & thou a lamb,
We are called by his name.
Little Lamb God bless thee.
Little Lamb God bless thee.

Blake (SI 1789, E, pp 8–9)

The Tyger

Tyger Tyger, burning bright,
In the forests of the night;
What immortal hand or eye,
Could frame thy fearful symmetry?
In what distant deeps or skies.
Burnt the fire of thine eyes?
On what wings dare he aspire?
What the hand, dare seize the fire?
And what shoulder, & what art,
Could twist the sinews of thy heart?
And when thy heart began to beat,
What dread hand? & what dread feet?
What the hammer? what the chain,
In what furnace was thy brain?
What the anvil? what dread grasp,
Dare its deadly terrors clasp!
When the stars threw down their spears
And water'd heaven with their tears:
Did he smile his work to see?
Did he who made the Lamb make thee?
Tyger Tyger burning bright,
In the forests of the night:
What immortal hand or eye,
Dare frame thy fearful symmetry?

Blake (SE 1794, E, pp. 24–25)

Plate 16
Fall of Satan
Thou has fulfilled the Judgment of the Wicked

Each man is in his Spectre's power
Until arrival of that hour,
When His humanity awake
And cast his Spectre into the Lake.[1]

(J. Pl. 37, E, p. 183)

I have quoted the three poems above as they encapsulate what I am trying to articulate as participation. The Rilke expresses the experience of participation in a binary form, stretching your strengths between two opposing poles, 'because it is inside human beings where God learns'. I see Blake moving towards the same idea with the poles of innocence and experience, expressed here as the Lamb − Jesus, and the Tyger − Wrath. Blake asks whether God makes both knowing full well the answer. For me this God is not necessarily a Christian one, although for Rilke I assume it to be so, but is experienced beyond our material sense.

In this image we see Yahweh casting out Satan and the spectres of Job and his wife. This is a personal and collective letting go, witnessed by Yahweh, the divine council and the angels who have protected Job throughout his journey. Satan and the spectres are falling into the fires of hell, which for Blake, as we have discussed, are the energy for life. In other words this is the heat of transformation that when surrendered to becomes loving compassion, and is not experienced as torturous suffering; as the lake of fire in the quotation above, from the epic poem *Jerusalem* (1820). At some point, the habitual left brained mechanisms by which we manage or filter experience need to let go, to perceive something new that is recontextualised by the right. Reason and rationalisation must give up to the context of the whole. In the Buddhist canon this would be seen as 'self-liberating': after sufficient practice appealing to the right brain and bodily context, the proximal fragmentary attachments of the left brain begin to self-liberate, to dissolve. It is only through this process that the new perception is formed that comes in Plate 18.

Whitehead describes such a context for the arising of the new, set in a sequence of events – he calls these 'occasions'.

Life is a bid for freedom: an enduring entity binds any one of its occasions to the line of its ancestry. The doctrine of the enduring soul with its permanent characteristics is exactly the irrelevant answer to the problem which life presents. This problem is, how can there be originality?

(PR, 104)

The originality he is curious about is emergent between the context and the processing of that context. It arises once the old, in Blake's terms 'self-righteous' or mechanistic understanding, has been let go, and the new perception is possible. Whitehead gives up the notion of Platonic 'metempsychosis', the transmigration of souls from life to life, that Blake accepted, to a more fluid flow of perishing and becoming, the flow of the whole that I see Ray (2008b) perceives in his experience of ensouling, which is nearer to a Buddhist construct than a traditionally Christian one. That of the soul as a felt sense of the becoming universe in the whole body and up the spine.

Solomon (p. 65) points to the form of a flower or chalice as consistent across Blakes' work, for instance, in 'A Vision of the Last Judgement' (1808), the image of perpetual falling and rising, that is now in Petworth house. He likens this to the grail, or flower image of the lotus, of the feminine, or of the created world, and of love and compassion. Here, this frame is formed by the angels/cherubim beside Yahweh at the centre. He also psychologises this plate as a confrontation between vice and the personal shadow,[2] suggesting the suffering created by inner conflict. By eating of the Tree of Knowledge, we become aware of our dual state, an ego separated from the whole, an objective mechanical 'me' separated from the subjective 'I'. Liberation would therefore mean a state of non-duality, as may be seen in Plate 18.

Satan's fall seems to penetrate the cloud that separates Yahweh from Job, forming a different participation after the advent and letting go of an ego. This is the process of reconnection with the whole, but now more openly perceived. In my experience this happens through compassion, not the hatred of the annihilated self. Hatred is still an attachment, which lends strength to 'Satan of the Selfhood', whether that is through self-hate or rigidly defining one's self through hatred of a fantasised other. A compassionate acceptance that the habits of one's behaviour are no longer appropriate or useful allows them to fall away. The experience here is more this allowing for, or letting go of the fixed image of self, to apperceive the creative process behind its imagination. Like the moment on the bench with the CORE member who knew he 'just had to stop', it wasn't me telling them they needed to stop, just that we both knew, not intellectually, but viscerally and relationally, it was time, and it was named. There the old self was liberated.

Raine (p. 238) comments that Satan is consumed in his own shame. Shame here would be cast as redemptive fire, as nothing exists outside the mind of God. Blake sees that the selfhood creates its own torments, which serve to initiate a process of change, which may be ultimately redemptive. In the *Proverbs of Hell* he expresses it directly: 'If a fool would persist in his folly he would become wise'. (MHH, P.17, l. 18: E, p. 36)

Satan exits from the story at this point, and Raine suggests we have to ask what role Satan has had in Job's enlightenment. Is the fall a *felix culpa*, a happy fault? Because without the fall, we have no 'Jesus of the Imagination'; we do not come to know. I think that this is the case, but for me it is no fault. It is through the breaking of things that we learn and make conscious, so that that we can form new relations. The old image moves almost instantly out of date and has to perish. The breaking apart and codification need to take place to make us aware; however, this codification takes place in a context to which it has to be returned. This is up lift, or *aufgehoben*, as McGilchrist points to (2009, pp. 203–207), is the most human of experiences: to break is to know, the foundation of the Kabbalistic myth of repair.

There is one more component that needs to be let go, as we will see in the next plate, which sits well with Nietzsche's insight that if God is dead, so is self (Barresi & Martin in Gallagher, 2011, pp. 43–44). The self falls first, which in this context is a sort of limit. If we return to Solm's (2021) and Panksepp, Biven and

Siegel's (2012) construct for the psyche, that turns classical Freudian theory on its head, seeing the conscious life in the Id (the undifferentiated unconscious) and the calming down in the ego; then the ego forms limit, the limit of the reality principle, but unfettered by context. The homeostatic balance that is sought becomes a tyrant, a Satan of the Selfhood, rationalising and defending against intolerable life.

In the Bible, Satan is one of the sons of God. This is not the case for Blake. Satan is the son of Time, mechanistic rigid linear time. Bohm and Peat (1987, p. 232) conceive of time as a very ancient social construct reified into a fact. For Blake there is no Satan, but a Satanic state of time-bound materialism. The son of God in Blake's sense is the 'True Man' – the imagination in all of us reflected in each other, the sum of human imagination.

We have come to the next stage of the process, a new perception – having suspended thought and propriocepted. We have perceived corporally and imaginatively, and we need to recontextualise our experience. This unfolds over the next three plates. For Blake, this is the fall of 'Satan of the Selfhood'. For us, this is the breaking down of the old ego-centric self-narrative. This fall happens in direct response to the revelatory moment of the previous plate. Through the perception of the participatory universe, the notion of selfhood is altered, its relationship changes and is ultimately lost. The organising principle in the universe is a creative, organic resonance, and self in this context is an emergent experience component in that process.

The 'sacrifice' of self is not the sacrifice of the subjective experience, but a re-contextualisation of the perception of self, so that we can recognise and experience its context. What we must forgo is the rigid reliance upon a fragmentary notion of a consistent selfhood, rather than self as a perceptual framework driven by context; personal, social and ecological; individual, group and planetary.

Blake constructs this image on the four Kabbalistic levels of becoming, which we met earlier: Eden, Beulah, Generation and Ulro. Error is cast out and 'truth' is accepted. As he says in 'A Vision of the Last Judgement' (1808): 'Whenever any individual Rejects Error & Embraces Truth, a Last Judgement passes upon the individual (VLJ E, p. 562). For Blake the Last Judgement is not the terminal moment of creation, but an ever present iterative cycle. Each moment we bring ourselves closer to the wider, conscious, apperceived experience of becoming. I see this as a letting go of the personality as a fixed object, as a reified thing, as 'me', and experienced more widely as an 'I' that is generated through the dualistic interplay of, for example, self and other, or conscious and unconscious, the homeostatic and compensatory experience of meaning-making as a reified object, rather than a fluid and perpetual process of continued emergent change, what Bohm (1980) sees as the unfolding implicate. The idealised self inevitably becomes compulsive, the contingent clung onto as necessary.

Group Vignette

At CORE we used a ritual to mark progress through the programme. It was based in a tradition that was established in the men's movement of the early nineties and adapted to the needs of the project. This was in keeping with the founders', particularly Jackie Leven's, thinking, but congruent with my experience as I left the theatre and moved into psychotherapy. Some of the practitioners came through that experience and added weight to the ritual in this context.

The ritual involved making a bundle that represented intent in life, a 'soul bundle', and it was memetic for a soul set in a community of souls. This was a material practice, gifted originally by a Guatemalan shaman, that evidenced symbol formation in a group, representing the individual in relation to the group. One could take this as metaphor or more literally dependent upon the attitude one has to the literal nature of symbol formation. I oscillate between the two, but err more, as I get older, to a reality of felt experience in the body, as I will discuss in relation to Plate 18. Any proximal image will carry with it the images that surround it, cultural, personal and archetypal, but the root felt sense I think has a commonality to humanity. Here I would point to what Blake sees as all religions being one, whilst for me retaining the diversity of their cultural context.

To bring the community together and foster a sense of belonging the first individual bundle was added to a larger bundle that was held by the community, as an act of mutual reception. This was a clear and volitional act of belonging that was witnessed in the community, which for the members had become a kind of home. This regular ritual provided a point of connection between community members, and marked the intent to lead a life free from addiction. As with all mysterious things one could approach it as literal, a material representation of a psychological abstract, or a creation of a symbolic alliance. As Colman (2016) argues, the formation of archetypal experience occurs in a social context. The local nature of this context would be set in the urban experience of using, and the desire to be free from that use.

What this did practically was set a frame for the humanisation of experience and the setting of that experience in a social, relational and I would say, sacred context. What was met in this space was wider than the atomised experience of the individual and focused on the intent to alter the identity one was attached to. It served to embed that identity in a shifting and fluid narrative that contained the letting go of the using self. The Satan in this context of identity is the user, so that a more nuanced and relational ego could form. To this end it was generally successful, as each of the psyches that were able to bear this became relational and intent on the management of this process. Everyone was struggling in the frame, and generous to each other in the atmosphere of letting go. Of course the choice to let go of using and embark upon a relational life was not always possible. The experience may well have been alienating, and felt like yet another community that could not be belonged to. But within the community this would be heard or seen, raising alarm bells that could be addressed in individual or group therapy. Pepe was an illustration of this, however, much we as individual practitioners or the community as a whole tried to bring him in, he was in the end unable to join fully and be held.

There is another example that comes to mind. A person who had experienced considerable abuse at the hands of a psychotic mother and had been in the care system. They spent eighteen months with us. I remember how difficult it was to contain their experience. It was as if we experienced in most sessions what Winnicott refers to as 'primitive agonies' (1974; Winnicott, Winnicott, Shepherd & Davis, 1989),[3] deep wounds to the early formation of the ego. Often this is experienced as falling for ever, but in this instance it was not so much an absence of holding but an impingement of a chaotic and violent mind. My countertransference experiences were of trying to hold this mind together whilst not losing my own in sleep, chaos or indeed identification with internal murderous rage or dissociation. Often I sat on the floor with this patient, to help them and me feel grounded, whilst I tried to hold them in mind. They were charming and personable, but also clearly murderous and self-destructive. They left the project after some success, stayed clean, moved on and began to enter a residential community. On the night before entry they took just enough heroin for it not to be clear whether they would wake or not. They didn't. I read the overdose as the ambivalence they experienced about their desire to live and the perpetual difficulty they would face staying alive.

We can see in Plate 16 the recording angels have stopped their record; they simply bear witness now for Job and Yahweh. All components of the psyche are becoming integrated in a new form. In the group process outlined above this was the case not only for individuals but for the community. The self as an ascribed function, a necessary fiction, is no longer necessary, and a more fluid relation can begin as part of the context. With addiction this is when the idea of the addict is let go of altogether, and one steps into a new, more open, more full, but simply human life.

Jung would see this as a change in the ego's relationship with the self, as Edinger (1986) articulates. The old ego structure is passing. The horseshoe of the life trajectory (Samuels, Shorter, & Plaut, 1986; Sharp, 1991; Washburn, 1994, 1995) and Buddhist thought, a trajectory from merger with mother at infancy, through to the formation of an ego, to trans-egoic consciousness, to a sense of oneness with all, but 'aware'; another term often used is 'awake'. In Jungian thinking I see this is expressed as ego formation, then individuation.[4] In Jung's view, no one is ever completely individuated. Whilst the goal is wholeness and a healthy working relationship with the self, the true value of individuation lies in what happens along the way. It is crucial to my understanding of Blake and his relevance to our current psychospiritual experience that we do not travel individually through one path to enlightenment, or towards redemption in heaven. It is not a linear process but about continually drilling into the consciousness that is eternally around us and within us, gradually opening our awareness of the ground or field of experience to include broader and less ego-centric forms of perception, to allow ourselves to open more widely to the creative process as it is happening relationally between people and context. So this is not a linear model, but one of growth or unfolding, opening to experience on all levels, in circularity; so unfolding and refolding as Bohm describes. This is a right brain experience, not linear and fragmented with occasional epiphanies, large or small.

Here in the Job narrative, it is the point at which Job lets go of any attachment to his old personality. Indeed, in the grand narrative towards enlightenment, this is the letting go of the personality to allow for what Buddhists might call 'pure awareness' – the letting go of a fixed self and an external God image, which we will see in the next plate before a full participatory experience of the divine whole which Blake articulates in Plate 18. I particularly like that Blake is clear that this is an incremental process, not one moment of enlightenment but a process that is continual.

> Whenever any Individual Rejects error and embraces Truth, a Last Judgement passes upon that individual.
>
> (VLJ, 84; E, p. 562)

From this sentence alone it would seem that he sees the last judgment as an immanent process which takes place from breath to breath, as much as the culmination of an entire life path.

When working with people there is a sense of narrative, however, this narrative is often experientially undermined. When we return to the past with our clients, when they regress, we revisit something of their experience, but not quite in a linear way. We are both there and here, and the two experiences are informing each other, creating a third. The top down and bottom up neuroscience of Solms (2015, 2021), frames this in the context of reconsolidation of neural pathways: a re-opening of experience in relationship that, for a period, can be reframed in the light of current experience, then reconsolidated, laid down as a new memory in a new form. In the left-right model it is recontextualisation of the left brain's perception by the right, but the lived experience is held in the moment between two or more, reflecting beyond the limit of that event.

In Tibetan Buddhist thought, there is the concept of relative and absolute truth, the incremental path and the journey which we have made. There is a narrative and there is an ending, and embedded in the absolute truth there was no journey, no time. It is just as it is, or was as it was. In Kabbalistic terms, this is the reflection of the divine in creation, as experienced by creation. In a mundane sense, this is present in each little epiphany, in the practice room or the group – the daily moments of the change of our personality, which I have described as paying attention to.

In my work with groups, these moments occur when there is a shift in an individual who becomes able to bear something of their experience that until then had not been consciously available. This shift, held by the group, alters the whole functioning of the group, not only in resonant recognition of the dynamic change but in their contextual relatedness. Each group member is informing each other member, and a third thing, the life of the group, is also forming and changing – I would call this the body of the community. This is not an experience that happens alone, or only in one person. It is also reflected in the wider community. Change is an emergent expression of the communal and collective process. An event such as the bombings in London (2005), that clearly had a global and cultural symbolic resonance, became negotiable across the community. These events passed into the psyches of the community and went further, into social, political and personal narratives. At CORE it was the group's capacity to contain that experience and not defend against it, but articulate the experience and bear it, that made the experience digestible and thinkable.

Plate 17
Surrender
I have heard thee with the hearing of the ear, but now my eye seeth thee

This is the final moment of letting go. The ego-centric self-image of the previous plate has gone, and now the image of the externalised and idealised divine is being transcended. The binary of subject and object is about to dissolve.

Blake's inscription on Plate 17 reads: 'I have heard thee with the hearing of the Ear, but now my eye seeth thee'. As we know from Plate 5 and Satan pouring poison into Job's ear as he hypocritically offers alms to a beggar, Blake believed that the ear was the spiritual organ. Now Job is in direct contact with the divine, as an internal and imaginal experience, and will embody 'Jesus the Imagination'. The text surrounding the piece raises the question of why God should be interested in humanity and answers it with this participatory experience of the divine within. Between here and the next plate, the divine is recognised as an internal participatory oneness, not an abstract objective experience out there to be attained or grasped, gained or envied, but a lived experience of the whole coherent with and coincident with our more mundane experience.

Although seemingly difficult for the comforters to engage with, this experience is fully entered into by both Job and his wife, as they both look directly into the face of God. In the cloud above, the question is posed to Job in a reductive way. "What is man that thou art mindful of him?" And is answered in the lower margin with an image of a female angel, which I can only see as a reference to the Shekinah,[5] the female counterpart to God in the Jewish and Christian Kabbalist context that Spector (2001b, pp. 42–43) describes. This was a context that Blake would know through his understanding of the Kabbalah and the Gnostic traditions. It is the female aspect of God that is missing from the Christian tradition, which Jung laments. Resonance with the divine feminine is the root through which this final transformation takes place. Raine (1982, p. 245) sees this as a Platonic image of Sophia and Psyche, making a connection through Athene and Beatrice as the inspirer of divine wisdom. We might conjecture that it is the figure that we have worked to re-incorporate into our psyche and culture over the last century. I read this in the context of the rebalance of that binary, its transcendence and, for that matter, all binaries.

So, here, and in Plate 18, we come to 'Jesus the Imagination'. This is the moment of release from contraction. Solomon (1993, p. 71) links this to the Jonah story, as a metaphor for the sacrifice of self. Jonah, cast into the sea, risks being consumed by Leviathan. With the sacrifice of the ego-centric self, Job has risked the disintegration of order, and the onset of madness – disintegration rather than deintegration (1985)[6] – to build a new but better form. Yet it is just this letting go of the personality and the identifications that sustain it, that is necessary to experience 'pure awareness': consciousness reflecting upon itself. So, having let go of 'Satan of the Selfhood', Job is letting go of self altogether, and he lets go of the image of a God external to him, who he once thought he had to please through a dogmatic adherence to Christian law.

So here Job experiences recognition of the interconnected nature of the divine experience, a fluid sense of wholeness beyond the boundaries of self and other, or subject and object. It is the point of final withdrawal of projections and thereby the recognition that consciousness is reflecting itself and the emergent process of the world. Not only have we let go of the ego as self, as in the previous plate, but we now let go of the projection of wholeness into time and space. We let go of the objective God image.

The scrolls at the bottom of the image carry the text from the Gospel of John, when Christ is at the eve of the crucifixion. 'I and my father are one. I am in my father & you in me & I in you'. There is a continuity of being between the individual human and the whole. For Blake, as he describes, 'The divine body of the saviour, the true vine of eternity, the Human Imagination'. (VLJ, 69–70, E, p. 555). This is a moment similar to the eve of the crucifixion.

There is reconciliation, but not a full re-integration of the psyche. This is left until the last plate. In Bohm'sterms there is a recognition of the implicate beneath the explicate, but it is not yet participated in fully. The new necessity is not yet perceived, which comes in Plate 18. In the context of Jung's transcendent function the symbol from the unconscious is about to present in the conscious mind. This is a deep moment of opening and also sacrifice. The letting go of ego in the last plate has to be embraced and borne so that something new can enter. The internal relation to God is available, but as yet not quite internal. This requires a move from a faith of punishment to a faith of compassion; not 'I must behave this way because it is the rule' but 'I will behave this way because it is right'.

In a group sense there is an internalisation of the moral authority of the group to form the inner and lived ethical strength, whilst recognising one's place in the group and in the wider community. One will no longer need to project moral authority onto an object – a tablet of stone, the Twelve Steps, or a wrathful God, but be able to participate in an agreed and dialogic process of becoming. In Sloan Wilson's (2015) terms this is embodying the altruistic need of the group, not following rules in order to act as if so.

GROUP VIGNETTE

At CORE we structured the work in the context of community. As I have described, individuals progressed through the project with levels of authority. These levels of authority were perpetually negotiated and examined, not given but earned through discussion. The more experience one had of letting go of using, and the hurdles it presented, the more authority one had to help others with similar struggles. To some extent this progress was marked through the rituals we held twice a year. There were clearly differing responsibilities between the staff members and the service users, but they still formed part of and were included in the community. Authority was gained through experience and authenticity: authentic actions by the staff relating to the experience of the service users and the service users themselves acting authentically with each other. It produced a profound relational containing based upon respect and experience. This authenticity was measured much as a felt sense, not as an as if, it was where someone's actions and words lined up with a sense of truth in the context they were living, here, for instance, in the context of CORE. In technical terms one might think of this in Winnicott's frame of the true and false self, relation between true selves being life giving, whereas the defensive false self structures are not, or as Bohm (1996) describes, as we move past tacit assumptions there is a felt sense in the body that is resonantly truthful. For me this is often experienced as beauty when coherent to the unfolding whole. There was a beauty to the care and compassion, to much of the group work, and the development and containing of the community at CORE. An example of the resonant reception I am pointing to in this book as a shift in consciousness.

During the progress through the service, people would gradually gain authority born from the experience they had of changing their lives, the development of insight and the ability they had to contain and articulate their experience. There would be a projection of authority onto the more experienced members of the community, which became internalised as members worked through the process of becoming clean. This means of bringing about change we found was far more effective in the long term than simply acting upon individuals as a staff team. Those who passed through the process of letting go were held by those who had recently achieved this. This experience of holding the new community members by those who had been there longer, and were further from using, in turn deepened the understanding of what it is to lead a life free from using. This was held in mind by the staff team and, of course, we made some of these interventions too. But it was the communal and relational group frame that made the interventions effective. It also taught often isolated individuals how to form and find community in the context in which they lived, which then had a real impact upon their capacity to remain drug or alcohol free after leaving the project.

During the final three months at CORE we held a group for leavers which ended with a leaving ritual. We worked for them to internalise the changes they had made to become clean and looked in practical and deeper psychospiritual terms at how they could sustain these changes in their communities of origin. This was set in a narrative of dependence, integration of relational experience, earned security and separation from that dependence, to a reliance on one's own psychological resources. All things having gone well, this would be the process that participants went through as they progressed through the project. They would have given up using, become relationally dependent on community members, staff and service users, and begun to separate from the project, internalising what they had learnt and gained communally.

With the ending of use and the replacing of the dead object with living relationships, there is a deep and human – I would say spiritual – learning, which I see described in Job's journey. The release to expansion in the next plate is profound. The opportunity to experience this in a functional community establishes the simply human relational experience of gift and receipt. The progress through the community made it possible to experience not only the receipt of generosity towards the suffering in the early stages of letting go of using, but the capacity then to receive those who struggled into mind, and hold them as they let go. When it worked, the mutual reception that was possible was life giving and truly altruistic. Of course, this was most profoundly felt during the three months of the leavers group, where the hurt of the imminent loss of the community made all too clear what it could offer. As we became more experienced at holding this group, we could better help the participants navigate this process and internalise what they needed. Every year we would hold what we ironically called a garden party in the yard outside CORE, to which everyone who had been there could come. This was to suggest that the leaving home was not permanent, and the parents could be visited.

Sloan Wilson's (2015) Darwinist metaphor considers that through the threat of 'survival of the fittest' group there is a transactional need for humanity to be altruistic (if we don't do this together, then we will fail). It is a good argument but misses for me the inspiration that Blake offers and Whitehead (Segall, 2013, pp. 16–31) describes with his symbiotic organic process of experience orientated to creativity. If it is by commandment that we must co-operate, then we are tied to the dead letter of the law, which we are ever there after searching for freedom from. Here is Job at the outset of this journey. However, if we are able to realise the whole coherent and coincident within us we are free to participate in a resonance with the unfolding whole. This is a freedom that opens to creative novelty and participation in the creative universe as a whole. Whitehead (PR, 350) describes this experience as the love of God, and Spector (2001a and b) refers to the collaborative nature of the Kabbalah God and humanity working together, pointing I think in the same direction. However (and here is the rub), we cannot own it; not because it is forbidden, but, because it is not possible. We can receive it, participate in it, but then the fixed event is past, it perishes. To own is to break as have seen in the first half of this piece. What we tried to hold and teach in the final three months at CORE was the perpetual process of perishing and becoming that can be danced with but not owned or commodified or bought, only suffered and loved in the faith that an unfolding will continue, until it doesn't.

As an example of this process in practice I will refer again to the man who felt in their final group a sense of enlightenment and a concomitant euphoria, which I worried turned a bit to mania. He came into my private practice seeing me several times a week for some years. Of course the mania dissipated fairly shortly and he became grounded and moved on with his life, career and family. The rhythm of the work settled in its usual seasonal frame, and he explored at depth his unconscious life. He was in my office at home, and I came to move, so we changed offices as part of that move. Firstly, my couch was by the window, then moved to the other side of the room by a radiator. The cold and the heat accessed very early experiences for him, as did the disturbances to the frame, but the rhythm of the year, the containing and the articulation of the suffering, mostly borne in silence between us, allowed for his gradual unfolding and opening into the process of his becoming. We articulated to some extent these processes but primarily we bore the suffering together and tried to receive creatively as best we could. Jobs came and went, children arrived and grew, the sharper angle of his personality softened with age and we paid attention to this through the frame of the therapy. I watched the Pigeons in spring, the sun in summer and the rain in autumn. Winters came and went and fold after fold of a crumpled psyche opened to reveal its jewels. Eventually of course the time came when the room and our work was no longer necessary and the conversation, in that form at least, ended he had taken in enough of that which was projected out that our shared journey could end. I might say that internalisation happened long before we did finish but something of the shared space offered deeper, more participatory, insight. For me this is even more so in the group. Life becomes in the space between, between people, between moments, between thoughts. It is there our infinite subjectivity is met but of course as Bohm would say (2008c) unnameable, unlimited hence the participatory silence. This then moves to Job's experience in Plate 18.

A New Context
Plate 18
Internal God (the infinite Subject)
And my Servant Job shall pray for you

This is the moment of the internalisation of God, for me an experience of the interconnectedness of all things. The image is clearly the acceptance of the divine and the transcendent experience into the body through the heart. The direct and divine experience is emanatory (as in the Kabbalistic and neo-Platonic tradition) and focused directly into Job's breast, his heart and indeed the self, the place of the sixth Sefirot of the Kabbalah. For me, this experience comes not only from the heavens but the earth, the ground where Job is so directly rooted. We see the arts of poetry, painting and indeed engraving. It is perhaps important that in Blake's imagination, music, the first of the arts to become conscious, is held by the six angels, which have replaced the recording angels in the upper margins, a reference perhaps to the auditory nature of his spiritual experience.

The key is the text in the lower margin. "And the Lord turned the captivity of Job when he prayed for his Friends." It is not the divine experience, nor the process that Job has undergone in a heroic context that has offered him wisdom. This has merely created the frame through which he can perceive, letting go his reified identification with self and God in the last two plates. It is his relationship to the context in which he finds himself and his fellows, and his capacity to bear direct apprehension of the numinous, that is founded upon his communal associations, which provides what Bohm (1994) call 'the creative perception of a new order of necessity' (p. 220). It is precisely because he has let go of personal identifications that he is able to bear this experience. This is not a process that is contained singly. It is with, and for, the community in which Job is contained, that of his everyday relations.

For me, this is the manifestation of the poetic moment, a participatory and immediate consciousness, which both Bohm (1996) and Ray (2016) describe, when all comes together and the sum is greater than its parts. In Plate 12 we had the echoes of this moment as it comes towards us, but the changes that have taken place in the intervening plates shift Job's perception of this context, making available to him this experience, which he is able to share with his community. There is clearly further to go on this journey and later, a wider group consciousness will be expressed in Plates 20 and 21. I perceive this as a resonant co-creative becoming but, for now, I see this image as the experience of 'the divine', in Blake's terms *within*, 'Jesus the imagination', the creative principle that both Whitehead (PR, 21) and Bohm (1998) point to as the fundamental experience of becoming alive and present within personal experience, which is a perception.

I liken this to the experience of Qi Gong, when the force from above and the force from below are brought together in the lower belly and thence throughout the body. This happens in meditation too. It is perhaps the root of 'transmission', the resonant experience of co-creative becoming that will be passively addressed in Plate 19 and actively addressed in Plate 20. With 'transmission' I am borrowing a phrase from Buddhist thought. To truly inhabit a practice one has to have been in a room with another who has known this practice and teaches it, opening themselves on an energetic level to share some of the content of their experience. Transmission is something of a corporeal exchange. I am stretching this term to incorporate the idea of a resonant connection between on a wider level. In psychotherapeutic terms one might see it as the field of intersubjective experience. However, I am mindful of Whitehead's (PR p. 276) caveat that consciousness is only the brightest spark in a great whole, echoing a great penumbra. Ray (2016) would liken it to the experience of the unalloyed joy of the universal becoming. He makes clear that this moment of enlightenment is not just the matter of eliminating self, as some erroneously understand the means to enlightenment, but replacing that frame, allowing it to 'self-liberate' – a process perhaps of dissolving into a wider perspective, becoming the infinite subject.

Set in a Jungian or transpersonal frame, this process is described as a separation of the ego from a merged and infantile state that, challenged in midlife, follows a path of individuation or return to the dynamic ground of becoming the greater self. It is the same in Buddhist thinking, although there is a differing context to the notion of self, particularly at the end of the process. There is a disappearance, not an annihilation, but a liberation, a transcendence of subject and object.

My understanding is that seasoned meditation practitioners are able to maintain the contextual perspective of pure awareness continually. I wonder if this is what Blake experienced with his coincidence with God – 'God only Acts & Is, in existing beings or men (MHH, Pl. 16, E, p. 40), which Ferrara (1997) seems to suggest. I have not found that expressed in this Job narrative. More I see a cyclic Kabbalistic model of perpetual fall and redemption, exile and return, building better the ineffable experience of the divine. It is a discussion beyond the remit of this book to try to decide a difference between the two. Blake as we will remember perceived all religions as one and my feeling is for that form of connection a resonant correspondence.

Suffice to say stories of self and context repeatedly deconstruct in the face of experience, until self is eventually replaced by an apperception of the co-creative process as a whole. I would see that one picks one's story, as to how much self is left after each round of this process. The emergent theory of mind, as expressed by Whitehead, offers a means by which we can begin to apprehend the process in conjunction with the material lens we have built through mathematics and physics. This construct is near to Buddhist thinking. After all, we have not stopped being human or part of the whole system, but simply look more and more clearly to one component of that system, our mind and, in McGilchrist's (2009, 2021) sense, the left brain component of that mind. I am not convinced by such objectification, but it has material impact on the world. We need to bring our experienced life up to this level of thought, as Bohm (1996) suggests in suspension and proprioception, to bring thought back to the right brain contextual perspective and not remain invested in the fragment.

To return to the Blake, the burning light here is in the centre of the body. This is the place of *Tiferet* (the 6th Sefirot of the tree of life, called amongst other things 'Beauty' and 'Self') and the heart chakra. In the moment of enlightenment, both a sense of self and ego are gone, and pure awareness is reflecting upon itself. The very small and the very large, the particular and the whole, are united in the connection of our spectrum of experience and our capacity to form symbol, Blake's 'entirety in a grain of sand'. Job has had to make this change, bringing himself into the poetic realm, recognising that the suffering experienced is the path to the new world of changed perception.

Yahweh has left the image. Because he is no longer an external projection, he is withdrawn and will not return. He is inside Job, inside us – Blake's divine humanity. Job is open to receiving the divine eminence and bearing it into his being. Job is now able to experience that there is no self and no other, only the ongoing creative process in which he and his community are participant.

All his friends and his wife are incorporated in his prayer, pointing to the inclusivity of this process. We could read this as an intra-psychic process, with the different internal actors, or archetypal structures of the psyche coming together, or as an external process of social and physical relations. Blake would take the former position, seeing the whole of creation as an internal experience, so this would be a narrative for an internal individuation process, but also a component of the systemic change to experience the group. So this image can also be read as being about group change, reflective of and resonant with individual change, as is my focus of interest; how what we perceive as internal experience is perceived in the context of the whole.

I look at this as the image of how we are affecting the system in which we live, our struggle with power, and the organisation of that power which cannot, for so many reasons, be organised as it has over the last 5,000 years. To construct this relationship as unilateral feeds the split and separation evident in the subject and object. Part of the recognition of our context is a re-recognition of our relationship to the whole, and a de-centring of the place of the individual human psyche, perhaps of humanity altogether, to move away from the religion of humanism to something less omnipotent, and more systemic and relational. These final plates offer a template for that process.

Whilst I was struggling with the conclusion to this book, I worked with a coach who used active imagination and visualising techniques to overcome blocks. The scene that came to mind was set on a rolling Sussex lawn, leading down to a marshy wetland, and in the distance, a levee. Trestle tables had been set out for a funerary tea. I had been the celebrant. The house was not in sight. I was talking to the family and finding it uncomfortable how, after having created a space for them to allow someone's 'passing', they were redrawing battle lines to fight over what was left behind, to contest the will.

I backed away from the group in despair, somewhat defeated by the lapse into greed. I noticed a figure sitting some distance from the group in a deck chair with a sun hat, sipping tea and looking out over the salt marsh, watching the wading birds feeding. I had not seen him at the funeral and was not sure who he might be. I slipped away from the group and went over to him. I could not see his face, as it was obscured by the hat, but I asked how he was. 'Enjoying the tea', he said breathing out an almost imperceptible sigh.

I leaned forward to see him better, but still I could not make out his face; it was clear to me that this was Hades, whose face one cannot see. I looked out across the wetland and the birds on it and the levee in the distance. It was as if something in him moved each time a bird pecked, that there was a recognition of the death of the tiniest creatures as they were eaten by the birds

"Interesting times" he said.

"How so?" I replied partly in wonder, and partly concerned that I might not wish to know what I was about to hear.

"My work is changing. You face the death of self … or species trauma, and then the death of self."

I blanched and had nothing to say to this, not sure quite what he meant. The birds skipped from tussock to tussock and the hubbub of familial conflict reached a crescendo then died away.

"I am happy either way. However, I am happy here in the late summer sun and enjoying this tea and as you can see I have more than enough work as it is."

He returned to his cup and looking into the distance and settled into his chair. The interview was over and we gazed at the beautiful scene before us.

This was alarming to experience, but I saw it in the context that Barresi and Martin (2011), Ray (2008b and c, 2016, 2020) and McGilchrist (2009) suggest, following the narrative I have tried to draw through Blake's images. Our individual relationship with the co-creative system is changing, and changing en masse. These changes are difficult to make, and it may take a great trauma to promote them. I saw that my imagination was attempting to show me this cultural tension through imagery outside of my individual frame. Addiction then is exactly this isolated deadly symptom that resonates with this cultural experience.

For many years, working in CORE, with its pluralist and syncretic model, I was wont to say that there is nothing left to have faith in but faith itself. This was difficult to understand but an experience that people suffering with addiction can readily appreciate. The existential construct that accompanies it is faith that the next moment will happen, until of course it doesn't, and we must consider all the complexities of meaning and non-meaning that come with that. However, given the context of the radical betrayal of everything, including oneself, that is experienced at the end of a habit, this was usually just a practical explanation of a lived experience. The only thing left to have faith in is the faith that life will unfold. To let go of using, one had to let go of death and chose to live, to let go of the petty death of relating to a dead but knowable object and have faith in the unknown possibility of the moment. This was done at rock bottom, as we saw in Plates 11 and 12, but there is another act of faith that comes later, one more subtle and more human. It is at this point, in Plate 18, where one lets go of the idea of the addict and has faith in one's own humanity and its becoming in context. What is faith if not the resonant connection between the stubborn facts of our becoming.

Addiction always leads towards death of a self, usually the death of an omnipotent self that has managed, through the using, to sustain some life to the point that it might be lived in a more creative way. The death can often be literal, but most often is not. It is the death of an old idea of self. The point of death of course is the point that the new life fully arrives. The old has been let go. The call of the habit, and the self that held an idealised form of habit in relation to a dead but dependable object is being let go. A new self is forming and in this instance it is a self that is negotiable, relational and fluid set in the context of the group as a whole. As Hillman (1992) suggests:

> My practice tells me that I can no longer distinguish clearly between neurosis of the self and neurosis of the world, psychopathology of the self and psychopathology of the world. Moreover, it tells me that to place neurosis and psychopathology solely in the personal reality is a delusional repression of what is actually, realistically, being expressed.
>
> (p. 93)

The final three plates show this process and its concomitants.

I harbour the idea that this is the image where Blake connects to his own work. It is the experience he inhabited – I assume on a good day – when he was making images and his art, evidenced, I would see, by graving tool, palate, brushes and poetic scrolls in the lower margin, the source and root of all his work. It is apt here, to remember the creative space made in the printing process that I described earlier. Blake portrays his artistic expression as the divine light of human imagination as it is constellated into our becoming.

Notes

1. The lake in question here is the transforming lake of fire.
2. This is Jung's notion of the other that opposes the every day personality, 'the thing a person has no wish to be' (CW 16, 1945, para. 470). This is the negative side of the personality, the sum of all the unpleasant qualities we want to hide (Samuels et al., 1986, p. 138).
3. Primitive agonies are unthinkable in that they cannot be thought about and are brought about by the trauma of too much impingement, destroying the self (Abram, 1996)
4. I am not directly equating the individuation process with Buddhist notions of enlightenment. However I am suggesting a resonance between and sense of wholeness aspired to through individuation and the felt sense of emptyness. A fullness experienced in the unfolding process of becoming as I would see it in the emptiness of Buddhist practice. To quote Sharp (1991)
   In Jung's view, no one is ever completely individuated. While the goal is wholeness and a healthy working relationship with the self, the true value of individuation lies in what happens along the way.
   The goal is important only as an idea; the essential thing is the opus which leads to the goal: that is the goal of a lifetime.["The Psychology of the Transference," CW 16, par. 400.] To quote Wellings 'In Buddhism 'emptiness' is the Holy Grail. The direct, unmediated experience of emptiness is synonymous with complete spiritual awakening. To know emptiness entirely is to lose the self in rapture!' (2023, p. 80).
5. The Shekhinah is the female counterpart to God, to the divine presence. In the fall she was separated from the godhead and exiled. They will be reunited in the final restoration (Spector, 2015, p. 15.)
6. Fordham believed a sense of self and formation of the ego came about through a separation of the 'primary self' which had psychosomatic unity. This disintegration formed a sense of mind and body. Disintegration is the extension of this process and the components of the psyche are experienced as flying apart.

Chapter 7

Participation

A Blessing

Just off the highway to Rochester, Minnesota,
Twilight bounds softly forth on the grass.
And the eyes of those two Indian ponies
Darken with kindness.
They have come gladly out of the willows
To welcome my friend and me.
We step over the barbed wire into the pasture
Where they have been grazing all day, alone.
They ripple tensely, they can hardly contain their happiness
That we have come.
They bow shyly as wet swans. They love each other.
There is no loneliness like theirs.
At home once more,
They begin munching the young tufts of spring in the darkness.
I would like to hold the slenderer one in my arms,
For she has walked over to me
And nuzzled my left hand.
She is black and white,
Her mane falls wild on her forehead,
And the light breeze moves me to caress her long ear
That is delicate as the skin over a girl's wrist.
Suddenly I realize
That if I stepped out of my body I would break
Into blossom.

James Wright (1990)

Plate 19
A Mutual Reception
Every one also gave him a piece of Money

I have chosen the poem above because it was one of the first that clearly articulated the notion of participation for me. I used poetry in groups to help others understand what it was that I was trying to bring them to experience and what I had begun to experience myself through working this way. Firstly, I did this with men suffering from addiction, but I drew the style across my practice. Occasionally I will read a poem now, but more I try to draw people's attention to the poetry of their own lives. This is the moment of beauty I have tried to illustrate in choosing to live. I think this is what Whitehead and Bohm are getting at when they talk about beauty, truth and creativity. For me it is almost a criterion upon which one can judge 'rightness'. If something is experienced as beautiful it is in alignment with the unfolding order of things, connected to the more subtle orders of our becoming, that Bohm points to behind our fragmentary thoughts. This is not beauty as a social construct, dead and linear, but beauty as an apperceptive experience that resonates with our present unfolding moment.

In the last plate, the participatory experience was seen in its receptive form: humble, listening and relational. Whitehead (PR, 345; Mesle, 2008, p. 75) places this kind of reception at the root of becoming. He believed that any actual occasion comes into being through reception: the seeds of becoming implicit in the historic occasion are constellated into the next occasion through a reception, a valuing, that is rooted in the whole, and is felt as the love of God. This is perhaps what Ray (2016) describes as discovery: 'that our own life, from the beginning, has been the free and joyful expression of the universe itself' (p. 28).

There is a restoration of the relational after the isolation and horror of an encounter with death. We are only so when seen and experienced as an intersubjective experience. The death that we have experienced is the death of attachment to a fixed idea of self and its necessary constraints. This is not a one-time experience for Blake, but an iterative and cyclical process. Raine (p. 251) points to Job having let go of his religiousness, and can now receive experience, not hold himself aloof, as separate, but participate.

This is the plate in which Job and his wife meet with communal rapprochement, where humility and a creative life is restored. Again, this is not the narcissism and false modesty of Plate 5, but a humble experience of true relating. It is Bohm's (1996, pp. xviii–xix) 'impersonal fellowship', beyond the needs of self, and how he describes relationship between participants in the dialogue group. Each of the community brings generous gifts as Job is restored to his previous place in the community and comes back into coherent relation with the whole, but altered, more able to participate, with a deeper and wider consciousness. The fig tree, wheat and date palms can be read as symbols of abundance, with the palm, the Christian symbol of suffering, bearing fruit. The perspective which was broken in Plate 4 has been restored.

At the centre of the image is a trinket held out by a woman – in the Bible it is an earring. I see this to be gold, in the form of a classic quaternary, reminding me of the four Zoas, as the image of completeness, or the image of Milton's Track (1811 M. P. 32). The comforters are now other figures of the community who themselves are inspired by their internal life and are receptive of Job, as can be seen by the hair of the woman to the far left. These figures may echo the level of Beulah and his daughters who are to appear in the next image – the world between heaven and earth, the world of the soul. A soul, the world of Beulah, is for Blake a bridge for divine imagination (FD, 2013, p. 45) filling the space created by the loss in the first half of this journey. In keeping with Hillman's notion of soul (Hillman & Moore 1989, pp. 15–91). The benefit Job has won from his ordeal, the access to a deeper wisdom and capacity, is not just for him, but for his whole community and humanity at large. The community is clearly receptive to this, recognising relationally the new context that Job and his wife bring.

Job is now restored, embedded and respected in the community of which he is component – bodily and materially freed from his spiritual blindness, and now able to inhabit his corporeal life anew. The community receives him, recognising the wisdom he brings to the group through his personal journey. They bring gifts. This is a mutual reception. Now, with the depth of his experience, he and his wife embody their becoming, which will be evidenced in the next two plates. This plate stands in contrast to Plate 5, where Job is giving hypocritically. Now his fortune is returned to him through the benefits of a more embodied living in the context of the group and the whole. These are not literal gifts, but spiritual gifts – the gold of the golden age representing Eden. Job and his wife now have abundant wheat and figs, 'autumn Fruits … When Grapes and figs burst their covering to the joyful air' (M.P 5. 32. E, p. 99). I read the vines in a more interconnected sense, as the moment between, the resonance between the components of self, and self and other as they unfold.

Job is holding his knees as a reminder of the journey, a reminder of the contraction, pain and suffering of the first half of this process. He has obtained knowing that is formed only from direct experience, the knowing formed of what it is to be human after addiction has passed. What Job and his wife have done for the group is received by the group. This I think is the meaning of the quotes in the margin: "Lord maketh Poor & maketh Rich. He bringeth low and Lifteth Up." Creation as a whole affects the process we dimly perceive in our flickering consciousness. I believe this is a reference to the relational power in our becoming, wounded and dialogic, not the unilateral exertion of might born out of our own wilful strength (the abuse of power and authority as done to Job by Satan). The resonant contact with this is through compassion, and the humble acceptance of what is perceived.

As we move into the next plate, we find ourselves at the end of this particular journey of individuality, where that individuality becomes a component within a wider process, material, social and spiritual. The system's awareness of itself shifts away from its presence, not merely in the individual psyche, but to the resonant relationship between psyches and their context upon the planet. Bohm (1996, pp. 97–108) points to this, referencing the beginnings of Homo Sapiens' shift to their place of primacy in the planet's development. The hunter-gatherers dream of their place in the system and allow that to directly inform their experience. I would suggest that through dialogue – the process of listening in group to our experience, psychological and corporeal – we can return to the capacity to perceive the co-creative process of the whole with this directness again, but in a new context suited to the time in which we live. It would appear that we are at a time where these ideas are returning, but in a different and more conscious form. Our fears about our relation to the planet and the impact we have on each other and our environment, made and given, bring this experience to the surface. The exploration of our psyche in the context of our social and material environments points to a systemic fluidity coming to the perception of a new interconnected necessity.

The point in the sacrifice of self is that it is volitional. Job chooses to undergo this process through his faith. Job could have given up and died, given up on himself or given up on his faith, but he chooses none of these. He stays true to his perception of his experience, confused perhaps, but not faithless. He is neither distracted by false dawns nor abandoning of his experience. He submits and surrenders to the process as it unfolds, between him and Yahweh, and between him and those who are around him; one has to trust in the process, as a colleague of mine will often say.

The critical appraisal of these narratives is a past-time of choice, whilst we still live in the decaying remnants of their hegemony, searching for a new vision, which is currently (at best) a vision of diversity, multiplicity, plurality and dialogue. I would argue for a little more faith in perception, the personal defeat of our becoming, the defeat and awakening that Job experiences and remains faithful to. Blake's *Job* can be viewed as a narrative frame for the apperception of a new necessity.

Plate 20
Transmission
There were not found Women fair as the Daughters of Job in all the Land & their Father gave them Inheritance among their Brethren

For me this is an image of transmission, the active form of the participatory experience, an image that is outside time and space, for the transcendent and trans-egoic; of the apperceptive, of direct communication and the bearing of the unfolding instant. Some might call this 'channelling'. If the last plate was passive receipt, this is active bearing, leading to the manifestation of becoming; in other words, the action that responds to the moment of arriving into a participatory life.

My approach to clinical work is organised around this idea. I sit with the experience as it unfolds within and between the participants in the therapy group, as I see Job here holding lightly the unfolding nature of the process; an apperceptive reception of relating infinite subjects. I have not abandoned theory, and I still organise work in the frame of therapeutic boundaries, but look to the most valuable possibility to become through the event in hand, and pay attention to that. The group at CORE around the bombings, the work with the client that came on into my private practice, the client on the bench, are all examples of such a creative moment, but held with varying attention.

Here is an example from my experience which shows the holding not in a psychotherapeutic frame, but in craniosacral therapy, and matches the event I refer to in Plate 15, where I meet the ringing living creature at the centre of the earth. In that plate I described a downward journey with my colleague in Wales to the bright orange ferrous being at the centre of the planet. Some weeks later it was suggested that I talk with a shaman in Odessa to start the upper process. This was not successful, but triggered an unfolding which I followed up in a session of craniosacral therapy. The therapist I have found is able both to hold the dynamic physical space, the psychodynamic and spiritual process as it unfolds, and is able to process what one presents. We used this treatment a lot at CORE. It would hold a space beyond the normal dynamic or material process, that often was unnameable, but impactful upon people beyond language, at a deeply vulnerable time in their lives.

This journey started with a normal ascent, upward into a light and profound place that become white and undifferentiated. This time there was a sense of going beyond what I had previously experienced, for instance, in a semi-dreaming or semi-waking state, after I had completed my training as a transpersonal psychotherapist. Here 'more' and 'other' were not really the right category of differentiation. The cosmic joke was meeting Christ as Neil Gaiman describes him in the appendix to the 10th anniversary edition of *American Gods* (2001), the conceit being that he is a vintner, mostly interested in grapes and terroir, tired by the projections as a result of the need to be everything to everybody. This I read as a psychotherapy gag, harsh on many levels, but collegiate to my limited thoughts. It was also, of course, my imagination throwing up reference to Blake's Jesus the imagination, the resolution to the dual problem, and what Ferrara links to Chan Buddhist thought.

We talked inconsequentially and we laughed. I rested for a moment and then he opened a door for me. I stepped out, first into a blinding light, and then the blue of what I imagine to be the Gnostic pleroma.[1] The felt sense was numinous and timeless and loving. There was a great stillness and opening to the possibility of event, of wonder and of incarnation. I could pay attention at any point and all points with which I was, if 'I' is the right idea, entirely coherent. This was an experience of what I would see as the infinite subject. The imaginings and the thoughts are what they are and no doubt resonant to much of my psychic life, history and the work I have done to produce this book, and of course my practice, but that was not the primary thing. The deepest felt experience was and is beyond literal language. I can describe it as a holding and a resting in the unfolding process, fully aware of the event in hand, but also the context in which that sits and primarily a coherence with it all. A oneness is accurate but does not do the experience justice either.

The colours blue for the heavens, and orange for the earth, are complementary and resonate with the aphorism for beauty being oranges in a blue bowl, part for me of the beauty and the humour with which the unconscious, and I would say the universe, expresses itself. The peace was profound and somehow beyond. There was event colour, room sensation, and a presence, an unfolding in which I was participant, constituent, coherent and whole. The return to a more ordinary dual conscious was reluctant but also necessary and open to the participatory and subtle beneath. This was a redolent and coherent experience of what I see as participation. My work has a flavour of this, but is, perhaps too often, caught with the dualistic events of the day.

Although transition to this perception took place in Plate 18, we see it here in its most direct and expressive form.[1] It matches Plate 19 in terms of its depiction of interconnectedness. The two will be synthesised relationally in the final plate as community in dialogue. Job is pointing to the events of his past experience, but it is as if they are in fact present to him and to his daughters. Job's expression is both peaceful and devoid of personality, as if life passes directly through and within him. he is transparent yet engaged and perceptive. Spector (2001b, p. 140) suggests that *Jerusalem* (1820), the epic poem he completed before *Job*, is the perfect Kabbalistic poem. Here Blake is able to align himself with what I would see as the unfolding process, that the 'form and content coalesce in the artistic representation of the divine vision'. It is here that she sees the liberation of Blake from self, as a mystic would experience.

The images on the wall that he points to reference Plate 3, the cataclysm, and 6, agony and ecstasy, framing his downfall. On the central panel, Plate 13 is referenced through the return of the divine presence. This is the kernel of the narrative compressed into one image – everything relating to everything, all the time, everywhere. His daughters are included in this process. There are three which could reference the dream world of the daughters of Beulah, who double for muses and graces. This is the level of the soul between the divine Eden and matter, the world of generation and Ulro.

Herein is an image of the co-creative ongoing and ever-present, synthetic and syncretic, the one and everlasting unfolding experience, the implicate as apperceived beneath the explicate. This is reflected in the instruments of the Lute and the Lyre, instruments given by Hermes, the imaginal, to Apollo, the logos, in Hillman's archetypal rubric. The image is surrounded by Blake's beloved vine, which represents the inter-connection between all things, now bearing fruit.

The quote in the margin, 'How precious are thy thoughts to me ... O God how great is the sum of them' (Psalm 139: 17) points to the idea that 'it is inside human beings where God learns', where through our capacity to symbolise we find the means through which the creative process is known and the novel is perceived. The evolutionary frame changes from blind fate to thought, to symbol and relationship as we move to its perception.

During my training in group work, I was interested in the notion of the transpersonal, both in a social group analytic context as well as in a Jungian archetypal and collective context. How and where do we emerge out of the whole, and how does that differentiation develop? As I saw it, through a Jungian lens, the shift was from the ground of 'being' to the archetypal, then on to the differentiated complexes of the unconscious, to conscious experience and self-formation. I imagined interrelating narrative streams on personal and group levels, conscious and unconscious interacting externally and internally. Self would be a slice through this complex process at any one moment. It would not be permanent, but a product of an emergent process.

The quotation in the margin: 'If I ascend up into Heaven thou art there ... if I make my bed in Hell behold Thou art there', which points to the sense of duality and its transcendence, which we struggle with in our limited experience of becoming and redundant ideas of good and evil. The transcendence of the egoic state of good and evil, and the binary of male and female. It is made clear that there is equality between Job's sons and daughters.

All division and limit are gone and exist at the same time. It is merely a matter of where in the frame of our experience we rest our attention. If we could let things go in Plate 6, then we could jump right here, but this does risk madness, as there is no experience frame to contain the unfolding process. I have worked with people who have tried to make this jump and it has been impossibly difficult. This attempt might be seen as the spiritual bypass. The rest of the journey is necessary to build a frame that can contain the experience. This is shown in the remaining plate. Addiction itself is an example. We use because we suffer and do not have the experience to mediate that suffering and imagine a life free from it. The experiences gained through the using and its letting go become the foundation upon which we can build a structure to live, build an ego that can then be transcended.

Raine (p. 255) points to the original text in which there are new children for Job as all his previous offspring died. However, in the Blake it is clearly recognisable that the sons and daughters in Plate 1 appear in Plates 20 and 21. Raine takes this as a relational death brought back to life by new insight. To look at this in terms of the transcendent function, it is the full arrival of a new image into experience, in a form that is usable and knowable. The manifestation of a new order of being first touched in Plate 18 received as a mutual reception and blessed communally. In Plate 19, this is now lived and inhabited. However, it is important to recognise in this context, and it is seen in this image, that the suffering involved in the process of creating the perception of a new necessity fills that experience with its lifeblood.

For instance, in the experience of a long analysis, which can often last up to twenty years, the process of becoming, through the recursive bringing to consciousness and re-imagining of our past 'errors' (in the sense that Blake might have understood them), re-visioning injuries as windows rather than walls, failings, as Hillman (1975a, 1983b, Hillman and Moore, 1989) might frame them, remain a part of the process to the end. The experiences, and their echoes, come readily to mind most of the time, however, our relationship to them, our experience of them, shifts, as does a great wine from sourness to depth of flavour. It is this depth, not the eradication of experience, nor the reframing of those experiences into some idealised form, that evidences and allows for change. Having undergone such a process of repeated suffering and despair, Job is open to a capacity of bearing, in a Winnicottian (1960, 1965a) sense, a holding that enables the creative process of becoming to unfold against the fixed moment of being.

I note that Job's expression seems to be open, personality-less, free of self, compared to other plates. We recognise what was before, the clothes, the hair, the body – which is now seen as the corporeal moment of experience as a frame, a tool for perception. I have tried to avoid pressing one religious thought over another. I have used God as a word throughout the book in Kabbalistic, Jewish and Christian contexts and also made reference to Buddhist thinking in Vajrayana, Mahayana and Dogzen frames. I have touched on Gnosticism, but have not pursued that imaginal frame, more out of time and space constraints than prejudice, and of course there is a secularist underpinning in analytic thinking. I am not a scholar in any of these religious disciplines. I have spent most of my time practising psychotherapy and building psychotherapeutic communities, but these ideas cross syncretically into Blake's work. So my perception of Job's face as empty of self perhaps falls into my particular experiential preference for an Eastern 'no self', open to a universe reflecting upon itself, in which my experience, my perception, is participant; rather than a Western and Jungian actualised self.

My personal view is that we are in the process of building a new imagination, a new symbol, a new necessity, to use Bohm's term, to live by, as our context has altered so rapidly and so totally. This necessity will include all those that have become recognised as contingent. If we look at this from Jung's view of the transcendent function we won't see this symbol until it gets here, and the process of its unfolding has the terror and difficulty that Blake expresses in the Job narrative. I cannot see what this is, but I have faith that it is unfolding. It is what I see in my practice as the people I work with their lives. I worry though that we are in a negotiation over price, like an addict negotiating over ending use. I am afraid, and this much I know, that it will be a hard boundary, there will be no negotiation, and the price will go up the longer you haggle.

Plate 21
Wholess/Pre-Fall
So the lord Blessed the latter end of Job more than the beginning

Plate 21 shows the resonant moment. All is in order and the symbols are in their rightful place between the eternal and the temporal. This is the perpetual boiling holomovement, with everything connected to everything and moving in flow. It has a clear Kabbalistic theme, all is held from top to bottom. The ten instruments that in Plate 1 were in the tree, unavailable to the self-righteous Job, are now in his hands and those of his family, who play together. The rightful flow of energy is restored from heaven to creation and reciprocated. The unfolding emergent is experienced and participated in. The music of the resonant whole is perceivable and embodied. This transforms, in Solomon's (p. 85) terms, the tree of knowledge of good and evil to the tree of life. Urizen, to the right, is in wonder, as are we all, at the numinosity of the moment. Job's daughters hold a book, a lyre and a scroll – the word, poetry and music – all expressions of poetic genius, or windows to the soul. The central figure looks out to us holding the poetic scroll.

"Marvellous are the ways of the lord God Almighty and Just and true are the ways O thou King of Saints" is quoted from the *Book of Revelation*, pointing to the experience of this moment of direct vision, the world revealed not reasoned. However, if you look to the image of the sheep and the cow at the bottom of the plate, they are inverted from Plate 1, suggesting that they go face to face, and act as keys, locking the plates together. This recognises that a state of blissful grace cannot be sustained, and the process moves on to a further fall, the end of one cycle and the beginning of the next. On the altar is written, 'In burnt offerings for sin thou has no Pleasure', recognising that the suffering experienced through this journey is not a pleasure to the whole, to God, but a function of the process echoed in Plate 5 and Yahweh's despair.

Plate 21 reflects the moment of perception, or the moment of apperception, at the end of the participatory process of incorporation, which is the experience of the whole and the divine interconnectedness of becoming. Raine points to this process as a journey of enlightenment, often seen as the emptying out of self, so as to experience the divine within. There is some truth to this, but the experience of the 'within' is full and reflexive of the flow of creativity witnessed through our relation in group. She comments on this (p. 262), that the harp Job plays represents that he has passed through the last judgement, that he is now at play in and with the universe. She links this instrument to a neo-Platonic lyre and its play as the universe. In this plate, we see the participatory becoming of relating infinite subjects. The image is very similar to Plate 1, referencing the cyclic nature of the process. However, here all is in coherent flow. The instruments are in use, the flock are awake and even Urizen, to the far right, is included.

Bohm and Peat (1987, pp. 169–177) understood that symbolism is a holographic[2] form i.e. all reflected in the one image. This is expressive of the implicate nature of context on ever more subtle levels, the context that everything is happening, everywhere, all at once, and is interrelated, non-local and non-linear (p. 183). We are the whole and the fragment in movement and process. Jung (Samuels et al., 1986, pp. 145–147) also suggests there is a numinous and ineffable core to symbol and would frame the deepening understanding of the infinite beneath, as the process of perception and transcendence of ego needed in order for that symbolisation to happen as a communal event. Colman (2016) points to the archetypal structuring of these events not as some a priori phylogenetic given, but socially negotiated over history. This leads me to Whitehead's notion of meaning being an event that is incorporated into the following events as predicates. Through this process we have to stretch beyond our self to apperceive a new experience, the 'poetic moment'. Our collective harmonics are resonant with an experience of the whole more openly received before we collapse again into the next contingent perishing event.

We could see this as abreaction (release of the repressed through reliving), in the context of a grand narrative from farming to now. This narrative begins with the move to operating on the earth and ends in the hubristic imagination of the 'conquest' of that earth. The arc of thought up to this point and the separation from the environment we inhabit would appear to be costing us a great deal. Clearly, we are part of nature, as is God, or at least the images we form for that experience of a containing environment. Our imaginations for this relationship I see as being between the particular and the whole and are socially negotiated. I am seeing in my practice a longing for the return of context, a longing for home and community, a longing to belong. This was a profound outcome of CORE. It provided a home in which the underlying struggles to let go of addiction could be held communally, a place where people could belong, could reimagine themselves and separate into their own creative lives. However, this belonging was not connected by rigid adherence to rule, which as we have seen in the first half of this piece would be hollow and empty. The community was built on mutual reception, agreement and negotiation. Not left brain logic, but right brain relation.

Using is an example of the desire to take in something and somehow belong, without the difficulty of relating to a living object. People in the pub look convivial but are in fact relating to the alcohol behind the bar. This is by degree of course. But the point is substantially true, therefore the antidote is real relation, but letting that happen may come with some difficulties. Most of us inhabit an alienated life in some form, certainly in busy western cities; however, it is how we dialogue that helps us live creatively. The football team, the allotment society, the church or the sanga, the Twelve Step meeting: the emergent process experienced in a narrative 'me' engaging with the emergent process in 'other' is the resonant and creative event that opens to the context beneath that we are all coherent with. If rules are incoherent to the unfolding process they take us away from the process of becoming. As Sloan Wilson (2015) argues, the rules simply frame the non-altruistic, the selfish to the needs of the group.

Through my work at CORE it was the group and the community that contained any change, as we have seen. There was always an appeal to the whole and the context in which the individual sits. Now I try to bear and explore this in a practice in central London. The state ran over CORE in its attempts to economically liberalise and regulate the addictions field. CORE was a small and domestic project of belonging, a home, not an institution, and the state wanted large institutions with which it could relate, to progress its addiction treatment on a manualised basis. CORE was dependent upon the actual human relationships that formed it and beautifully inefficient for that. The new managerial agenda of manuals and bureaucracy found this abhorrent, as it could not be bureaucratised or systematised in the way the mechanistic efficiencies of 'scaling up' demand.

I would see this as an acting out of the left and right brain split. The mechanised left brain model could not see the necessity of a more holistic right, inefficient relational frame. A model and mechanism was required, preferably a medical one, rather than the fact of simple human care. This dilemma is so effectively argued and expressed by Hillman (1964) in relation to suicide, and perhaps is an example of the horrors McGilchrist points to with our left brain hegemony (2009, pp. 429–462).

I left CORE at the point I felt we could no longer take people through the journey they needed to release themselves from addiction. I had probably stayed too long as it was. Others took on the project and successfully steered it through those turbulent times, merging with a larger and more bureaucratic organisation in an attempt to share skills and capacities. It lived for twelve years after I left. I spent some years in the wilderness, then formed another communal project, working in a more psychotherapeutic model, but nonetheless syncretic and diverse. The founding of number 42, a psychotherapy and well-being practice in central London, brought together the ideas developed at CORE, and grounded them in a practice that tried both to accommodate the emerging of new sensibilities and recognise the past from which they were born. To bring value to the emerging moment.

The project is held in a dialogic frame that owes much to the work at CORE and the ideas of Bohm, Whitehead, Group Analysis and Jung, as well as a myriad of other ideas the practitioners bring to the practice. We use group to contain the practice. We have a weekly dialogic group to process the ongoing dynamics, and a large group twice yearly to bring the practice together. Some of these will be discussed to illustrate the ideas I have put forward, however, below is a vignette illustrating the process of the large group.

VIGNETTE

The twice yearly days are usually structured with three groups that are often theme based. The day starts with a dream matrix that evolves into an open large group, then there are three smaller groups before lunch to process some of the work that arises in that group, then an extended lunch, so that people can meet each other more socially, then a final large group that concludes the day.

One such group opened with a series of dreams ranging from streets of Palladian architecture in central London to convivial basement workshops, to the German idealists dressed as middle aged skinheads unsuccessfully trying to destroy the community violently, to a tiger roaming along a fence, with us on the outer side, nervous at its presence. The tiger found a gate and came in, or out of its enclosure. No one was hurt. The group associated to the dream with regard to the struggle and difficulty bringing feelings to life. I made no reference to Blake. There was discussion of our multidisciplinary work, and how we worked together as a diverse community of therapists. These themes were addressed in the small groups which I do not attend.

In the afternoon much was raised about what we contain. The uncomfortable social feelings that come to the work, although difficult to bear, are held in the practice. The transference knows no boundaries. It will manifest in the group to be processed by the group. To some extent in this group there was a processing of polarised experiences in relation to race, gender and sexual orientation, class and accessibility to a white middle class profession. What it was like to be a woman in a patriarchal culture was particularly voiced, and what indeed it was like to be from a minority. As a white man I felt bruised at the end of the day, as if beaten by the 'lardy idealists', as the German Philosophers had become described and wondered about. Although I wanted to polarise through identification or through othering I remembered being told in other situations that were not dissimilar that you have to take it, but not take it personally. The good will, the fellowship, to use Bohm's term, in the room, enabled the containment and exploration of these tensions and experiences. There was not resolution, there could not be, but there was an acceptance, a human acceptance, and what I understand as a mutual reception. A colleague of mine with considerable group experience said "it doesn't get better than this" as we closed, at which I felt some despair, as I had hoped for something more convivial!

To perceive the experience of the component in the whole, as I perceive me in you and you in me, we in us, we participate in a moment of becoming resonant to the whole. For me, this is play. As soon as we enter the division of literal thought or feeling, imagination and self, we enter the arena of the separate, the objective; the left brain's processing and division. Yet in so far as we enter that together we constellate the space for the creative whole to emerge into consciousness, the perpetual dance, where, as Blake would have it, 'the morning stars sang together' (Plate 14).

When we step back from the fragmented ordering of our perceptions and we participate, we allow the dance to move us to the music of our relations, divine or otherwise, to sing in the great chorus of becoming. This is the key to experience, both mundane and numinous. It is experienced through the resonant forming of the participatory whole in the event. This is 'Jesus of the Imagination' that Blake so clearly inhabited and brings to us directly in his work, exampled through the process of these plates as perpetual resonant experience.

The focus and breaking up into parts, as Job has experienced on his mythic journey, is the act of perception duplicitously informed by memory's fragmentary echo that divides us into self and other. It is necessary to organise the day but does not easily allow for the unfolding perception of a new necessity and openness to the whole of life. So Blake offers us in this final image a perception of the group, and the group in contact with each other, resonant and creative, returned to the whole, bringing new understanding to that space, transitional and resonant. Between us he shows how an apperception of the holomovement might be, how a resonant consciousness might be. Of course it is full of suffering, full of discomfort and the broken toys of our desire, as much as joy and excitement, the 'uplift' of McGilchrist's (2009) *aufgehoben*.

Conclusion

It is the conceit of this book that Blake's *Illustrations of the Book of Job* point to the expansion of our consciousness by the recognising that each of us is a Job in process. However, that individual process is itself a group formation, a group of cells, of organs of archetypal structures within narrative streams. This individuality is also set in a process in groups where as individuals we are able to perceive a wider unfolding process in dialogue – relationally participating in and conscious of the underlying co-creative process of a universal becoming. A consciousness of resonance. I see this in symbol formation, in which we are participant. We imagine into life the unfolding experience in which we participate.

Each theorist I have brought has offered a frame for symbol formation between and within personal experiences – individually and in the group. The frame I offer forms a narrative that articulates the consciousness of the individual in the group, informing the process that individuality emerges from. Blake sees this as an iterative process of falling and rising, and focuses upon it as an internal experience – an internal perception. He has used a syncretic model to articulate a personal, collective experience, as I have tried to.

I have shied away from getting too deeply involved in spiritual models and stuck principally with the models of Whitehead and Bohm, both scientists, but both deeply connected to the experience of the divine whole and its unfolding movement. Any meaning system is only proximal adaptation, in Sloan Wilson's (2015) view, for a root collective human experience which is perpetually in a process of flux, searching for a new frame to match our expanded experience.

The perception that I have offered is that of a creative emergence. I share Bohm's perception: the idea of the infinite subject is congruent with the apperceptive felt sense. The unfortunate aspect of the finite experience of becoming is the destruction that goes with it, the death and rebirth cycle, of course rooted in ideas of our own mortality, which is more focused in the moment than the actuality of the end of our body. To paraphrase the Finnish poet, Gösta Argen, death's secret is that as life ends so does death. To hang onto any one dogma is to limit experience. The same is true of self, which can become a limit that forms its own transcendence.

The central shift of consciousness that I see humanity making is the same one that we have struggled with since we became conscious of our capacity to symbolise – to bear and participate in that symbol and its repercussions in the context that it is formed, and live with its numinosity and its impermanence. For me, the crucial negotiation for our time is the group as a species and that species set as a component in the context of the planet. Within which, of course, there are many complex and competing group structures and systems that Whitehead frames in an organic and evolutionary model. How can we try to build a symbolic frame that will recognise these processes and their necessity? This is the beauty of Sloan Wilson's perception that evolution is altruistic at the level of the group and involves the recontextualisation of self in that context. We are both individual and part of the whole, depending upon which perspective one is taking.

With the number of us that there are on the planet, and the technical capacity we have, the means by which this formation will take place is evermore in our hands, but the issue is just the same. I have found through my work with addiction that the psychic changes needed to address addiction and let it go are the same as are needed to let go of our consciousness of exploitation, and move to a consciousness of resonance, experiencing our coherence with the unfolding whole. To recognise our shifting place in the order of things and to participate in that resonant dance is shown here in Plate 21. So now, as Blake suggests, we start again – once more with feeling.

Notes

1 The Gnostic pleroma is the fullness out of which creation emerges. In Christian Gnosticism it might be seen as the heavens.
2 A holographic image contains information of an object in three dimension. This is done by encoding the interference of coherent light waves upon each other as they reflect from different surfaces. When decoded, the image of the differing surfaces appears, like with a television signal that is encoded into digital form that when decoded represents the picture filmed. This digital form can then be transmitted over time and space and watched seemingly independently to the event.

Chapter 8

Endnote
Three Rituals and Two Groups

You see, I want a lot
Perhaps I want everything:
the darkness that comes with every infinite fall
and the shivering blaze of every step up.
So many live on and want nothing,
and are raised to the rank of prince
by the slippery ease of their light judgments.
But what you love to see are faces
that do work and feel thirst.
You love most of all those who need you
as they need a crowbar or a hoe.
You have not grown old, and it is not too late
to dive into your increasing depths
where life calmly gives out its own secret.

Rilke (1905, Trans. Bly, 1981)

The primacy of imagination

We mine for grief in different seams
Under the earth away from the light.
Fragments of dirt glister, pyrite, or diamond.
The ordering of parts, neat piles, or
Slippery sheets suggest worth or value,
All fragments struggling to partake.
The longing in absentia, that hole in the heart
That shines light beyond imagination, is the glue
I hand to you as we dance, aging, step by step.
The silver thread runs deep to our ferrous core.
Slips through the spine consecrating divine will.
We work with our hands and we tread with our feet
But the beat of our existence turns all from death to life.

Wright (2022)

DOI: 10.4324/9781003354642-9

The two poems above one mine and one Rilke's, as translated by Robert Bly (1981), talk to an apperceptive understanding of the imagined life through symbol. The inhabiting of that is our incarnation in the moment. I do experience this in the body. Not as the materialist argument might go, as the only thing, but as the outfall, the consequence of Whitehead's value, as in the last two lines of my poem. Below I set out some events with which I try to elucidate what we have just been through in the main body of the book.

As I write we are living through turbulent times. There is a general sense of instability after the global coronavirus pandemic, Russia's invasion of Ukraine, which is particularly anxiety provoking in Europe, and the prospect of a recession following these events. Disease and war are drawing our attention to old rigid narratives of self and statehood. These narratives seem to take a much more complex form, orienting around traditional notions of splitting, polarisation and duality (East versus West, good versus evil) but with a nuanced postmodern sensibility (perhaps NATO's expansionist policies are partly responsible for Putin's aggression), which expanded on the thoughts I had about the bombings in London, presented earlier in the book. These narratives and the political turmoil created by them presage a change in our social order. I have suggested this is driven by the numbers of us alive and the means of communication we have developed, by our success as a species (at least in proliferating) and our connections.

In Jung's rebirth paper (CW9i, 1939, para 225), he described groups as tribal and regressive. Clearly, I disagree. I think we are moving towards recognising our group needs more consciously. However, one might have thought at the time, living in Switzerland, just as the Second World War was starting, that he was right. His model draws the consciousness of the collective into the individual psyche through myth. Group analytic theory would point to that as a social phenomenon; the individual is born out of the group, positing a social unconscious. Bohm (1980, 1996) and Whitehead point to this socialising at a deeper level, of experiential events forming societies of events leading to percipient moments, connecting the whole to the single event, all consciousness resonant in the one perceived experience. Whitehead is inverting the relationship between matter and experience, offering a pan-experiential organic whole. I tend to this view, as I sit in the room with groups and individuals. All of us are coalescences of sub-atomic energies thinking they are a 'me'. I see the frames for imagination of how we are social or individual as fragments of an unfolding whole. This will not make them inaccurate, only not ubiquitous, necessary, but contingent upon the imaginal context.

So to follow the thread I have tried to pursue, we struggle with our place in the middle of the food chain. Social and psychodynamic structures of ownership and power, mine and yours, better and lesser, are played out in a new context. It is less important whether we are going to prey upon or be preyed upon, what we must consider is how we fit together and how we receive each other into a mutually creative becoming, perhaps how we transcend these ancient dynamics, which become more redolently visible as we crowd the planet. Flickeringly, we see how we lack the majesty to bear our responsibilities, our ability to respond to our newly perceived circumstances. We can look and we can bear love, but we can't keep its products in this world of continual movement, continual reinvention. We can only move with the unfolding process. The perpetual falling and perishing, folding and unfolding, of life's experience precludes fixed ownership. To use Blake's metaphor, Job's self-righteousness is his downfall, it is Satan who through his deprivations offers the opening to a deeper and wider experience, a more communal experience beyond the fantasy of selfhood.

I have argued in this book that this context points towards a shift from a consciousness of exploitation towards a consciousness of resonance; not the exploitation of an external objective world, but a resonant relational unfolding within which one's experience is coherent. This is a participation in rather than ownership, and it is, I believe, what Job discovers, at least in Blake's telling.

If what Blake saw is to be believed, this coming turbulence will threaten our rigid and hollow identities, particularly in the West. I see this as true both in the context of self and the nation state, which to my mind are increasingly redundant organisational symbols as we recognise something more communal as the organising structure going forward. Five years ago, when I started to write this book, I felt this process of change before us, but the time it has taken to write, and the turbulent events we have lived through, has pushed me nearer to seeing the beginnings of a wider change, not only in a political world order, as we polarise our thinking and head towards war, but through our increased technological capacity to communicate and relate, augmenting our capacity to cooperate around symbol. How hard it will be and in what direction is, as always, impossible to say. I am not a futurologist, except to say that the construct of time and space can be transcended, as can any organisational structure. As Bohm and Peat (1987, pp. 223–227) make clear we could revivify more timeless, nonlinear and nonlocal perceptions of our experience in this new context. A better apperception of that complexity would help us. As I have tried to show, Bohm and Blake point to a deeper order that channels our becoming in the context of the whole.

What suffering stands between us and a new and wider perception remains our choice. Like a user, we could just stop our habits, but this would mean facing what compels us towards ownership and thence destruction, as we identify with that which perishes, the order of matter, and that is very difficult as it feels like making contact with death. Blake makes that process clear, Job must wait and suffer through his impoverished perspective, indeed wish he was dead, in Plate 8, until a new necessity is perceived – Bohm's limited opening to the limitless. Job trusts the process until through experience some new necessity unfolds from the implied whole. I would see this as a relational experience, not an aspect of rational materialism that Blake so eschews, a matter of simple human trust in the simple human capacity to bear and allow experience in search of its most creative outfall. It is our capacity to cooperate. 'It is inside human begins where God learns' (Rilke, 1924).

Blake and Linnell and Concluding Events

I will end with some notes on Blake and Linnell, who's relationship brought the *Job* into being. Then I will present three rituals that illustrate participation in the becoming moment and its context. Finally, I will describe two groups that illustrate our shared capacity to articulate and bear our becoming, allowing for a creative and resonant experience. These examples also tie together the individual and group narratives of the book, and I believe show in different ways the synthesis I have tried to describe.

Linnell's arrival in Blake's life opened a final phase of five years or so that saw him understood and lauded by a small group of young artists and enthusiasts who styled themselves 'the Ancients'. They were Samuel Palmer, Fredrick Tatam, Edward Calvert and George Richmond. They were young, aged 15–19, and Calvert was 25 (Bentley, 2001, pp. 400–401). Linnell offered him some acceptance into the academy, from which he negotiated a stipend for Blake and offered him the finance to survive to his death in 1827. Like Blake, John Linnell was also a dissenter and holding a deep but not conformist Christian faith. However, he was a successful artist and earned well from a young age, allowing him to fund the production of the *Job*. He was far more able to manage his relationship with the academy, and he continued to fund Blake in the production of the Dante illustrations, even though he was becoming ill and unlikely to complete the work. He said he would have continued to fund him even if he had not been able to work.

After Blake died he helped Catherine, Blake's wife, keeping her in his house as a housekeeper. He secured a £84 payment from Lord Egremont for the *Faerie Queen*. However, she did not trust him, and he stepped back as Tatam took possession of Blake's works (Bentley, 2004, pp. 554–560), saying he was executor to his will. There was an unedifying dispute about the veracity of the will, when Tatam tried to take possession of the Dante (Bentley, 2001, pp. 445–446; 2004, pp. 538–543). Linnell tried to promote Blake's works, particularly the *Job* and Dante. Tatam also tried to sell what he possessed. It is thought Tatam destroyed works he felt were not good, or Satanic, after falling under the thrall of the millenarian preacher Edward Irving (Bentley, 2004, p. 560). I see Linnell's resonance with Blake enabled between them the manifestation of not only the *Job* but the Dante. From reading the discussion between Blake and Linnell about the *Job* it would appear Linnell's input was close in a way that few others except, I think, Catherine, had been allowed. Between them, through Blake's vision and Linnell's acumen, we have access to Blake's mythological experience very directly. I would see this as a relational achievement.

Later in life, Linnell supported the Pre-Raphaelites, who pick up Blake's work, particularly Rossetti, who saw him as a man of genius (Bentley, 2004, pp. 711–712). I see a direct reference between Holman Hunt's *Light of the World* (1854) and the frontispiece of *Jerusalem*, but this is conjecture on my part, an intuitive felt sense. However, I am told that they would have both agreed upon the spirituality of landscape and there is certainly evidence of their relationship in an early biography of Linnell.[1] These links I would see as providing a thread to Yeats' picking up and championing Blake in the last century. So there is something of the direct transmission I refer to earlier, from Plates 19, 20 and finally 21, which could be seen to lead from Blake to Linnell and on to us. To see the crowds that flocked to the two great Blake exhibitions at the Tate over the last twenty years is testament to that last plate and our participation in his work.

Linnell's own work succumbed, to some extent, to disappointment, seeing himself more as a craftsman than an artist (Linnell, 1994). The fervour of his own vision was hidden beneath the need to support a family of nine. He is rather harshly credited with dulling Samuel Palmer's vision. It is thought that he suggested that Palmer paint like him. I think this is better interpreted as David Linnell (1994) does, that he said that if Palmer wanted to make money like Linnell had, he would need to paint more like him.

I would argue that in life we all too easily take Linnell's path of material security, as opposed to Blake's of spiritual exploration. An eye ever to the practical and the efficient is an eye to the limited, representational, and leads to spiritual impoverishment. I see this direction taking us to addiction and the use of matter, or the use of substances, to be consumed, to replace the often unbearable felt experience of becoming. However, when allowed, when received, those difficult feelings will at root settle in the creative whole as both Whitehead and Bohm suggest and Blake has here illustrated. This is the divine and antientropic resonant whole expressed as Sloan Wilson (2015) sees in the altruistic group. This apperception I would see as the antidote to our middle of the food chain anxieties, not based simply on the hypocrisy of socially organised religion, seen from Plates 1 to 12, but the apperceptive reception of the becoming moment, to which we surrender the old image of our selfhood and open to the new, from Plates 12 to 21. However, this cannot be owned, only lived and loved.

Perhaps such a structure in the social group, as we see between Linnell and Blake, is the process that McGilchrist (2009) points to, of ordering, and gestalt in negotiation, that brings about the creative possible. In this example, Linnell takes the place of emissary, a guide and refiner of an open vision. He receives that vision and supports it to form. This is perhaps the dialogue McGilchrist describes between the left and right brain. If we take Sloan Wilson's (2015, p. 14) lead and look at one human as a functionally organised group the correspondence is not so difficult to make.

This leaves me with the question of how we create a communal and internal life that opens to this process. Blake would be clear that it is not the line of rational materialism which gives us this, but a correspondence of resonance. In Plate 21, even Urizen can be seen to have his place amongst the cast but only his place not the whole cast. The hegemony of reason finds its place in the dialogue of the whole. This is important as that place is only a fragment and as Bohm (1994, pp. 3–10 & 19–20) would say to identify with it is the error.

In these vignettes I express some of this in process across a range of frames – personal, individual and group – spanning different times and contexts. Each was an experience of receiving into life and allowing the emergent new to arise, illustrating a co-creative and as I would see it, anti-entropic process of poetic becoming.

Ritual One – A Poetic Moment

This ritual involves the poet I mentioned at the beginning of the book. We had worked together for a few years and she decided she wanted to have a child. She wanted to make some steps to mark this transition, as she attempted to become pregnant. I offered to help, to hold a ritual of transition for her, which she agreed to.

My office is close to the Thames and we walked from there to the foreshore on the south bank of the river near the Globe Theatre. Hidden behind a jetty is a secluded spot which retains the resonance of old London, the docks and to some extent the liberty. The Liberty of London was a part of Southwark, in south London, that neither fell under the jurisdiction of the City nor the Sheriff of Surrey, but was under the jurisdiction of the bishop of Winchester and enjoyed greater freedom. Particularly late at night one could still sense this quite strongly, until fifteen years ago, when the area began to be heavily redeveloped.

I wanted to use the river to carry away a symbol of her old life and bring in something new. There is a trick that works well on the turning of the ebb tide, where it seems that the water can let things go and call in the new. Just before the low point, one casts an offering, then one waits for the turn, and when the tide comes back one makes an offering symbolising what will be brought into life: the offerings travel in different directions and the intent for change is marked.

We clambered across the stones and the beach to the water's edge. She had brought a little wooden sailing ship, some grain, tequila, wine, flowers and tobacco. All this was to make the boat beautiful and represent the things she wanted to let go. The perishing parts of her life that we hoped would leave space for the new. I suggested she might want to keep the steering oars back, which she did, and the boat was loaded. I said a few words to note the event and she walked to the water's edge. She made a statement of intent and launched the boat into the river. The stage manager in me had noted that water rituals need a lot of preparation. They are fragile and open to the capriciousness of that element. I was therefore a little anxious as to how this would go.

It was a clear sunny summer's day, but the river was not without wind. The boat headed out into the waves a little way and turned, as the current took it, and then headed into the sea. However, it was so loaded with a cargo of past addiction and family tensions it hung low in the water. I noticed some way off down river two vibrant male Mallards paddling up stream as if engrossed in conversation. The ship tilted a little and then steadied, then sailed on for a few moments. I wondered what was to become of her and the flotilla of ducks. A water bus passed out in the river with some wake that worked its way towards the shore. I wondered at the poetry of the moment, anxious that the beauty of the ritual would carry the poet's intent a little further. But one has to surrender to the becoming of the world. The wake and the wind unfortunately capsized the boat and the ducks dived for its contents, opportunistically feeding on the grain and the tequila. We laughed out loud. A great part of the work we had done together was to help her reconcile the early break up of her parent's marriage and then the generous love of two fathers. The ducks we imagined were the merrier for their feast. We marked the closing of this part of the journey and walked back to the river wall, thanking what spirits had been with us. We crossed the threshold back to the ordinary world of tourists and the bustle on the south bank of the Thames.

It is best to wait an hour or so, for the tide to turn; however, we remained in ritual space, not unlike Winnicott's notion of analytic or potential space.[2] It is good to use this time to reflect on what has been and what is to come. We found a restaurant a few streets away. I ordered a salad and she had confit de canard, which surprised me. I did not remark on this. It seemed an excellent way to address her father complex. She, it appeared, was entirely unconscious of the symbolism. We talked of the boat, what was lost, what had foundered, what brought about suffering and for me what Whitehead sees as the tragedy of the event: the smallness of the actual in the face of such infinite possibility, and how that bears with beauty in the value of each event. I gave her time to prepare for the next part of the ritual, making a list of what she wished to come, using the oars and some flowers to make a beautiful offering for the future. The oars I thought might help her represent something of our work together, using the past to steer the future. We walked onto Southwark Bridge, made the appropriate representations and cast the object into the river. We watched it float to the West for a full ten minutes, until it could no longer be seen. I'm sure we both wept a little, closed the space and went our separate ways.

For me, as with Whitehead (1933; Cobb, 2008, p. 79) and Bohm (1998, pp. 57–58), it is the beauty of the event that shows us its coherence with actual becoming, reflecting something of the implicate order out of our limited view: the magic of chance, the wind, the ducks, the confit – the grace notes of experience – that highlight the moment and reflect the infinite beneath. They leave room for the imagination to offer the possibility of the new and for that greater awareness to arise. I experience this as the component in the event which takes your breath away and resonates beyond the sense of beauty as a mere social construct to the evolving resonance of all in which we participate. The poet and I participated in the suffering of the perishing moment and the opening into the new for a couple of brief hours which I hoped would allow for a new life.

Ritual Two – A Burial at Sea

The second ritual expresses a communal holding over time, over some twenty-five years. As I said in the last chapter, CORE as we built it struggled to conform to the new managerial agenda and had to adapt to that model. I left when I felt I could no longer deliver the work. The project eventually came to an end some twelve years after I left. However, at that point, the conundrum arose as to what to do with the bundle that represented all the rituals we had made to foster the sense of belonging and the need to let go of using. There were people still in the project who knew the importance of this. We had thought to bring together a large group of ex-CORE participants to mark this ending, but it didn't come to be. This was not to be an omnipotent moment of exhibited grief but a ritual marking the passing of the old to allow for the new. With the colleague who I had most closely held CORE with, we decided to take the bundle to Graves End and cast it into the river.

Collecting the bundle from the project was as much like a drug deal as it could be. I pulled up in a car on Lisson Grove, a busy London thoroughfare, and it was hustled out of the gate into the boot. Brief and furtive pleasantries were exchanged and I headed off at quick speed, slightly euphoric with the intent of release and renewal. This was exactly the intent at the roots of CORE. The next day we travelled early to Graves End to catch the turn of the flood tide. It has been said that Graves End is named because it is the last place on the Thames before you reach the city where you can have a sea burial. I believe this is probably not true, but the name is an adaptation of an older name.[3] However, it seemed a fitting place to let the project finally perish and let its ideas open more to those who had used them and who had chosen to live.

We found a park next to the river and set out the big bundle to make one final ritual pass, remembering those who had put so much into this now quite substantial object. Memories jostled in our minds, past events and people. There was some anxiety that we would be questioned or moved on, but we were pretty much left alone. This was in keeping with the outsider nature of the project and echoes the projections we as a society put into the using community, placing our own weaknesses and denials into those least equipped to bear them. I have returned to an understanding that addiction is the expression of our defensive grasping against the horror of life. We enslave ourselves to matter because we can't bear the impermanence of our perpetually unfolding experience. With the bundle ready, and high tide passing, we moved to the water's edge, ready to cast it in. We said a few words and thought not only of the project's past, but our relation to it now, then we threw it into the Thames.

Again, it was a water ritual, so one must think ahead. Although heavy – cotton, maize, tobacco, chocolate and flowers filled the bundle – it was not dense enough to sink, well not until it became water logged. It made a great splash, but as it was unweighted it bobbed to the surface. I imagined it looked back at us with some grief. A Sikh in a dayglow orange jumper walked past, reminding us of a particularly strong member of the early community and we laughed. Gradually the tide started to take the bundle. It bumped past a group of small yachts moored close to the shore and built up speed on the ebbing tide. We did not see how far it would go, as it soon passed out of sight behind pleasure yachts and dinghies.

We returned to the car, mostly silent and with some grief. We left the river and went back to central London. We were in Tower Bridge before we found a place for breakfast. As we sat we began to remember the people who had passed through the project, as if the large bundle were breaking up and each individual soul was liberated to something new, the community bearing itself to the world, as so many had done from this great port. Here, through memory and intention, something was born in the meaning between us, something that recognised not only the work of the project and the people in it, but the unfolding experience that connects us out of the whole across time and space. 'When the morning stars sang together and the sons of God shouted for Joy', Pl 14.

The Tragedy of the Personal Event

This final ritual event is congruent to Blake's thought that we fall and fall again in a progressive cycle of change, which is Whitehead's (Cobb, 2008, pp. 75–76) perpetual perishing and becoming. If we had the wit, we could jump straight from Plate 5 to 19, but we lack that. Often, with our wish to grasp the moment in hand, we forgo the depth of generosity needed to receive, so we fall ever further into the ecstatic agony of Plate 6 and thence the whole process through Ulro and loss to a new context. This is particularly so with the story of addiction.

As might be imagined, the struggle with the writing of this book has had itself a Jobian quality. I am wont to say, and believe, that the Job narrative is the narrative of our time, leading, as I think Blake's version does, to a participatory consciousness, resonant but from a position of expanded volition – as seen in Plate 21. Addiction, and the movement away from it, is a symptom and symbol for this process, an example of how by grasping onto something dead we hold ourselves back from the capacity to bear actual relatedness, infinite subject to infinite subject. By shifting primacy from matter to experience I see Whitehead returns us to the aliveness Blake articulates in the face of the dead hand of empiricist rationalism.

This writing experience is one such moment, in which I am addicted to my difficult prose. Right at the very end of writing this I couldn't find how to conclude the piece, having been through various choices. I could not in some way let the project go, although the process had been completed for some time. I could not bear to let it be the imperfect representation of what I have tried to articulate. I went to a writing coach with the first two chapters, who said not so unceremoniously I needed to rewrite the whole thing and that I couldn't punctuate. The latter is probably true the former it turns out from a later conversation I made up. However to rewrite struck me to the quick. I hadn't the energy to do it all again. All I wanted to do was go to the sea and throw myself in – clearly I didn't. However, the following morning I drove to Tilbury, where my wife feels the river begins to turn to the sea and went for a long walk along the corroding sea wall. I could see the park in Graves End on the other bank where we had, a few years earlier, let CORE sail to new lands. The bracing January air quickened my lungs. The guns of Tilbury fort built to defend from Napoleon and Hitler stared into space down the river, and the odd cargo boat chugged in and out from the port. The Thames seemed very small.

I walked for an hour or two, calmed down, then went into a nearby pub, 'The World's End', for a coffee, before returning to London and a Sunday at home. The pub had a violent feel to it, dark and full of the history of the Essex shore. I was shaky, full with the unease of defeat, sea air and confusion. I spilt the coffee on my notebook. All I could think was that this has to the end, which I scribbled on one of the sodden pages and resolved to let the whole thing go. I found a hat in the boot of the car, a brochure from an exhibition of Tracy Emin and Munch's art, which seemed to have a fitting Blakeian intensity, and resolved to cast all into the sea as an offering, a letting go of the whole endeavour, and more importantly my attachment to it.

I stood on the wall for a few moments gathering my thoughts. Next to me stood an Eastern European fisherman with four rods. "Better than watching the television," he said. I flung the hat as hard as I could into the incoming tide. Just at this moment, the wind picked up, the hat and contents sailed high into the air, altering its arc, and blew back towards me, foundering on the rocks below the sea wall. There it sat, dejected and abandoned at the water's edge, eyeing me, I imagined, with resentment. I had to wait, a full twenty minutes of utter defeat, for the tide to come in and claim it, taking it up stream to London and then on the turn out to sea. I returned to my car unsure whether this task would ever be complete and headed back to my home.

As I drove away a memory started to form from *Heart of Darkness* (1906), Conrad's short and devastating novella about the horrors of empire and its oppression. This is in some ways an expression of the resonance between oppressor and oppressed, a confrontation with the shadow. I began to smile. I set this event, this final subjugation, at the place Conrad sets that collective imperial confrontation with the shadow of empire in Africa. It was a story told on the ebb of the tide, telling of the darkness, of hatred, exploitation and dehumanisation. Back with Edinger (1986), my first encounter with the Job, and the dark vestiges of imperial selfhood we are working through en-masse, it felt like a pulling together of this work's themes in one grand circle.

The event can never be what is imagined in potential, forever it comes to meet us and we are inadequate to the task. Freedom is our surrender to the process, to the receipt of the moment and the unfolding possibilities it augurs. This I see expressed in Blake's *Job* and articulated in Whitehead's work, and indeed lived and examined in the work of psychotherapy. It is the attention and intention with which we receive the decaying moment into new life that gives us freedom, not so much freedom from our suffering, but a freedom to become anew. It is not what we do to make life, but by how we receive into life which tells all, as with the experiences above.

In the illustrations it is how Job bears the agony and ecstasy of becoming that enables change. Blake's plough, which we see in Plate 20, is the preparation for the new age, for the seed, turning us over and over in the context of and supported by the whole. This I see as being held in group, by all, not only people and humanity, but the whole of the planet, if we were but to lift our head from our personal sorrows and notice. This is the lived and known experience of becoming in process.

A Large and a Small Group

In these last illustrations I shall give an idea of this in practice. Number 42, the psychotherapy and wellbeing practice that I found and manage, has been held as a communal and group organisation, the practical basis for which has been a process of dialogic group holding. This manages and thinks about the life of the practice and the context within which each practitioner and practice sits. To quote a colleague, "the context is all." To this end there are a series of group frames: formal, informal and administrative, clinical and social, which allow the practice to dialogue. The two principal groups are a weekly open group and a twice yearly large group. This vignette is from one of those large group days. There was a particular event in December 2021, at the point we felt we were becoming free from the strictures of the COVID pandemic. It had been nigh on two years since the practice had met in person and the tensions during this time had been difficult to contain, particularly with only the internet to hold the community.

The usual format for the day is a morning group starting with a dream matrix, then smaller groups to process some of the work, an extended lunch for people to meet each other, as some may work at different times and not be well acquainted, and finally a formal large group. The day is often themed. This one had no formal theme but the return to the room and the building was a strong undercurrent, and what would it be like to be back together.

There were differences to this day, we were meeting in an unusual setting, in a different part of London, and of course the context had shifted greatly through the pandemic. We met in the morning and exchanged dreams. Not much usually is made of the interpretation of them, certainly not on a personal level, but they are seen more as a dialogue of the proximal symbols in the unconscious of the practice. The dreams offered in that context are images in the community, from the body of the community, in dialogue with themselves. There were descriptions of what one might expect, tensions and difficulties about being in or out of the room, working online or in person, how the practice had changed. How our practices had changed. How we had changed.

The group moved on towards a coming together, a renegotiation of the space, psychic and physical, that we were to inhabit. A woman spoke about a darkly aspected new moon. Previously she had brought a dream about a tiger, which although initially fenced off, away from the group, finds a way around the fence. As we know, the tiger for Blake is wrath, powerful and destructive, part of the corrosive fire which can be transformed to the spiritual and inspired energy for life. In the poems from *Songs of Innocence & Experience* (1789), quoted above at the beginning of Chapter 6, it matches the lamb as the innocent poem of joyous creation. The poem is often misunderstood, out of context, as representing a lust for life. The poem actually questions how God can make something that is both hateful and destructive and a beauteous creation. One might see the Job as the description of Blake's answer.

By bringing the idea of a darkly aspected new moon, which was not to be resolved until Christmas Eve, my colleague shared again this kind of naming. How do we bear the fall, the perishing, the darkness of Ulro, from which the creative arises. She also brought CORE, as this is where she had started her training placement. Desiring to make good, I no doubt defensively met this with a metaphysical response, surely referencing Whitehead, Bohm and many of the cast of characters that have peopled this book.

We both love this symbolism and began to riff off each other. I know I had wanted to make the interpretation about the tiger so no doubt I brought that to. We must have been losing our audience, because one of the more experienced group analysts simply said, "I don't want your high faluting metaphysics. This is my first time out in a group for nearly two years. I want to hear what people are actually about."

I felt somewhat chastened, brought right down to the ground, but it was the right moment for the group, landing our experience in the lived moment. How do we bear to receive ourselves into life, bear the infinity in the human breast together, but in the group? We must participate in our becoming through relationship. This is born in the body of the community, where there is space enough for any individual psyche to fall apart and come together held by the whole group, as Job is held in the context of his community throughout this work. Together we can allow the creative to become and for freedom not from what we fear, but towards the possible, that itself collapses towards the tragedy of each actual event. All we can do, all we need to do, is bear that collapse and its value, and live in the beauty of the experience.

The group picked up and ran with this, and developed a dialogue of the difficulties we had faced through the pandemic, and how difficult it felt to return with fears of death and a slight agoraphobia, from being so long inside. The small groups discussed aspects of this, and we went together for a lunch in a local restaurant, simply enjoying the pleasure of human contact. The afternoon group, which can be a difficult time, where tensions in the practice can come to a head, was much informed by a good lunch and the relief of re-establishing a secure as can be shared context. The group was convivial and shared the optimistic thoughts of our return to the building and the possibility of change that could follow the difficulties that we had been through. The difficult exploration of our differences could wait until another day

Blake points to 'all is alive in the human breast'. Whitehead (1927) would frame this as perceptual, as does Bohm. I share this view and see that it is the reception of that experienced perception and its infinite possibility that allows for the new and creative, the symbolic reference between the arriving event and the imagined experience of the world. In so far as the incoming perception is unknown, imagination is possible, a poetic imagination, or direct access to poetic genius; behind which Blake would point to the divine 'Jesus of the Imagination', who is not so far, as Ferrara (1997) says, from a Buddhist perception of the universe reflecting upon itself, beyond the proximal resistance of our selfhood.

The personal event at Tilbury reflects something of that reception. The idea at root in this book was apperceived five years ago, before the unfolding context that we are now living through, as a view of what might be before us and how we might let it unfold to allow for the most creative possibility. Now it seems there is a perpetual crisis, projecting us towards a wider vision. The waiting is uncomfortable. I had to wait for the event of the book to finish itself, repeating endless rounds of this Jobian cycle. As with therapy, we have to wait for the process to come to its own conclusion, suffering with our patients and caring for their renewal; something that is not quite in the hands of either psyche, whatever the books might say, but emergent between two or more lived lives.

A Final Small Group

I have suggested through this book that these illustrations chart an individual and social process of unfolding change, recognising an evolute and resonant experience in the context of the whole. Throughout his work Bohm offers the technology to explore this, bringing this experience to light, as does Blake; the primacy of experience before matter, as Whitehead suggests, an iterative process of perishing and becoming, fall and return in which all previous events have a component.

As number 42 began to return to the building more fully, after almost exactly two years, the small groups began to meet again in person. The first group was very small, only three, but the apologies were more. However, this was none the less reflexive for the whole. I was somewhat apprehensive as the two members attending had been in conflict. The conflict had ranged across race, age, class and personal disagreement. It had focused on room allocation and group work, a conflict over space, symbolic I imagined, for the discomfort of return. This was being experienced as harder than the sudden retreat two years earlier. It is not unusual that such difficulty would be expressed and thought about in a dynamic, over something so concrete. Often boundary difficulties are expressed in this arena. The conflict was put aside and understood quite easily with an open recognition of correspondent family dynamics in the history of the two participants, which echoed the unfolding process of the wider community. This recognition and the good will attached to it allowed space for the conflict of being together again to be aired. The three of us remarked upon the smallness and the disappointment that so few had been able to be here on the first of these groups, yet also these few had generated the capacity for intimacy that might not have been there in a larger group. It seemed that the small group had worked through something for the larger, as Job does for his whole community.

We discussed the context of the return, which included the developing war in the east. Quoting from the minutes we thought about the 'Felt sense in the room'. The possible new. How can we find it? How to actually care and make that known. 'How might we be seen by others in the moment that it all comes together?' This was an articulation of a wish for simple human trust, and trust in the process of relating, towards an apperception of our lives in context: an explicate coming together, coherent with an implied whole, felt within and between in human relation, an example of the resonant emergent moment experienced within and between, which then perished for the next to arise.

Notes

1 Private conversation with Professor Geoff Quilley.
2 A note on boundaries. Often I have been asked how I can set my boundaries so openly, for instance, that I could sit and have lunch with a client. The answer is principally experiential. Whilst leading CORE as an open community my life was more visible than in a traditional setting. As is always the case with addiction everything came down to the negotiation of boundary, first of course the boundary not to use and then the boundary between life and death, finally the boundary between self and other. This complex negotiation I have tried to show in the course of the book.

3 The origin of any place name is open to debate. The town of Gravesend and the Borough of Gravesham are no exception. It has been remarked that the Borough name of Gravesham – adopted in 1974 – is a version of the town name Gravesend. But that is by no means so! The Domesday Survey of 1086, where it was called Graff-ham. Later, during the Middle Ages, it was a known interchangeably as Gravesend or Gravesham. Thus, the name has a very firm base in history. There are two main schools of opinion as to the true origin of the name itself. The view with which most scholars agree was expressed as early as 1576 by the historian, William Lambarde, in his book entitled "Perumbulation of Kent". Lambarde claimed that:

> The original cause of the name of this place lies hid in the usual name of the Officer lately created in this town - he is commonly called Portreve, but the word anciently and truly founded in Portgereve, that is to say, the limit, bound or precinct of such a rule or office.

The early scholars who subscribed to Lambarde's view added as a crowning statement that the word 'ham' meant a homestead or village that would have inevitably grown gradually into a town. So we have Grevesham. The second – and slightly less popular theory – is that the prefix of the place name 'Grave' probably came from the word 'Greva' used in the Domesday Book. This signified a coppice or small wood or grove – as in the Latin 'Grava'. Either theory completely rules out any possibility of the name Gravesend being linked in any way with the town's waters being the furthest point for burials at sea, or Gravesend having any connection with the Black Death when, it was suggested, bodies of plague victims were brought to the area to be buried to avoid spreading the disease in London.
  http://www.discovergravesham.co.uk/about-gravesham/what-s-in-a-name-gravesham-or-gravesend.html

Bibliography

Abram, J. 1996. *The language of Winnicott: a dictionary of Winnicott's use of words*, London, Routledge.
Ackroyd, P. 1995. *Blake*, London, Sinclair-Stevenson.
Astley, N. 2002. *Staying alive: real poems for unreal times*, Tarset, Bloodaxe.
Atmanspacher, H. & Fuchs, C. A. 2014. *The Pauli-Jung conjecture and its impact today*, Exeter, Imprint Academic.
Barresi, J. M., & Martin, R. 2011. History as prologue: Western theories of the self. In: Galagher, S. (ed.) *The Oxford handbook of the self*. Oxford, Oxford University Press.
Bentley, G. 2001. *The stranger from paradise: a biography of William Blake*, New Haven, CT & London, Yale University Press.
Bentley, G. E. 2004. *Blake records*, New Haven, CT & London, Yale University Press.
Bergson, H. 1910. *Time and free will: an essay on the immediate data of consciousness*, Montana, SD, Kessinger Publishing Company.
Bion, W. R. 1961. *Experiences in groups, and other papers*, London, Tavistock Publications.
Bishop, P. 2002. *Jung's answer to job: a commentary*, Philadelphia, PA; Hove, Brunner/Routledge.
Blake, W., Ellis, E. J., Yeats, W. B., Linnell, J. & Lessing, J. Rosenwald Reference Collection (Library of Congress). 1893. *The works of William Blake, poetic, symbolic, and critical*, London, B. Quaritch.
Blake, W. & Yeats, W. B. 1910. *Mr. William Butler Yeats introduces the poetical works of William Blake: born in 1757, died in 1827*, [London], G. Routledge & Sons.
Bly, R., Hillman, J. & Meade, M. 1992. *The rag and bone shop of the heart: poems for men*, New York, Harper Collins.
Bly, R., Knoepfle, J. & Wright, J. 1993. *Neruda and Vallejo: selected poems*, Boston, MA, Beacon Press.
Bohm, D. 1980. *Wholeness and the implicate order*, London, Routledge and Kegan Paul.
Bohm, D. 1994. *Thought as a system*, London, Routledge.
Bohm, D. 1996. *On dialogue*, London, Routledge.
Bohm, D. 1998. *On creativity*, London, Routledge.
Bohm, D. 2008a. *Towards wholeness*, Toms, M. (ed.), Santa Rosa, CA, Audible: New Dimensions Media.
Bohm, D. 2008b. *Parts of a whole*, Toms, M. (ed.), Santa Rosa, CA, Audible: New Dimension Media.

Bohm, D. 2008c. *Essential reality*, Toms, M. (ed.), Santa Rosa, CA, Audible: New Dimensions Media.
Bohm, D. 2008d. *Creativity, natural philosophy and science*, Toms, M. (ed.), Santa Rosa, CA, Audible: New Dimensions Media.
Bohm, D. & Peat, F. D. 1987. *Science, order, and creativity*, Toronto; New York, Bantam Books.
Britton, R. 1998. *Belief and imagination: explorations in psychoanalysis*, London, Routledge.
Campbell, J. 1949. *The hero with a thousand faces*, New York, Pantheon Books.
Churton, T. 2014. *Jerusalem: the real life of William Blake*, London, Watkins Media Limited.
Cobb, J. 2008, 2015. *Whitehead word book*, Anoka, MN, Process Century Press.
Colman, W. 2016. *Act and image: the emergence of symbolic imagination*, New Orleans, Spring Books.
Damon, S. F. 1966. *Blake's job*, Providence, RI, Brown University Press.
Damon, S. F. 2013. *A Blake dictionary: the ideas and symbols of William Blake*, Lebanon, NH, University Press of New England.
De Mare, P. Piper, R. & Thompson, S. 1991. *Koinonia: from hate, through dialogue, to culture in the large group*, London, Karnac Books.
Edinger, E. F. 1986. *Encounter with the self: a Jungian*, Toronto, ON, Inner City Books.
ERDMAN, D. V. 1988. *The Complete Poetry and Prose of Willliam Blake*, New York, Doubleday.
Ferrara, M. S. 1997. Ch'an Buddhism and the prophetic poems of William Blake. *Journal of Chinese Philosophy*, 24, 59–73.
Ferrer, J. N. 2002. *Revisioning transpersonal theory: a participatory vision of human spirituality*, Albany, NY; [Great Britain], State University of New York Press.
Fischer, K. 2004. *Converse in the Spirit : William Blake, Jacob Boehme, and the Creative Spirit.* Madison: Fairleigh Dickinson University Press.
Fordham, M. 1985. *Explorations into the self*, London, Karnac Books.
Foulkes, S., H 1983. *Introduction to group-analytic psychotherapy: studies in the social integration of individuals and groups*, London, Karnac Books.
Gaiman, N. 2001, 2011 *American Gods.* London: Headline.
Gallagher, S. 2011. *The Oxford handbook of the self*, Oxford, Oxford University Press.
Garre, A. 2006. Whitehead and pythagoras. *Concrescence: The Australian Journal of Process Thought*, 7, 3–19.
Gendlin, E. T. 1978. *Focusing*, New York, Everest House.
Gendlin, E. T. 1996. *Focusing-oriented psychotherapy: a manual of the experiential method*, New York, Guilford Press.
Gill, R. 2014. Addictions from an attachment perspective: do broken bonds and early trauma lead to addictive behaviours?: *The John Bowlby Memorial Conference monograph 2013*, London, Karnac Books.
Harari, Y. N. 2014. *Sapiens: a brief history of humankind*, London, Random House, Vintage.
Harari, Y. N. 2016. *Homo Deus: a brief history of tomorrow*, London, Random House, Vintage.
Harari, Y. N. 2018. *21 Lessons for the 21st century*, London, Random House, Vintage.
Helmont, F. M. V. & Spector, S. A. 2012. *Francis Mercury van Helmont's "Sketch of Christian Kabbalism"*, Leiden; Boston, MA, Brill.
Higgs, J. 2021. *William Blake vs the world*, London, Weidenfeld & Nicolson.
Hiles, D. 2001. Jung, William Blake and our answer to Job. *Paper resented to Collegium Junianum Brunense*, Brno, CZ, 25.

Hillman, J. 1964. *Suicide and the soul*, London, Hodder & Stoughton.
Hillman, J. 1975a. *Re-visioning psychology*, New York, Harper & Row.
Hillman, J. 1975b. *Loose ends: primary papers in archetypal psychology*, Zürich, Spring Publications.
Hillman, J. 1979a. *Puer papers*, Irving, TX, Spring Publications.
Hillman, J. 1979b. *Peaks and Vales: Hillman, et al., Puer papers*, Irving TX, Spring Publications, 1979, pp. 54–74.
Hillman, J. 1983a. *Healing fiction*, New York, Station Hill Press.
Hillman, J. 1983b. *Archetypal psychology: a brief account*, Dallas, Spring Publications.
Hillman, J. 1992. *The thought of the heart and the soul of the world*, Dallas, Spring Publications.
Hillman, J. 1994. *Healing fiction*, Dallas, Spring Publications.
Hillman, J. 1996. *The soul's code: in search of character and calling*, New York, Random House.
Hillman, J. 2004. *A terrible love of war*, New York, Penguin Press.
Hillman, J. & Moore, T. 1989. *A blue fire: selected writings*, New York, Harper & Row.
Hillman, J. & Pozzo, L. 1983. *Inter views: conversations with Laura Pozzo on psychotherapy, biography, love, soul, dreams, work, imagination, and the state of the culture*, New York, Harper & Row.
Hoxun, S. 2004. *Spontanious movement for health and happiness*, Bristol, Haarlem.
Hopper, E. 2003. *The social unconscious: selected papers*, London; Philadelphia, J. Kingsley Publishers.
Hopper, E. 2009. The theory of the basic assumption of incohesion: Aggregation/Massification or (BA) I: A/M. *British Journal of Psychotherapy*, 25, 214–229.
Hopper, E. & Weinberg, H. 2018. *The social unconscious in persons, groups and societies: mainly theory*, London, Routledge.
Jung, C. G. 1916/1958. The Transcendent Function in: Read, H., et al. (eds.) *Collected works: 8 structure and dynamics of the psyche*. Princeton, NJ: Princeton University Press.
Jung, C. G. 1931. *Psychological types*, Princeton, NJ: Princeton University Press.
Jung, C. G. 1936. Individual Dream Symbolism in Relation to Alchemy. In: Read, H., et al. (eds.) *Collected works: 12 psychology and alchemy*. Princeton, NJ : Princeton University Press.
Jung, C. G. 1939. Concerning rebirth. In: Read, H., et al. (eds.) *Collected works: 9i The archetypes and the collective unconscious*. Princeton, NJ: Princeton University Press.
Jung, C. G. 1946. Psychology of the transference. In: Read, H., et al. (eds.) *Collected works: 16 practice of psychotherapy*. Princeton, NJ: Princeton University Press.
Jung, C. G. 1952. Answer to job. In: Read, H., et al. (eds.) *Collected works: 11 psychology and religion*. Princeton, NJ: Princeton University Press.
Kalsched, D. 1996. *The inner world of trauma*, London, Routledge.
Korzybski, A. 1933. *Science and sanity: an introduction to non-Aristotelian systems and general semantics*, Englewood, NJ, Institute of General Sematics.
Lancaster, B. 2005. *Approaches to consciousness: the marriage of science and mysticism*, Basingstoke, Palgrave Macmillan.
Linnell, D. 1994. *Blake, Palmer, Linnell and Co: The life of John Linnell*, London, Book Guild.
Martin, R. & Barresi, J. 2000. *Naturalization of the soul: self and personal identity in the eighteenth century*, London, Routledge.

206 Bibliography

McGilchrist, I. 2009. *The master and his emissary: the divided brain and the making of the Western world*, New Haven, CT, Yale University Press.

McGilchrist, I. 2021 *The Matter with things: our brains, our delusions, and the unmaking of the World*, London, Perspectiva Press.

McWilliams, N. 1994. *Psychoanalytic diagnosis: understanding personality structure in the clinical process*, New York, Guilford Press.

Mesle, C. R. 2008. *Process-relational philosophy: an introduction to Alfred North Whitehead*, West Conshohocken, PA, Templeton Foundation Press.

Miller, J. C. 2004. *The transcendent function: Jung's model of psychological growth through dialogue with the unconscious*, Albany, State University of New York Press.

Mulhern, A. 2015. *The sower and the seed: reflections on the development of consciousness*, London, Karnac Books Ltd.

Panksepp, J., Biven, L. & Siegel, D. J. 2012. *The archaeology of mind: neuroevolutionary origins of human emotions (Norton Series on Interpersonal Neurobiology)*, New York, W. W. Norton.

Peat, F. D. 1996. *Infinite potential: the life and times of David Bohm*, Reading, MA; Harlow, Addison Wesley.

Quinney, L. 2010. *William Blake on self and soul*, Cambridge, MA, Harvard University Press.

Raine, K. 1968. *Blake and tradition*, Princeton, NJ, Princeton University Press.

Raine, K. 1979. *Blake and antiquity*, London, Routledge and Kegan Paul.

Raine, K. 1982. *The human face of god: William Blake and the "Book of Job"*, London, Thames and Hudson.

Ray, R. A. 2008a. *Touching enlightenment: finding realization in the body*, Boulder, CO, Sounds True.

Ray, R. A. 2008b. *Your breathing body. Volume 1, beginning practices for physical, emotional & spiritual Fulfilment. Sounds True audio learning course*, Boulder, CO, Sounds True.

Ray, R. A. 2008c. *Your breathing body, volume 2: advanced practices for physical, emotional, and spiritual fulfilment Reginald A. Ray*. Boulder, CO, Sounds True.

Ray, R. A. 2016. *The awakening body: somatic meditation for discovering our deepest life*, Boulder, CO, Shambhala Publications.

Ray, R. A. 2020. *Somatic descent: how to unlock the deepest wisdom of the body*, Boulder, CO, Shambhala Publications.

Rilke, R. M. 1981. *Selected poems*. Translated by Robert Bly. New York, Harper and Row.

Rilke, R. M. & Bly, R. 1981. *Selected poems of Rainer Maria Rilke*, New York, Harper & Row.

Roethke, T. 1966. *The collected poems of Theodore Roethke*, Garden City, NY, Doubleday.

Roy, D. E. 2017. Can whitehead's philosophy provide an adequate theoretical foundation for today's neuroscience? *Process Studies*, 46, 128–151.

Samuels, A., Shorter, B. & Plaut, F. 1986. *A critical dictionary of Jungian analysis*, London; New York, Routledge & Kegan Paul.

Segall, M. D. 2013. *Physics of the world soul,* Morrisville, LULU.

Sharp, D. 1991. *Jung lexicon: a primer of terms & concepts*, Toronto, ON, Inner City Books.

Solms, M. 2015. *The feeling brain: selected papers on neuropsychoanalysis*, London, Karnac Books.

Solms, M. 2021. *The hidden spring: a journey to the source of consciousness*, London, Profile Books.
Solomon, A. 1993. *Blake's job: a message for our time*, London, Palamabron Press
Spector, S. A. 2001a. *Glorious incomprehensible: the development of Blake's Kabbalistic language*, Lewisburg, Bucknell University Press.
Spector, S. A. 2001b. *Wonders divine: the development of Blake's kabbalistic myth*, Lewisburg, Bucknell University Press.
Stengers, I. 2011. *Thinking with Whitehead: a free and wild creation of concepts*, Cambridge, MA, Harvard University Press. Cambridge Massatucets
Story, A. T. 1892. *The life of John Linnell*, London, Richard Bentley and Son.
Stukeley, W. 1740. *Stonehenge, a Temple restor'd to the British Druids*. By William Stukeley, M. D. Rector of All Saints in Stamford, London.
Suzuki, T. D. 1991. The Buddhist Conception of Reality. In Frank, F. (ed.) *The Buddha eye: An anthology of the Kyoto School* (pp. 89–110, p. 99). New York: Crossroad Publishing Co.
Tweedy, R. 2013. *The God of the left hemisphere: Blake, Bolte Taylor, and the myth of creation*, London, Karnak.
Washburn, M. 1988. *The ego and the dynamic ground: a transpersonal theory of human development*, Albany, NY, Suny Press.
Washburn, M. 1994. *Transpersonal psychology in psychoanalytic perspective*, Albany, State University of New York Press.
Washburn, M. 1995. *The ego and the dynamic ground: a transpersonal theory of human development*, Albany, State University of New York Press.
Weber, M., Parsons, T. & Tawney, R. H. 1930. *The protestant ethic and the spirit of capitalism*. Translated by Talcott Parsons. With a foreword by R. H. Tawney, London, G. Allen & Unwin.
Wellings, N. & Mccormick, E. W. 2000. *Transpersonal psychotherapy*, London, Sage.
Wellings, N. & Mccormick, E. W. 2021. *Present with suffering: being with the things that hurt*, Woodbridge, Confer Books.
Wellings, N. 2023, *Dzogchen, who's who & what's what in the great perfection*, Mud Pie, Oxford.
Whitehead, A. N. 1925. *Science and the modern world. Lowell lectures, 1925*, New York, The Macmillan Company.
Whitehead, A. N. 1927. *Symbolism, its meaning and effect*, New York, Macmillan.
Whitehead, A. N. 1933. *Adventures of ideas*, New York, The Macmillan Company.
Whitehead, A. N. 1938. *Modes of thought*, New York, The Macmillan Company.
Whitehead, A. N., Griffin, D. R. & Sherburne, D. W. 1978. *Process and reality: an essay in cosmology*, New York, Free Press.
Wickstead, J. H. 1971. *Blake's vision of the Book of Job*, London, J.M. Dent and Sons.
Wilson, D. S. 2015. *Does altruism exist?: Culture, genes, and the welfare of others*, New Haven, CT; London, Yale University Press; Templeton Press.
Winnicott, D. 1974. Fear of breakdown. *International Review of Psychoanalysis*, 1, 87–95.
Winnicott, D. W. 1965a. *The family and individual development*, London, Tavistock Publications.
Winnicott, D. W. 1965b. *The maturational processes and the facilitating environment. Studies in the theory of emotional development*, London, Hogarth Press; Institute of Psycho-Analysis.
Winnicott, D. W. 1971. *Playing and reality*, London, Routledge, 1991.

Winnicott, D. W., Winnicott, C., Shepherd, R. & Davis, M. 1989. *Psycho-analytic explorations*, London, Karnac.
Winnicott, D. W., Winnicott, C., Shepherd, R. & Davis, M. 2018. *The squiggle game: an amalgamation of two papers: one, unpublished, written in 1964, the other published 1968 1. Psycho-analytic explorations*, London, Routledge.
Wright, J. 1990. *Above the river: the complete poems*, New York, Middletown, CT., Farrar University Press of New England.
Wright, J. 2014. Addiction: Treatment and its Context. In: Gill, R. W., Kate (ed.) *Addictions from an attachment perspective: do broken bonds and early trauma lead to addictive behaviours?: The John Bowlby Memorial Conference monograph 2013*. London, Karnac Books.
Yates, F. 2001. *The occult philosophy in the Elizabethan age*, London, Routledge.

Index

Note: Page numbers followed by "n" denote endnotes.

addiction 1, 5, 9, 19–21, 25–27, 32–33, 45–46, 52–55, 59, 67–69, 72, 79, 82–83, 85, 87, 89, 96–97, 99, 107, 116, 119, 135, 150–151, 162–163, 167–168, 172, 176–177, 180, 185–186, 188–189, 194n2
Adishanti 119, 125n4
agony 85–87, 101, 120, 172, 189–190
Alexander, F. M. 102n2
Alexander technique 16, 96, 102n2
American Gods (Gaiman) 171
Anima Mundi 112, 125n1
apperceive 10, 44, 54, 114, 148–149, 172, 176, 192
archetype 4, 8, 35, 38, 112, 114
Argen, G. 179

Barresi, J. M. 30
Bergson, H. 113
Beulah 52, 55, 58–59, 63–64, 69, 133, 135, 149, 167, 172
Bion, W. R. 10, 31, 76
Blake, W. 1, 24–29, 45–47, 87n3, 184–186; All Religions are One 2–3; coherence 34–35; and community 31–34; Crabb Robbins 66; divine humanity 30, 161; felt sense of experience 34–37; *The Four Zoas* 48, 65–66, 85, 87n3, 167; frontispiece 38–44; *The Marriage of Heaven and Hell* 71, 140; *Milton* 2, 107, 167; neo-Platonic 30, 47n4, 52, 57, 158, 175; Poetic Genius 2–4, 7, 42, 51, 59–60, 64, 71, 120, 124, 174, 192; polarisation 27, 33; Porphyry 47n2, 87n9; *Proverbs of Hell* 71, 148; psyche 37–38; Satan 17, 21, 40, 54–55, 57–69, 72, 75, 77, 83–85, 101, 105–108, 110, 116–117, 129, 140–141, 146–150, 154, 168, 183–184; 'Satan of The Selfhood' 4, 8, 17, 21, 35, 45, 52, 55, 58, 65, 72, 106, 117, 140, 148–149, 154; 'The Sea of Time and Space' 40; *Songs of Experience* 52–53; *Songs of Innocence* 53, 107, 191; *Thus did Job continually* 49–54; transmission 22, 116, 160, 169–174, 185; True Man 2–4, 6, 26, 30, 37, 51, 53–54, 56, 59–60, 64, 71, 101, 110, 119, 124, 133, 149; Ulro (spiritual blindness) 3, 26, 48, 52, 55, 58, 63, 69, 80, 84, 88–102, 119, 133, 136, 172, 189, 191; 'A Vision of the Last Judgement' 40, 46, 59, 147, 149
Bly, R. 182
Bohm, D. 2–3, 5–8, 10–13, 15, 17–22, 34, 125n1, 130, 135–136, 139, 141–142, 149, 151, 155–156, 158, 160–161, 167–168, 173, 175, 177–179, 183, 185, 191–193; on creativity 121–125; *On Dialogue* 93–94; explicate 5–6, 8, 22, 23n5, 30, 34, 42, 44, 46, 49, 93, 95, 130, 155, 172, 193; fragmentary nature of thought 74–75; impersonal fellowship 167; implicate 5–6, 8–9, 15, 17, 22, 26, 30–31, 34, 40, 44, 46, 49, 60, 67, 93, 95, 130, 136–137, 149, 155, 172, 175, 187; proprioception 60, 62, 75–82, 84–85, 94, 110, 161
Bohme, J. 29, 51, 133

Britton, R. 26–27
buddha nature 130–131, 143n1
Buddhism 8, 61, 63, 97
Butts, T. 28, 38, 129

Campbell, J. 114
Churton, T. 4, 28, 65, 93
Colman, W. 112, 150, 176
community 10, 12–13, 16–17, 19, 22, 31–34, 36, 40, 67–69, 73, 76, 82–83, 87n5, 97, 110–112, 114–117, 120, 136, 138, 150–152, 155–159, 161, 167–168, 171, 173, 176, 178, 188, 191–193
consciousness 1, 3, 5, 8–11, 19, 21–22, 26, 28–29, 35–37, 42, 51, 59, 61–64, 70, 72, 74–75, 84, 89, 109, 112, 116–117, 121, 123–124, 125n5, 128, 130–133, 135, 139–142, 151, 154, 156, 158–160, 167–168, 173, 178–180, 183, 189
CORE Trust 16–17, 31, 61, 67–69, 72–73, 79, 82, 84, 89, 94, 96, 108, 110–112, 115–117, 119, 121, 124, 128, 131, 142, 148–149, 152, 155–157, 162, 169–170, 176–177, 187–189, 191, 193n2
creativity 7–8, 18, 20, 22, 110, 114, 118, 121–125, 131, 136, 138, 140, 142, 157, 167, 174

Damon, S. F. 18, 40, 65, 71–72, 87n6, 107
death and rebirth cycle 4, 20, 38–41, 46, 59, 179
De Mare, P. 10–11, 16, 22–23n3, 48–49, 77
denial 3, 7, 45, 65, 69–74
Descartes 10
despair 33, 36, 48, 64, 72–73, 76, 82–83, 85, 87, 90–97, 100–101, 118–119, 162, 173–174, 178
destruction 19, 27, 36, 49–54, 71, 73, 77, 87, 116, 140, 179, 183
dialogue 2–3, 5, 8–11, 13, 19, 30, 33–34, 36, 40–41, 44, 48–49, 68, 72, 91, 93–97, 100, 122, 135, 137–139, 141, 167–169, 171, 176, 179, 185, 191–192
disintegration 30, 84–85, 122, 154, 164n6
divine (God) 6–8
divine order 66, 97, 131–134
Divine Vision 130
dreamt 120–121

ecstasy 85–87, 172, 190
Eden 52, 55, 58–59, 63–64, 69, 80, 133, 135–136, 149, 168, 172
Edinger, E. F. 8–9, 151, 190
Ein Sof 17–18, 23n7, 51–52, 63, 95, 133, 135
Elihu 117, 119–120, 129
Eliphaz 99–101
endogenous 62
exogenous 62

Ferrara, M. S. 130, 160, 171, 192
Ferrer, J. N. 2–3
Fordham, M. 9, 164n6
Foulkes, S. H. 10

Gaiman, N. 171
Gebser, J. 125n5
Gendlin, E. T. 62
Gnostic pleroma 171, 180n1
Griffin, D. R. 13
group 3, 5–6, 9–14, 16–18, 22–23n3, 26–27, 29, 31–34, 36, 40–43, 48–49, 53, 60–63, 67–68, 70–71, 73, 75–77, 80, 82–84, 89–96, 99–101, 107, 110–112, 114, 116–117, 119–121, 124, 130, 135, 139–141, 149–152, 155–162, 166–169, 172, 174, 176–180, 182–185, 190–193

Harari, Y. N. 25, 37; *Homo Deus* 61; *Sapiens* 61
Helmont, F. M. V. 17, 59
Higgs, J. 28, 93
Hillman, J. 1, 16, 22n2, 23n3, 30–31, 35, 45, 47n4, 67, 74, 97–98, 120, 125n1, 128–129, 142, 163, 168, 172–173, 177; *Peaks and Vales* 128; poetic basis of mind 120; *Suicide and the Soul* 98–99
Hopper, E. 31, 76, 112
humanism 53, 161
hypocrisy 80–82, 108, 120, 185

Internal God (the infinite Subject) 158–163

James, W. 30
Julian of Norwich 28
Jung, C. G. 1, 3–5, 8–10, 12–13, 15, 22n1–22n2, 31, 34, 38–39, 44, 61, 64–68, 72, 80, 84, 92, 95, 102n1, 105, 108–109, 112, 117, 125n1,

128, 137, 139–140, 151, 154–155, 160, 163n2, 164n4, 172–174, 176–177, 182

Kabbalistic thought 2, 9, 17, 19, 21, 27–29, 43–44, 51–53, 56–57, 59–60, 64, 66, 68, 72, 84, 133, 137, 140, 148–149, 152, 158, 160, 171, 173–174
Kalsched, D. 26, 105–106
Korzipski, A. 35

Lambarde, W. 194n3
Lancaster, B. 9, 18, 23n7, 60, 117
Lawrence, D. H. 24
Leven, J. 16–17, 149
Linnell, D. 185
Linnell, J. 2, 27–28, 101, 184–185

Martin, R. 30
McGilchrist, I. 6, 9, 11, 26, 30, 49, 61, 65, 74–75, 117, 123, 125n3, 133, 137, 148; *aufgehoben* (uplift) 9, 11, 148, 179; brain lateralisation 11, 41; left and right brain 6, 9, 11, 26, 28, 30, 37, 41, 44, 48–49, 55, 61–62, 65, 74–75, 89, 94–95, 97, 113–114, 117, 120, 123–124, 129, 136, 140, 147, 151–152, 161, 176–178, 185
McWilliams, N. 22n2
Mesle, C. R. 130
Miller, J. C. 9
Moore, T. 67
Mosaic law 55, 58, 87n2, 105
Mulhern, A. 1, 21, 135
mutual reception 8, 15, 44, 133, 150, 156, 166–169, 173, 176, 178
myth: Christian 3, 28–29, 51, 59, 140, 142; Kabbalistic (*See* Kabbalistic thought); Lurianic 17–18, 51, 59, 77; and ritual 114–115

nadir 86–87, 89, 105–110
neo-animism 1, 97, 129
neuroscience 11–13, 152
Nichol 94, 124, 135, 139
Nietzsche 4, 21, 148

Otto, R. 128

Palmer, S. 27, 184–185
participation 13–15, 21–22, 29, 38, 40, 67, 75–77, 135–137, 139–140, 147–148, 157, 165–180, 183–185
The Past Order 134–137

Peat, F. D. 42, 149, 175, 183
Pepe 82–85, 90, 111–112, 121, 124, 150
Perumbulation of Kent (Lambarde) 194n3
Phaedo 43
Plato 13, 20, 38, 43, 45–46, 47n2, 56–59, 62, 83, 89, 93, 97, 105, 112, 120, 128, 131, 133, 142, 147, 154
poetic moment 40–42, 46, 75, 131, 158, 176, 186–187
presentational immediacy 5, 121, 132–133

Raine, K. 2, 8, 19, 21, 45, 48–53, 55–56, 58, 63–64, 66, 83, 85, 87n1, 89, 92–93, 97, 99, 101, 107, 117, 119, 128–129, 131, 133, 148, 154, 167, 173–174; *The Human Face of God* 128, 139–140
Ray, R. A. 6, 11, 13, 30, 36, 61–63, 74–75, 94, 117, 120, 132, 147, 158, 160, 162, 167
resonance 1, 3, 5, 7–8, 18–19, 21–22, 29, 36–38, 41–44, 59, 61–62, 64, 67, 73, 93, 97, 99, 101, 112, 114, 116, 124, 135, 149, 152, 154, 157, 164n4, 168, 179–180, 183–187, 190
Rilke, R. M. 36, 144, 147, 181–182
ritual 52, 68, 76, 80, 82, 89, 115–116, 142, 149–150, 155–156, 186–189
Roethke, T. 27, 126, 128

scorn 101–102
Segall, M. D. 112
self 9, 13–15, 26, 29–46, 48, 52–56, 59, 66, 112–114, 116–117, 120–123, 125n3, 149–156, 160–163, 168–174
self-liberate 147, 160
self-righteousness 19–20, 45–46, 48, 53–56, 59, 64–65, 75, 79–80, 87, 102, 105, 120, 122, 129, 136, 141, 147, 174, 183
Sharp, D. 10
Shekhinah 164n5
Sherburne, D. W. 13
Socrates 43
Solms, M. 9, 61–62, 152
Solomon, A. 18, 26, 52, 66, 70–72, 79–80, 85, 101, 135, 147, 154, 174
soul 5–6, 13, 16, 20, 24, 26–28, 30, 38, 43, 45–46, 52, 55, 58–59, 62, 74, 83, 85, 89, 98–99, 112, 120, 128–129, 131, 133, 139, 142, 147, 150, 167–168, 174, 188

Spector, S. 2, 17, 19, 28, 43, 49, 51, 59, 89, 93, 95, 125n3, 154, 157, 171; *Jerusalem* 2, 4, 7, 28, 52, 65, 69, 80, 83, 87n1, 87n3, 97, 147, 171, 184
spiritual emergency 27, 128
sunrise 115–117
surrender 153–155
Swedenborg, E. 4, 29–30, 49, 51–53, 56, 58, 72, 129
symbol 2–10, 12–15, 22n1, 25, 28, 31–33, 35, 37–38, 42–44, 49, 52, 54–56, 58–60, 63–66, 68, 74–77, 80, 84, 87, 89, 95, 97, 99, 102n1, 107, 109–116, 128, 132–133, 135–136, 139–141, 150, 152, 155, 161, 167, 172–176, 179–180, 182–183, 186–187, 189, 191–193

Taylor, T. 29
Timaeus 43
transcendent function 4, 8–10, 15, 44, 64, 72, 80, 84, 99, 109, 119, 140, 155, 173–174
transitional phenomena 44, 47n3
transpersonal 6, 22, 43, 49, 68–69, 112, 116–117, 120, 124, 160, 170, 172
Tweedy, R. 26, 41, 65
Twelve Step movement 36, 54, 79–80, 106, 108, 155, 176

unus mundus 112, 125n1

vision 4, 20–21, 28, 38, 42–43, 58–60, 65, 67, 72, 79, 89, 97, 99, 108–109, 126–143, 169, 185
Von Bingen, Hildegard 28
Von Helmont, F. M. 17, 59

Weber, M. 52–53
Whitehead, A. 2–3, 5–8, 10–16, 18–20, 22, 23n5, 28, 30, 34–35, 40, 42–44, 46, 53, 56, 59–60, 63, 67, 76, 92–93, 97, 110, 112–114, 116, 118, 120–125, 129–130, 132, 135, 138–139, 142, 147, 157, 160, 167, 177, 179–180, 182, 187, 189–193
wholeness 6–7, 121–122, 151, 154, 164n4
Wilbur, J. 120, 125n5
Wilson, D. S. 6, 12–13, 15, 34, 37, 114, 116, 138, 141, 155, 157, 176, 179–180, 185
Winnicott, D. 26, 36, 40, 44, 67, 75, 89, 119, 150, 155, 173, 187
Wolfe, C. 16–17
Wright, J. 165, 181

Yahweh 9, 15, 17, 20–21, 29, 31, 38, 48, 58, 60, 63–66, 72, 83–85, 90, 97, 105, 116, 129, 133, 135–136, 139–141, 147–148, 151, 161, 169, 174
Yates, F. 45, 47n4
Yeats, W. B. 3, 88, 185

For Product Safety Concerns and Information please contact our EU representative GPSR@taylorandfrancis.com
Taylor & Francis Verlag GmbH, Kaufingerstraße 24, 80331 München, Germany